*The
American
Spirit
in Theology*

The American Spirit in Theology

Randolph Crump Miller

*A Pilgrim Press Book
from
United Church Press
Philadelphia*

Library of Congress Cataloging in Publication Data

Miller, Randolph Crump, 1910-
   The American spirit in theology.

   "A Pilgrim Press book."
   Includes bibliographical references.
     1. Theology, Doctrinal—History—United States.
2. Empiricism. 3. Process philosophy. I. Title.
BT30.U6M54   230'.0973   74-11099
ISBN 0-8298-0285-1

United Church Press, 1505 Race Street,
Philadelphia, Pennsylvania 19102

Dedicated to
Henry Nelson Wieman

In memory of
Douglas Clyde Macintosh
and
Daniel Day Williams

Contents

Preface

DURING THE LAST CENTURY, A SLOWLY DEVELOPING SCIENTIFIC consciousness has infiltrated the thinking of many people. As science has become more dominant in our culture and as its application through technology has radically changed the conditions of living, many aspects of these developments have penetrated our consciousness and our religious thinking. This has been a very gradual process, so that religious thinking, especially, has lagged behind the thinking in other areas. Changes took place in philosophy, for example, that reflected scientific insights long before similar alterations took place in theology. There were conflicts between science and religion, but each discipline tended to remain in its own camp. Of course, there were some who responded more quickly to the challenge and made accommodations with the scientific view of the world, but the first attempts by theologians did not find widespread approval among most religious people.

This has changed to some extent in recent years, so that there is what Harold Schilling calls "a new consciousness in science and religion." This has been due to the success of scientific theory as a description of events and of a total world view. We know now that observable events operate in a dependable way, although there is room for chance and novelty. We can manage many aspects of nature. We see new life emerging from that which perishes, with some expectation that evolution will continue to exhibit some increase of good. In this process, even among human beings, we can expect novelty. The interrelationships of man and nature indicate that the rule of life is not simply the survival of the fittest but that criteria of morality and intelligence are indicated. These conclusions are evident without regard for religion, but they provide a basis for thinking that the processes of creation and redemption can be identified with what traditional religions have called God.[1]

The expanding horizons of the human consciousness indicate that traditional concepts of God may have been both too small and too grandiose. The universe is too large for many anthropomorphic concepts of God. Yet a God who is an absolute monarch offends the moral sense and contradicts the basic insight that God is love. The sense of mystery points to the inexhaustible element in our seeking to know God, and our sense of wonder at being loved gives evidence of a persuasive God of love.

This has led to what I have called "the American spirit in theology." There has developed in the American consciousness an approach to life and its problems that reflects American culture. It is not the spirit found in conventional American theology, which has multitudinous roots in its traditional, ethnic, and national backgrounds. It is, rather, a spirit that emerged first in the thinking of some philosophers who became symbols of the American spirit. The prime example was William James, but closely related were Charles Sanders Peirce, John Dewey, and, at a later date, Alfred North Whitehead. Certain dominant themes are clearly evident in these philosophies: radical empiricism, pragmatism, and a metaphysics that reflects both pluralism and process. It is this emphasis that I deem to be the American spirit, and my purpose is to show how it has emerged in the development of American theology.

I was first exposed to William James while in college. I was struggling with the problem of suffering and evil and found in James's limited God a religiously satisfying way of thinking. In courses with Robert Denison at Pomona College, I also became aware of John Dewey and Henry Nelson Wieman. At Yale I studied under Douglas Clyde Macintosh, and my dissertation dealt with empirical theology. In

---

[1] See Harold K. Schilling, *The New Consciousness in Science and Religion* (Philadelphia: United Church Press, 1973), pp. 224-25.

1941, my *What We Can Believe* was an attempt to develop this kind of thinking, but this was at the beginning of World War II and of a resurgent orthodoxy and neoorthodoxy. Only in the last decade, since the God-is-dead movement, has there been an opportunity to make an effective reexamination of the themes of radical empiricism, pragmatism, and process metaphysics. Only in 1971 did I begin to offer a seminar in empirical theology at Yale Divinity School; yet this is the school in which Douglas Clyde Macintosh was dominant from 1909 until his retirement in 1942.

In my opinion, now is the time to turn to those who have developed this kind of thinking, for they have much to say in this culture to this generation. Their writings have always attracted me, and the writing of this book has been a labor of love. My early exposure to this kind of thinking from my father, who was an Episcopal clergyman, and from the writings of James and the teaching of Macintosh, has provided a consistent approach to theology which has been evident in my writings in Christian education and especially in my recent *The Language Gap and God.*

I owe much to some of my students in the seminars and especially to those who offered critical comments, David Stinson and Larry Axel. My colleague, William A. Christian, has helped with his expertise on Whitehead. Just a month before he died, Daniel Day Williams checked the chapter on his position; in many ways he incorporated in his writings the major thrust of this book. My wife, as usual, has helped me gain some clarity and style and kept reminding me not to claim too many certainties just to satisfy religious needs.

The dedication of this book to Henry Nelson Wieman, now living in retirement, is an acknowledgment of how much he has contributed to both my thinking and my faith, chiefly through his writings. It is also a memorial to Douglas Clyde Macintosh, who as a great teacher introduced me to the intricacies of epistemology and to the ways in which empiricism can be used responsibly; it was under his direction that I wrote my dissertation at Yale. Finally, it is a memorial also to Daniel Day Williams, who embodied in his theology and person the American spirit in theology, and whose death at the age of sixty-three left all of us empty-handed, for we were waiting for those books on God and Christ based on an empirical process method.

I am indebted to the publishers who have granted me permission to quote from their publications, as acknowledged in the footnotes.

Randolph Crump Miller

The Divinity School
Yale University

The American Spirit in Theology

CHAPTER 1

THEOLOGY IN AMERICA HAS BEEN A MIXTURE OF MANY TRENDS. JUST AS ethnic groups have come to these shores with their cultural traditions, they have also come with their religious roots, and as time has gone by ideas from their original cultures have continued to be imported. This has led to a combination of characteristics reflecting both the melting-pot ideal and religious pluralism. Without merging these traditions, the American scene has resulted in new variations due to cultural and religious factors.

Dominant in these developments has been an appeal to experience, often more emotional than intellectual, so that we have had revivals, as well as new cults based on insights derived from the experiences of Joseph Smith, Mary Baker Eddy, and Alexander Campbell. Salvation has been experienced in emotional terms, conversion has led to new forms of moral behavior, and religion has been fostered because it works. Experience, often romantically interpreted, was central to the theologies of Jonathan Edwards and Horace Bushnell, and this led some thinkers in the direction of studying the psychology of religious experience at the end of the nineteenth century. This latter development provided some raw data for the development of theological concepts based on the findings of religious experience, as in the thought of William James.

At this same time, within American culture as a whole, certain characteristics of philosophical thinking developed. Philosophy, like theology, had tended to be systematic, abstract, idealistic, and intelligible primarily to other professional thinkers, but there now developed a new spirit that sought to relate philosophical thinking to ordinary life. The appearance on the scene of William James, who wrote in a nontechnical style that appealed to the average educated reader and whose writings had relevance to the American way of life, was symptomatic of the times. His ideas had a cutting edge that could be applied to human problems. His philosophical method caught the spirit of those who were influenced by certain aspects of American life. Always near the center of his thinking was a nontraditional but vital concern for religion.

James's thinking responded to scientific experimentation and theorizing, to the test of ideas by the way they work, to the appeal to experience as a basis for all knowledge, to the relativity of ideas, to the need for relevance in our thinking, to individualism, to man's capacity to work out his own salvation, and to religious faith. These ideas were not dominant in religious thinking at the time, and did not become so in competition with continental and biblical religious teachings, yet they provided a peculiarly American philosophical foundation for theology.

The Focus of American Theology

American theology after James began to deal seriously with some of the same ideas. Theologians began to take science seriously, to test ideas according to pragmatism, to appeal to experience, to develop an empirical methodology, to accept a degree of risk and tentativeness in their beliefs, to stress the importance of the individual, and to call upon some consensus of the community of leaders in formulating a theology. Each of these developments is worth looking at.

Americans are not distinguished from other people in taking science seriously. The effects of scientific experimentation and theorizing pervade most cultures of the world. Such thinking has changed man's cosmological views so that he has difficulty conceiving a God at work in such a world. It has provided ways for man to solve problems without divine aid. It has led to many blessings for mankind while threatening him with ecological disaster. It has supplied new ways of thinking in every field, including theology. In 1919, Douglas Clyde Macintosh titled his book *Theology as an Empirical Science*, and in it he attempted to construct a theology that utilized scientific methods and established scientifically valid principles. As we shall see, there were serious weaknesses in this approach, but Macintosh exemplified an attitude that was significant for theological development. Theology could no longer bypass or ignore the scientific spirit if it hoped to point to a deity that exists; such an approach could eliminate the irrational and outdated theological superstructures of belief while establishing an empirical base for religious theorizing.

The American spirit is also pragmatic. Such thinking was established in philosophy by Charles Sanders Peirce and William James. Sometimes pragmatism means only what will work in a crass political or materialistic sense, but it may be applied to the working out of beliefs, principles, and values in everyday life. One tests an idea by the way it works out in practice, and if it does not work it is probably false. We can test it, or we can imagine the conceivable results, or we can accept the observations of others. Sometimes our tests are practical in the sense that something may work "for all practical purposes" but needs more precision for more specific purposes; therefore, we settle for what is needed at a particular time rather than seek perfection. Ideas are significant, as Dewey insisted, when they assist us in solving problems. It is in this limited sense that we can understand James's discussion of the "will to believe."

Americans have tended to be somewhat naïve about experience. We make judgments based on a single experience taken out of context, or we accept experience at face value without adequate critical controls. We get caught in various forms of subjectivism. Experience is always selective and partial and therefore is abstracted from a broader possible experience. Experience is not knowledge, but there is no knowledge that is not the result of reflection on experience. Furthermore, experience may be in terms of sense data or a broader appropriation of stimuli or, as Whitehead suggested, there may be a nonsensuous perception of the whole. Both philosophers and theologians rely on experience, and there is a likelihood that every thinker is telling the story of his experiences however he may disguise them in abstract formulations.

The appeal to experience, in other words, does not make one an empiricist. Empiricism is an important element in American philosophy and theology; some would say it should be the dominant element. Empiricism has to do with method, with the way in which we handle and interpret experience as a basis for the construction of truth. An empirical method starts with data selected from experience, the selection depending on the end in view. These data need to be classified and evaluated. There must be opportunity for reflection and for the formulation of hypotheses derived inductively from the data. Then the hypotheses need to be tested by a return to experience and by a check with other interpretations for consistency and coherence. Much depends on the presuppositions of the original observer, his criteria for selecting data, and the way in which the data are interpreted. As a check, he needs also to know how to account for those data (selected or not) which seem to run counter to his conclusions.

In the field of theology, some empiricists take seriously both mysticism and religious experience; they refer back to religious experience as a form of verification; they use moral values and attainments as one kind of test; they check the data derived from their own religious tradition against those of other traditions and religions; they insist that the conclusions be checked against findings from other types of experience. But there are other empiricists who believe that religious experience is only a reflection of the religious consciousness and is therefore subjective; by rejecting this form of experience, they are therefore ready to examine experience in general to discover what works to transform human beings, or to explore the structure of all experience (as in phenomenology), or to appeal to experience as recorded in history or interpreted through social psychology or even to restrict theology to the data of anthropology.

There is, then, a variety of empiricisms or empirical methods, and the exploration of these differences is essential to an overall view of the American spirit in theology. Some empiricists insist that the whole range of human experience must be taken into consideration, and therefore they make use of the social sciences or political and economic interpretations as part of their methodology. Others turn to history and the Bible and see in the direction of historical events the working of God.

What is common to those using empirical methods is that they take the data of experience seriously as the primary source of human knowledge. When empirical theologians speak of revelation, they interpret it as those activities which can be observed through which God reveals himself in the processes of history and daily life. They are not likely to restrict this interpretation to a single tradition, not even to the Bible, although they take the biblical evidence with great seriousness.

Empirical methodology is an essential ingredient of the American spirit as applied to science, philosophy, and theology. It is more than an appeal to experience, which every philosopher and theologian accepts at least covertly. Even if the experience being interpreted is private or in one's solitariness, it provides data which are open to public inspection. In principle, at least, everyone can see for himself or herself what the theologian is talking about. Because the testing is open to inspection, it is self-correcting. Because any empirically based theory must be consistent with the rest of experience and coherent in itself, it is modified and adapted so that it fits in with an overriding theory of experience beyond the particular data that have been abstracted for testing. The meaning of experience in the last analysis is tested by how it works out, and thus empiricism and pragmatism remain wedded in American thought.

The American spirit has included an element of risk. The conclusions of American philosophers and theologians are to be understood in terms of tentativeness. Because truth is based on empiricism and pragmatic testing, it is open to correction. Doubt and skepticism are embedded in the American mind, so that questioning faces all conclusions, which may be considered only relatively certain. A kind of tentativeness runs through any empirical theology, for all the evidence can never be in. This is as it should be, for the certainties of commitment can be held and practiced consistently with the continuous revising of concepts and beliefs.

There is an open-ended element in such theology, for all the data do not point to a closed universe. Yet there is a tradition in both philosophy and science that points to determinism, which has been enforced by modern technology, that denies the elements of novelty, chance, and freedom. We find explications of fixed laws, activities determined, freedom denied, and fatalism the result. In contrast to this, discoveries in modern physics associated with relativity and quantum theory point to elements of chance. If we take experience seriously, we become aware of unpredictability, novelty, and chance in a world where human freedom seems to be an empirical fact, however limited it may be. Such thinking led James to belief in a pluralistic universe and in a God of limited power; F. S. C. Northrop derived the categories of chance and God's playfulness from the Heisenberg principle of indeterminacy;

Whitehead's approach to creativity stressed the concept of novelty. To some extent, this may reflect the experience of the American people with democracy as a fact of everyday living, with the adventures of the frontier in a nation in the making, and with the experience of genuine freedom in the process of growing up.

When empiricism and pragmatism are wedded in the American spirit, this leads to a demand for relevance in philosophical and theological thinking. If proposed beliefs do not make sense in ordinary life, they are likely to be dismissed. We have seen this as a problem in educational theory, and Dewey's instrumentalism in philosophy led to a problem-solving approach to an education that makes sense to the learner. Whitehead was in favor of teaching few but significant ideas and of insisting that unless beliefs make connection with experienced reality they would not be assimilated by the learner.

Some empiricists have been accused of not being hardheaded enough. There was a fundamental faith in progress running through Dewey's philosophy that reflected the times. But James was more realistic in his doctrine of meliorism, by which he meant that perhaps things were meant to work out well but that whatever man did would make a significant difference. The universe did not automatically guarantee progress, even with God intending it, unless there was intelligent commitment by mankind to the increase of good in the world. Therefore, James and his followers have always taken evil and sin seriously, even though they did not accept the usual Christian interpretation of the fact and meaning of man's fall.

Empiricism in philosophy and theology has looked carefully at the experiences of the individual and yet has insisted on some kind of corporate verification. James stressed the importance of the individual, while Peirce claimed that there needed to be a community of empiricists to share in the evaluation of the evidence, although this is not a final guarantee of freedom from error. It is easier to gather a community of scientists who share an empirical outlook than it is to form a community of empirical theologians, for the latter tend to remain rugged individualists in spite of their claims of a universal appeal to experience. Even Macintosh and Wieman, who were closer to each other than most in their claims for empiricism, never saw eye to eye in their interpretation of experience.

On the philosophical side, the spirit of American thinking has been favorable to religion. Peirce, who like James was interested in connections between things and activities, was not afraid of speculation about a world view derived from an evolutionary interpretation of nature, and this led him to speak of a God of love moving reality toward increased creativity and value. James began with religious experience and out of his radical empiricism was able to develop an idea of God as a divine "More." This was more important than his "will to believe" approach, which was much earlier. Even Dewey was able to talk about God as the relation between the ideal and the actual.

In the hands of such theologians as Macintosh and Wieman, this approach led to more fully developed discussions of the nature of God, although Wieman attempted to stay within the limits of his empiricism in his interpretation, while Macintosh built a superstructure to account for what James called "overbeliefs." The empirical method in theology found its strongest adherents in what we now call the Chicago school between 1900 and 1940.

Empirical Theology

There have been three steps in the development of empirical theology. First, Schleiermacher is usually called the father of empirical theology because his appeal was ultimately to what we call religious experience. In the religious consciousness there is a relation between the reality which we call God and our own sense of absolute dependence. This very important insight, however, was only one source of data for theology, and it did not approach what we might call empirical method. What Schleiermacher was pointing to was nearer to Rudolf Otto's description of the sense of the holy or numinous.

Second, as early as 1890, Lewis F. Stearns sought to develop *The Evidence of Christian Experience.* William Newton Clarke followed a similar approach to theology through experience, but for both men there was a primary appeal to the subjective element in religious experience as a basis for supporting Christian claims. Shortly thereafter, the Chicago school came into being with the historical and sociological approaches of Shailer Mathews, Shirley Jackson Case, George Burman Foster, and Gerald Birney Smith.[1]

---

[1] The best story of the Chicago school is found in Bernard E. Meland, "The Empirical Tradition in Theology at Chicago," in *The Future of Empirical Theology*, ed. Bernard E.

Third, the interpretation of experience moved from the subjective to sense data and then to the experience of relationships. This last step is what made empirical theology possible, for it assisted one to get beyond individualized experience of sensed things to experience in relationship. It was not the experience that provided the knowledge but the reflection on the experience through both induction and deduction.

Empirical method is the study of how something works, how the object of experience behaves, responds, or processes. Thus we find God by the way he functions. For the strict empiricist, the working of God is the reality of God. By means of observation, analysis, and interpretation, we are enabled to develop concepts that refer to reality. In spite of some claims, this is not a scientific method but is an adaptation of the scientific spirit to the data available for conclusions about religious beliefs. A concept held as a hypothesis is checked against reliable but not controlled data.

The strictest kind of empiricism limits experience to sense data, but under pressure no empiricist seems to remain there. Even Wieman, who is among the most rigorous, wrote that

perception, including sense experience, can carry with it appreciation most profound, intuition most penetrating, imaginative insight to the heights, personal relations most ecstatic, awareness of deity most transforming, corporate Christian experience most powerful.[2]

What he did was to enlarge the sphere to "perception, involving sense experience," which opens up the area of what Meland called the "appreciative consciousness." [3] But then where is the rigor of testing by experience?

Meland (Chicago: University of Chicago Press, 1969), pp. 1-62; see also Daniel Day Williams, "Tradition and Experience in American Theology," in *The Shaping of American Religion*, ed. James Ward Smith and A. Leland Jamison (Princeton: Princeton University Press, 1961), pp. 443-95; and in Harvey Arnold, *Near the Edge of Battle* (Chicago: Divinity School Association, University of Chicago, 1966). Others who could be considered members of the Chicago school were Edward Scribner Ames, A. Eustace Haydon, Henry Nelson Wieman, Bernard E. Meland, Bernard M. Loomer, and Daniel Day Williams. From the philosophical side, see Darnell Rucker, *The Chicago Pragmatists* (Minneapolis: University of Minnesota Press, 1969).

[2] Robert W. Bretall, ed., *The Empirical Theology of Henry Nelson Wieman* (New York: Macmillan, 1963), p. 42.

[3] See "The Appreciative Consciousness," in Bernard E. Meland, *Higher Education and the Human Spirit* (Chicago: University of Chicago Press, 1953), chap. 5.

If empiricism is interpreted too broadly, so that it cannot be clearly distinguished from other methods, such as the dialectical or rationalistic, we are in danger of what has been called "the fallacy of the suppressed correlative," [4] for no method is outside the empirical realm. As we shall see, there is a great variety of empiricisms and some of them approach this inclusive form, but others are simply ways of being factual and cautious in the appeal to public verification leading to tentative conclusions.

It is not always possible to discover the hidden presuppositions of specific examples of empirical method. For some thinkers, the task is obviously apologetic and their own tradition is a given which is to be demonstrated. For others, there is a naturalistic metaphysics which serves as the framework in which the findings of experience are to be interpreted. For still others, the lure of the supernatural is so strong that they move immediately beyond the empirically given to claims that cannot be verified. Some work entirely within the Christian tradition, and others seek evidence from the religions of the world. For some there is a use of relative values to interpret absolute values, which logically if not empirically is confusing. Others seriously consider history as providing empirical evidence and some almost completely ignore it. Metaphysically, many empiricists lean toward process philosophy as either a metaphysical framework or a metaphysical conclusion.

We can see the connection between empiricism and metaphysics if we examine the way in which James worked. He referred to his position as a "metaphysics of radical empiricism." The presuppositions of his empiricism, in terms of the stream of consciousness, the realism of his epistemology, and his pragmatism, led toward a dynamic view of emergence and process. The connection between James and Whitehead becomes obvious when the experience of the whole is considered more fundamental than the experience of particulars. When empiricism is restricted to sense data and to particulars, it does not lead to process metaphysics, and we will see that Dewey refused to speculate about metaphysics; but the sense of a dynamic whole as pointing to the structure of experience makes some kind of emergent evolution,

---

[4] J. Loewenberg, "What Is Empirical?" *Journal of Philosophy*, vol. 37 (May 11, 1923), p. 282; cited in James Alfred Martin, Jr., *Empirical Philosophies of Religion* (New York: King's Crown Press, 1945), p. 3.

philosophy of organism, or process metaphysics a normal development.

One needs to work with presuppositions. The problem is to clarify them so that one may either utilize them effectively or make adjustments for the bias that is present. Wieman, for example, was quite clear in his assumption of naturalism as the metaphysical framework for all his interpretations. Macintosh spent a great deal of effort in establishing a theory of knowledge that he used for his interpretation of the data of religious experience. At other points, however, we are not sure of what is presupposed and what is discovered as a result of careful consideration of the data. Sometimes we are not clear as to the nature of the data, yet we must be aware of the data if we are to understand the conclusions reached.

The appeal is to see for yourself, but for this to occur there must be openness about both the data and their methods of interpretation. We can test a hypothesis through observation, agreement, and coherence, we are told. If we take action on similar data, develop our skills of observation, and then examine the outcome which has been predicted, we have knowledge that is tentatively acceptable by ourselves and others. The concepts are tentative, but they point toward a reality with which we can have relationships. The idea of God so developed is an operational one that guides us in our relationship to the reality and keeps us open to richer concepts. Such an operational concept becomes a guide to action.[5]

Religious Realism

The earlier empirical theology shared many of the presuppositions of liberal theology. Liberalism as an attitude tended to be open to new knowledge from any source and was particularly important as an aspect of the development of biblical scholarship. But liberal theology as such reflected views about the natural goodness of man and the inevitability of progress that could not stand up against broader views of what was happening in history; it also tended to take the subjective aspects of experience as a basis for traditional supernaturalism. Shailer Mathews, for example, rejected the term "liberalism" in favor of "modernism" in order to emphasize a more critical use of empirical method.[6]

---

[5] See Henry Nelson Wieman and Walter Marshall Horton, *The Growth of Religion* (Chicago: Willett, Clark & Co., 1938), pp. 258-59, 343-45.

[6] See Meland, *The Future of Empirical Theology*, p. 10.

By 1931, this led a number of thinkers to cooperate on a volume entitled *Religious Realism*.[7] Macintosh, the editor, wrote that religious realism places God in experience but that God exists independently of such experience. By reflection on both experience in general and religious experience, we can gain knowledge both of God's existence and to some degree of what his nature is.[8] Another contributor, Robert L. Calhoun, stressed the attitude of being critical and level-headed in facing one's environment and of not being dogmatic about conclusions reached.[9] Wieman, in a later article, classified realism under four headings: (1) Metaphysically, it is the belief that events, things, and forms exist independently of God; they are the materials through which and with which God works. (2) Epistemologically, the realists are divided into two camps; there are the neorealists and the critical realists, both claiming, in agreement, that the object exists independently of its being perceived or known by a mind. (3) Evil is recognized as a definite fact to be considered. (4) There is a sense of urgency, for realism is predominantly practical and is willing to act before all the data are gathered.[10]

Religious realism served as a purge for the false optimism and easygoing complacency of the period. It was willing to deal with the facts of sin and social evil. It tended to interpret God as one who is struggling against opposition in order to bring about higher values. It saw God, values, evil, persons, and the world as objective elements or processes. This approach was a way of verifying some aspects of what man already knows in other ways. Some realists were more strictly empirical than others, of course, and there was always the temptation to go beyond the evidence. Wieman was the watchdog who tried to keep within a narrow interpretation of the presumed facts, while others insisted on overbeliefs.[11]

It is not always clear that process theology is grounded in empiricism and is related to the thinking of James and Henri Bergson. Whitehead clearly made use of both the concrete data of particular experiences and

---

[7] Douglas Clyde Macintosh, ed., *Religious Realism* (New York: Macmillan, 1931).

[8] Ibid., p. v.

[9] Ibid., pp. 195-96.

[10] See Henry Nelson Wieman, "Types of Theism," *Christendom*, vol. 1, no. 1 (Autumn 1935), p. 199.

[11] See "Religious Realism in America," *Modern Churchman*, vol. 27 (Dec. 1937), pp. 495-507.

the broader concept of the vision of the whole, as did James and Bergson. But Whitehead saw the limitations of particular experiences abstracted from the wider areas of perception, although he did not eliminate them. His position was, as Meland put it, "empirical with a difference." [12] This broader interpretation of experience, including nonsensuous experience, is clearer in the writings of Schubert Ogden or Daniel Day Williams than, say, of John B. Cobb, Jr., but is basic to the thinking of all of them. This development was not evident in most of the pre-World War II contributions, except for Meland, but it is significant for understanding more recent ways of using empiricism in theology.

Empiricism and Beyond

Many of the pre-World War II empirical theologians agreed pretty much on their conclusions, which were limited. They could point to a process in man's experience which makes for values, leads to transformation of persons, or is the creativity at work in our midst. Whether one examined the data of religious experience per se, looked at experience in general, examined history or social processes from an empirical viewpoint, or considered the findings of mystical experience and awe before the holy, it was hard to get beyond a process that helped to produce personality. The objection of the nonempiricists was that this is not the deity of revealed religion or even the God that man needs in order to worship and be obedient.

There were two possible responses to this objection. The first was that this is the only God there is, and that if we cannot see the religious values in commitment to "the growth of meaning and value in the world" it is the fault of our wishful thinking and the projection of our needs on the universe. It is possible, from this viewpoint, to stick to a careful empirical analysis from the standpoint of philosophy of religion. Certainly religious language is full of poetry, myth, and anthropocentric thinking, but it has only emotive value and is not necessarily related to things as they are. There was a kind of religious positivism in this position that anticipated the criticisms of the language philosophers at a later date, except that the empiricists claimed that such linguistic criticisms did not touch the empiricists at the point of verification.

Other empiricists took their clue from James and his "overbeliefs,"

---

[12] Meland, *The Future of Empirical Theology*, p. 54.

which go beyond the evidence. Empiricism strictly interpreted, they said, did not provide an adequate concept of God, although it is important to have an empirically verified minimum concept of God as the foundation upon which one can build a theological superstructure that is consistent with the empirical findings. Macintosh did this through what he called reasonable beliefs and permissible surmises, which enabled him (according to his critics) to bring into this theological superstructure the whole of his Baptist tradition. Others claimed that once the empirical foundations are clear there can be proper rational and logical developments. If one broadens the uses of empiricism to include the vision of the whole, as do the Whiteheadians, it is possible to develop a process theology that is consistent with the empirical basis.

The empirical approach, then, is relatively simple. It begins with the question of how God works, or what working in the world has the value of deity. It is a functional approach through experience, is pragmatic in its testing, and is metaphysical in its implications. One can start with any concept of God as a hypothesis and then follow through with an analysis of what is happening in particular or in general terms which can be applied to God. It may be that what we discover in and through experience does not dovetail with traditional doctrines, and this is exactly what we find in the writings of James, Wieman, Whitehead, Hartshorne, and others. Then the problem is to find ways of redefining God so that the concept fits what can be discovered and tested through empirical methods. Through this approach, there is enough evidence based on the data of experience to establish the hypothesis that there are processes or is a process which brings values into the world, which transforms human beings, and which as creativity makes human life dynamic and worthwhile. It does much more than this, but if it establishes an immanent deity in these minimum terms, we have a basis for reflecting on this evidence in order to construct a full-fledged theology.

Empiricists can claim that they are fulfilling the role traditionally given to natural theology. In natural theology it is claimed that man can have a natural knowledge of God and that this is the basis on which one can develop a revealed theology. This same pattern is used by many empiricists, who maintain that empirical theology is logically prior to any development of theology in a rational superstructure. It can be related to any religious tradition, not just Christianity. But because

Christianity is operating in a culture which has been influenced by empiricism at all levels, empiricism can serve more effectively as a check on Christian theology, as a basis from which its thinking starts, and as a way toward a reconstructed theology for today.[13]

The pre-World War II empiricists did not get this far, but they started in this direction. During the long period when forms of supernaturalism dominated the theological scene, not much attention was paid to the empiricists; however, since the impact of the God-is-dead movement, there is a new awareness of the significance of the need for what Ian T. Ramsey called the "empirical fit" for today's thinking.

Empiricism was one fundamental element in the American spirit. It was applied in many different ways, as we will see, usually in conjunction with pragmatism. Pragmatism is even more uniquely American, and some claim that it is the only unique contribution that America has made to philosophical thinking.[14] It originated primarily in the creative thinking of Peirce and soon after that was popularized by James. It became the basis of a school of thought under Dewey at Chicago and, in turn, affected not only philosophy but also educational theory.[15] Under James it led to a pro-religious pluralistic metaphysics and later to the process philosophy of Whitehead. Under Dewey it led to a more scientific outlook that was skeptical of any metaphysics and of most religious claims about reality. Empiricism, pragmatism, and pluralism, then, we see as significant elements comprising the American spirit, and they have affected religious thinking through the years.

The Interlude

Somewhere about 1940, the sheen had worn off the empirical and pragmatic methods in both philosophy and theology. Instead of taking empiricism seriously as a basis for understanding reality, philosophy turned away from its American heritage to European imports. From the continent came existentialism, with its emphasis on the interiority of experience and the meaninglessness of the outside world. From Great

---

[13] See my "The New Naturalism and Christianity," *Anglican Theological Review*, vol. 22 (Jan. 1940), pp. 25-35; also, my "Wieman's Theological Empiricism," in Bretall, *The Empirical Theology of Henry Nelson Wieman*, pp. 38-39.

[14] See Edward C. Moore, *American Pragmatism: Peirce, James, and Dewey* (New York: Columbia Press, 1961), p. vii.

[15] See Rucker, *The Chicago Pragmatists*.

Britain came a concern for logical positivism which focused primarily on philosophy as a brilliant analysis of the use of words. This led to a profound skepticism about any knowledge at all. As logical positivism eliminated any logical status for metaphysics and God-talk, so the reduction of pragmatism to a way of examining social and political policies effectively eliminated it from moral and metaphysical questions. Of course, there were complex factors at work in our culture and in the concerns of philosophers, and to this extent the change was a legitimate part of the American scene, but the Golden Age of American philosophy was tarnished.

Something similar happened to theology. Out of the nihilism of post-World War II Europe came a recovery of supernaturalism, reacting more against German religious liberalism than against empiricism and pragmatism as such, so that the names of Schleiermacher and Ritschl vanished from theological discourse, and we heard the voices of Barth, Brunner, and Bultmann. In America, the giants were the Niebuhr brothers and Tillich, while the voice of empiricism was heard from Wieman, who kept at work while aware of the developments around him, lecturing constantly in the Midwest and Southwest, from Meland, and from a few of their students. The contributions of those influenced by Barth, from a later empirical approach, were evaluated as both a needed corrective of some of the findings of empiricism and as an unnecessary obfuscation of the basic issues. The God-is-dead movement focused on supernaturalism, because of supernaturalism's lack of concern with verification as well as for various cultural reasons, such as dissatisfaction with its claims about the nature of revelation, and this led to the emptiness of the period immediately afterward when a group of theologians said that even the foundations for theology were gone and all we could do was to take soundings.

But if we are to take soundings in the post-Barthian period, they need to be empirical and pragmatic ones that lead to a world view that is consistent with scientific thinking, as illustrated most clearly in the thought of James and Whitehead. There is a call for a broader and more comprehensive interpretation of experience that will not be less rigorous than the pre-World War II type but will have a richer dimension than, for example, the thought of Dewey. If we are going to have a reason for the faith that is in us and learn to trust reality, and if there is a correspondence between what we experience, think, and do, we need an investigation that begins with a reconsideration of experience. A more refined and sophisticated interpretation of experience and its working in practice, within the framework of an adequate metaphysics, needs to be reworked as a basis for a theology for today.

After World War II, there was a brief period of surging confidence in theology, based primarily upon neoorthodoxy. But then came the attacks of the death-of-God movement and a rise of skepticism about any theology at all. This led to a renewed interest in empiricism and process thinking, especially as expressed in the thought of Whitehead and Hartshorne, and developed in specifically Christian ways by Schubert M. Ogden and Daniel Day Williams.

In order to understand this development, it is necessary to go back to its beginnings in the thought of James, and to see how Dewey, G. B. Smith, Ames, Mathews, Wieman, and Macintosh made contributions to what can now be seen as a movement in theological thinking. After a critical evaluation of these variations of empiricism, we can look to the contemporary scene stemming from Whitehead, Hartshorne, Ogden, Williams, and others.

Radical
Empiricism
and Pragmatism

THE AMERICAN TEMPER HAS BEEN EMPIRICAL, PRAGMATIC, AND activistic. Philosophy, until the time of William James, rarely dwelt on these themes, because it was looking for something more stable and settled. But James approached philosophy with a skepticism about anything that was fixed and any beliefs that were considered permanent. While he did not reflect the pious attitudes of evangelicalism, he did have a pious father. And although he was trained in science, he did not fail to appreciate the wider scope of experience. Furthermore, although he never had a profound religious experience, he had what he called a "mystical germ" that made him appreciative even of the more extreme types of experience.

This most thoroughly American of philosophers had been educated partly in Europe and had returned there from time to time as an adult. One would expect a fully home-grown type such as Josiah Royce, who was born in Grass Valley, California, to be the typical American philosopher, but Royce was more at home in the traditional views of idealism. It was James, with his irregular education, medical degree from Harvard, and early interest in biology and psychology, who developed a philosophy based on radical empiricism, pragmatism, and pluralistic metaphysics, and who became a champion of religious beliefs based on such methods.

Nothing was beyond James's interests. His sister recounted an occasion when "William expressed himself and his environment to perfection when he replied to my question about his house in Chocorua. 'Oh, it's the most delightful house you ever saw; it has fourteen doors, all opening outwards.' His brain isn't limited to fourteen, perhaps unfortunately." [1] He was interested in everything that could be experienced, including séances and morbid psychology and laughing gas, and to everything he brought a sympathetic yet critical attitude. He was always looking for new alternatives of interpretation, taking nothing for granted, especially conventional habits of mind and the idealism of such philosophers as Hegel and Bradley, to whom he was temperamentally opposed.

The center of his way of thinking he called "radical empiricism," which was an approach through "pure" experience, something prior to consciousness and self. He was not always clear about this, as we shall see, but it was here that he found the raw data for his philosophy. He believed that someone could be a radical empiricist without being a pragmatist, or a pragmatist without being a radical empiricist, but in his own thought pragmatism became the method by which to develop the meaning of experience, and the outcome was a pluralistic universe.

In experience the self is not passive but active, and therefore consciousness and will make a difference. The self approaches and selects from experience with a purpose, for by being partial and selective experience can serve human purpose, and thus life becomes concrete and ideas have "a cutting edge." Philosophy, for James, was supposed to be significant for daily life, not a hothouse flower protected from reality as experienced.

He realized that such knowledge was limited and that men moved beyond the limitations of empiricism and pragmatism in religious knowledge into what he called "overbeliefs." But he allowed for the same extensions of knowledge in other fields. Sometimes we cannot have immediate knowledge, and then we have to settle for something not as satisfactory. Most of our so-called knowledge is indirect, but at

---

[1] Ralph Barton Perry, *The Thought and Character of William James* (Boston: Little, Brown & Co., 1935), vol. 1, p. 411; see also James Dittes, "Beyond William James," in *Beyond the Classics? Essays in the Scientific Study of Religion,* ed. Charles Y. Glock and Phillip E. Hammond (New York: Harper & Row, 1973), pp. 291-354; and William A. Clebsch, *American Religious Thought: A History* (Chicago: University of Chicago Press, 1973), pp. 125-87.

crucial points we have data from experience by which we ground ourselves in the real world which exists independently of our experience of it.

The side of James which was most obvious in his philosophy was his activistic, healthy-minded approach to life, but the other aspect must be kept in focus. James suffered from various kinds of ill health, mostly nervous, and from about 1900 on he was restricted in his activities because of a heart condition brought on by overexertion. He knew times of extreme depression and exhibited what he called the "sick soul" approach to life. Both elements of his character are evident in his approach to religion. He was sympathetic with those who leaned on their religious faith and saw the comfort that is experienced, but he also saw religion as the great energizer of persons and thought of man as cooperating with God for the achievement of great moral ends. He never had what he would have called a mystical experience (although in his letters there is evidence of experiences that others might identify as mystical).

James stressed the personal aspect of religious experience to the neglect of any corporate element. He saw the fruits of private religious experience in corporate moral action, but he never dealt with the nature of the church or with traditional Christian beliefs. Yet there is an impression that he was both sympathetic to religious insights and had a religious faith of his own.

Radical Empiricism

In *A Pluralistic Universe*, James wrote, "Let empiricism once become associated with religion, as hitherto, through some strange misunderstanding, it has been associated with irreligion, and I believe that a new era of religion as well as of philosophy will be ready to begin." [2] Experience is rich in its fullness and therefore can lead to what seem excesses, but "without too much you cannot have enough, of anything." [3] Furthermore, because religious experience is personal, its interpretations are likely to be highly personalized.

Until the time of James, empiricism was usually interpreted in terms

---

[2] William James, *A Pluralistic Universe* (New York: Longmans, Green & Co., 1909), p. 314; also *Essays in Radical Empiricism* (New York: Longmans, Green & Co., 1912), p. xii.

[3] Ibid., p. 316.

of subject and object and of discrete experiences that were separate in nature. Sense data were paramount, and no connections of data were considered part of the experience. To this empiricism James brought some radical notes: consciousness is a function in relation rather than a substance, pure experience is prior to everything else, and experience of relations is as important as the objects being related. Let us look at these claims.

Much of what James wrote about consciousness and pure experience was anticipated in his *Psychology*, but it came out as a basis for knowledge in his *Essays in Radical Empiricism*. Consciousness is not made up of *stuff*, but rather is a relationship that holds together both subject and object. The subjective realm of the mental order and the objective realm of the physical order are modes of experience and are related in what we call consciousness seen as a function in which the mental and physical orders overlap. "Consciousness connotes a kind of external relation, and does not denote a special stuff or way of being." [4]

Underlying consciousness is pure experience, "the immediate flux of life which furnishes the material to our later reflection with its conceptual categories." [5] Like the experience we assume in a newborn babe, it is a *that* without a *what*. It can be only relatively pure, however, because we give it some sort of verbalization even in talking about it. It is the flux from which we choose our particular experiences, including all the disjunctions and conjunctions.

James did not always leave pure experience in the state of flux, however, for it is also a methodological principle which says that

nothing shall be admitted as fact, except what can be experienced at some definite time by some experient; and for every feature of fact ever so experienced, a definite place must be found somewhere in the final system of reality. In other words: Everything real must be experienced somewhere, and every kind of thing experienced must somewhere be real.[6]

Basic to this approach and unique in James's thought at the time was

[4] James, *Essays in Radical Empiricism*, p. 27; see William James, *Psychology* (New York: Henry Holt & Co., 1890), vol. 1, p. 225.
[5] James, *A Pluralistic Universe*, p. 348.
[6] James, *Essays in Radical Empiricism*, p. 160.

his insistence on the experience of external relations. This is what made his empiricism radical: "The relations that connect experiences must themselves be experienced relations, and any kind of relation experienced must be accounted as 'real' as anything else in the system." [7] Relations, whether conjunctive or disjunctive, keep changing, and the experience of continuous transition makes it cognitive. "Relations are of different degrees of intimacy." [8] They can be continuous or discontinuous. Ultimately, they include a relation of one to all the others. The continuous transitions can be seen in a number of contexts, both mental and physical, and in all such contexts we can establish an objective reality. As we move from moment to moment, we feel the continuous transition. But we also experience discontinuity, as when we seek to move to an experience which another has had; for we move from "a thing lived to another thing only conceived, and the break is positively experienced and noted." [9]

"My account of truth is realistic," wrote James, "and follows the epistemological dualism of common sense." [10] The pragmatic empiricist asserts that reality simply is, and concepts or beliefs that point to reality in a satisfactory way are in so far true. Because the test of the truth of an idea always involves its capacity to function satisfactorily in relation to an object or context of other experiences, epistemological realism is considered essential to this approach. We are still dealing with a world and life which consists of transitions that are experienced as relationships, and even when a terminal point seems to be reached, new processes carry us further. In this sense, there is a "beyond" in our future. Such a philosophy fits in with pluralism, novelty, indeterminism, moralism, and theism.

Pragmatism

James's epistemological realism was established by his empiricism and the resulting knowledge by acquaintance with experience. But this is a very limited area, and most of our explorations are in the domain of what he called knowledge "about." Because we have knowledge by

[7] Ibid., p. 42.
[8] Ibid., p. 44.
[9] Ibid., p. 49.
[10] William James, *The Meaning of Truth* (New York: Longmans, Green & Co., 1909), p. 217; see pp. 190-216.

acquaintance, we can be sure of our assertions concerning existence, and we are therefore free to make similar claims for knowledge about existence. Here pragmatism becomes an essential method. James said that one could be a radical empiricist without being a pragmatist, and vice versa, but for James pragmatism filled out the empiricist picture of the world of reality. Beyond pragmatism he also held that men could hold overbeliefs in the light of their right to believe beyond the evidence in specific circumstances.[11]

If truth happens to an idea, if it becomes true because it is verified in events, we need to know what James meant by verification. We look at the consequences as they work out in practice, which may lead through other ideas and events to the end of a sequence. True ideas established in this way may be used in the immediate situation, or they may be stored away for future use. Just as bank notes are acceptable so long as they are either not challenged or meet the challenge, so ideas have a similar cash value. They can be verified if necessary, but for most of our lives we live as if our accepted ideas are true until questioned. It is all right to assume the existence of Israel or Timbuktu, even though one has never been there. The idea works for us. We know that such an idea is verifiable, because it has been verified by somebody.[12]

This seems perfectly straightforward for verifiable physical facts or events or relations, but there are also mental facts and abstract ideas. Such purely mental ideas, said James, are principles or definitions and are obvious, so that sense verification is not necessary. Relations between numbers, colors, or even cause and effect would qualify. Such mental objects, once established as true, have an "eternal" character, but one can put them in their place only by means of concrete things, for otherwise there would be an error in naming or classifying.[13]

This brings us to the question of "leading." We have a body of truths as part of our inheritance, and we need to establish agreement among tradition, abstract ideas, and concepts verified by their working in experience. There is a demand for consistency. This kind of agreement, said James, is "an affair of leading—leading that is useful because it is into quarters that contain objects that are important."[14] This results in

---

[11] See Ralph Barton Perry, *In the Spirit of William James* (New Haven: Yale University Press, 1938), pp. 71-72.
[12] William James, *Pragmatism* (New York: Longmans, Green & Co., 1907), pp. 201-9.
[13] Ibid., pp. 209-10.
[14] Ibid., p. 215.

the pragmatic requirement that there has to be verification by sensible experience somewhere along the way. Thus we can take scientific formulae that only speak as if something were so—say, electrons—and the test is whether the idea works, although we do not believe literally in electrons. There can be relations between thoughts in the intellect as well as between ideas and percepts, and both are open to a pragmatic test, although this may be very remote. Knowledge may be more indirect than at first suspected, for the truth of an idea may lie in its "satisfactory adaptation" rather than in any kind of resemblance with the object.[15]

A pragmatism such as that of James, interpreted in terms of a pluralistic universe, does not lead to the Absolute, or even to a supernatural deity in charge of the whole works. It is at the opposite end from a faith that rests on a supernatural revelation. Pragmatism is not authoritarian about its assertions, although very close to it in what it denies. What it claims is that the hypothesis that God exists works in practice, but that this proposal needs constant refinement in the light of practical experience within the larger framework of a pluralistic metaphysics.

Truth has to do with ideas as they relate to experience. A true idea is one that is workable in experience. One starts with objective facts and claims and then discovers which claims work and which do not. Ideas both point and lead. They may point toward other ideas or to the actual experience, and they lead us from one moment of experience to another that is worthwhile.[16]

But truth claims are always provisional and open to further testing and revision. They may be the most complete possible statement at the present time, but the future experience may turn these ideas in new directions. Nothing is absolutely fixed; we live in a universe of experience that is constantly changing and in which there is novelty. Yet, when we come upon a new experience, there is a sense in which it was always there for us both to create and find. "Pragmatically, virtual and actual truth mean the same thing: the possibility of only one answer, *when once the question is raised.*" [17]

---

[15] See James, *Pragmatism*, p. 454.
[16] See James, *The Meaning of Truth*, pp. 44-45, and *Pragmatism*, pp. 204-5.
[17] James, *The Meaning of Truth*, p. 101; see pp. 90-100.

Experience is a wide-open domain, constantly being enriched in itself and being expanded as a result of leading and pointing ideas. Empiricism combined with pragmatism results in conclusions by which we can live, but remains open to both new evidence and new ideas. When applied to the evidence of religious experience, the resulting concepts are of significance for our total being.

Religious Experience

"The plain truth is that to interpret religion one must in the end look at the immediate content of the religious consciousness." [18] This is what James accomplished in *The Varieties of Religious Experience*. He opened the many doors of his mind outward as he sought to analyze and classify the ways in which religion is experienced. Even then, he restricted himself. Acknowledging that religion may be expressed in corporate and institutional forms, he looked for religious experience in individuals as the basis for this particular study. [19]

He was quite clear that this was not a scientific study, for both religious experience and persons' responses are so varied and vague that he was dealing with borderline questions. To sharpen the issue, his purpose was to look at religious experience in its extreme forms, "as in a sense a study of morbid psychology, mediating and interpreting to the philistine much that he would otherwise despise and reject utterly." [20] But he was clear that the significant element in these experiences was not its psychotic origins (if that is what they were) but its pragmatic results.

Furthermore, he did not consider the extreme forms of experience and belief as the norm. "By subtracting and toning down extravagances we may thereupon proceed to trace the boundaries of its legitimate sway." [21] His empiricism and pragmatism were thus brought to bear in a critical manner upon the question of the truth of religious concepts as tested in experience.

He distinguished between the healthy-minded and the sick soul, between the once-born and the twice-born, between the optimists and

---

[18] William James, *The Varieties of Religious Experience* (New York: Longmans, Green & Co., 1902), p. 12 note.
[19] Ibid., p. 29.
[20] Perry, *The Thought and Character of William James*, vol. 2, p. 325.
[21] James, *The Varieties of Religious Experience*, p. 50.

the pessimists, and between the tough-minded and the tender-minded. These distinctions were not always the same, for there is a tender-minded optimism which is open to mind cures and remains healthy-minded, to which the Lutheran doctrine of salvation by faith and the Methodist emphasis on free grace are related, along with Emerson's Oversoul.[22] The sick soul, on the other hand, has a strong sense of sin and pessimism and needs comfort more than encouragement; through conversion his divided self can be made whole.

The great chapters on "saintliness" point to the fruit of religious experience and faith. James analyzed many kinds of saints, saw the weaknesses of those who lacked one quality or another (and some so-called saints were stupid), and then pointed to the obvious life fulfillment of the greatest saints. Even the lesser saints have much to be said for them. If we are to be saints, we have to do it in our own way and in terms of our own unique qualities. This is the pragmatic truth of religion in terms of its results among human beings.

Religious experience operates in the area which Frederick Myers called the "subliminal" consciousness. One finds all sorts of strange things going on in this area, including silly ideas and distorted memories; but it also may be the seat of genius, where various religious experiences have their origin and from where they invade conscious life. James located prayer, conversion, and mystical experiences in this realm.[23]

James responded to mysticism with great sympathy, although he claimed never to have had a mystical experience. Such invasions from the subconscious that control the conscious mind lead to a "sense of union with the power beyond us," and this "is a sense of something, not merely apparently, but literally true." [24] At this point we have religious data or facts and not merely ideas, and these data lead to a pragmatic verification of religious ideas.

In a biting letter to James H. Leuba, a psychologist who reduced all James's claims to subjectivism, James responded by referring to his "mystical germ. It is a very common germ. It creates the rank and file of believers. . . . Once allow the mystical germ to influence our beliefs, and I believe that we are in my position." [25]

---

[22] See James, *The Varieties of Religious Experience*, p. 111.
[23] See James, *The Varieties of Religious Experience*, pp. 231-36, 511-12.
[24] Ibid., p. 513.
[25] Perry, *The Thought and Character of William James*, vol. 2, p. 351.

The Will to Believe

James not only sought to demonstrate the objective element in religious beliefs, he was willing to admit that much of what we hold is subjective. For this situation, he was willing to borrow Leuba's term, "faith-state." This state may not have much intellectual content, even when it is associated with beliefs dogmatically held. Even without further justification, religion has a sufficient and permanent function.

But faith does not stop there. It seeks a greater certainty. It prefers to risk seeking truth rather than to avoid error at all costs. If something really ought to be true, and there is no strong contrary evidence, we have a right to consider it true for us. Here James was dealing with probabilities of a statistical sort, as with a fire insurance company. If the odds are 2 to 1, we do not go halfway with someone; we have to make a choice.

James's melioristic universe was much like this. There are odds that human purposes (and divine ones) may work out, *if* man does his share. If religious experience provides the direction and the transforming energy that make possible man's cooperation, he has no right to refuse. We are to trust the powers that be and do our best.

> We can *create* the conclusion, then. We can and may, as it were, jump with both feet off the ground into or towards a world of which we trust the other parts to meet our jump—and *only so* can the *making* of a perfected world of the pluralistic pattern ever take place. Only through our precursive trust in it can it come into being.[26]

The statement just quoted is from "Faith and the Right to Believe," a later interpretation of James's famous and often misinterpreted and misused essay, "The Will to Believe." In this earlier work James made it clear that he would not have used the argument at a meeting of the Salvation Army, for it would be inappropriate in terms of the members' options. But for the scientific community that James was addressing, which refused to move on anything unless all the evidence was in, his pragmatic approach to the need for belief and action was significant, for

---

[26] William James, *Some Problems of Philosophy* (New York: Longmans, Green & Co., 1911), p. 230; see pp. 221-31.

it meant that persons would not be paralyzed when faced with forced, living, and momentous options. It was not a matter of denying or ignoring the data or of being foolhardy, but of knowing when to act in the light of incomplete evidence.[27]

John Dewey was helpful for James at this point. There have been discussions as to whether James should have said the "will" or the "right" to believe. Dewey said that if "will" means "active personal participation" we have the correct formulation. What is demanded is not a conscious intention or a logical right to believe, but a personal response by taking a stand or making a move.[28]

Normally James kept his empiricism and his pragmatism in a dual balance, with the weight in favor of empiricism, but he was always aware that much of our knowledge cannot be empirically verified, although often it can be worked out pragmatically in terms of satisfying experiences. In this case, where empirical evidence was not conclusive, he asserted that it is possible to test the pragmatic consequences of belief in God in terms of living out one's faith.

God

J. Seelye Bixler suggested that there were three stages in James's development of the idea of God.[29] James's earliest articles, going back to the period 1880 to 1895, as found in *The Will to Believe*, were in the strenuous mood, meeting man's need for support as he sought worthy goals. In "The Sentiment of Rationality" he sought to interpret faith as believing beyond the evidence and contributing data to add to the evidence, thus creating its own verification. So man stands on his own feet in faith; God responds. We discover that the universe is moral.

But already James was moving beyond this point. Not only is there a mind who cares for our purposes, but perhaps God is not the only mind. So James began at an early date to think of pluralism as a possibility, a multiverse, perhaps, in which God has plenty of difficulties.

James's empiricism and pragmatism were much more in evidence

[27] William James, *The Will to Believe and Other Essays in Popular Philosophy and Human Immortality* (New York: Longmans, Green & Co., 1897), pp. 25-29.

[28] John Dewey, *Essays in Experimental Logic* (Chicago: University of Chicago Press, 1916), p. 328.

[29] See J. Seelye Bixler, *Religion in the Philosophy of William James* (Boston: Marshall Jones Co., 1926), pp. 122-65.

operating in tandem when he moved into his second stage, exemplified by his Gifford Lectures on *The Varieties of Religious Experience*. His empiricism seemed to be open to almost any kind of evidence, especially that of the extreme variety that made clear the difference between religious and ordinary experience. The task of empiricism was to work comparatively with this richness of data and to spell out a philosophic base that eliminated the extravagances and stressed the verified conclusions. By now James was more aware of the passive as well as the strenuous mood in religious living, and therefore he indicated the ways in which the fruits of religious experience were evident in both the healthy-minded and the sick-soul types. We not only can be strengthened in our tasks but also be saved from wrongness due to our relationship with higher powers. For some this may be a sudden experience, for others it may be gradual, and for some it may be part of all their lives. Here, says James, is what happens:

> *He becomes conscious that this higher part is conterminous and continuous with a MORE of the same quality, which is operative in the universe outside of him, and which he can keep in working touch with, and in a fashion get on board of and save himself when all his lower being has gone to pieces in the wreck.*[30]

To all of James's case studies this description would apply. There is, then, some empirical evidence that the MORE exists and acts. James believed that most theologians would agree but would not stop at this point. Here is a divine something of which we can say that the idea of it is literally true.

In the third stage, according to Bixler, James brought together the arguments from the *Varieties* and his earlier pragmatic approach within a more thoroughly worked-out view of a pluralistic universe. By escaping from metaphysical monism and a deity who is responsible for everything including evil, we should "assume that the superhuman consciousness, however vast it may be, has itself an external environment, and consequently is finite." [31]

At this point, James leaned toward a view that reality is made up of minds or psyches, in what is called panpsychism, pluralistically con-

---

[30] *The Varieties of Religious Experience*, p. 508 (James's italics).
[31] James, *A Pluralistic Universe*, pp. 310-11.

ceived but based on idealism. Here he was in the area of overbeliefs; although he was attracted to this position he never gave his consent to it. He remained a pluralist, and yet God was in everything without being identified with everything. Seeing that God has an environment, his view was close to panentheism, in which God is in all but is also beyond the all.[32] He reasserted his empiricism in relation to religion in the final chapter of *A Pluralistic Universe* and remained a realist in his theory of knowledge.

In the last chapter of *Pragmatism*, he formulated his doctrine of meliorism, which "treats salvation as neither necessary nor impossible"[33] but "as a possibility." Man and God can move to bring about the necessary conditions by working together, but God acts by persuasion and man may overrule God temporarily.

James thought that overbeliefs could go in different directions, depending on the makeup of one's personality or temperament. The really tough-minded do not think that they need any religion, for they tend to be self-sufficient. The tender-minded, who are sometimes referred to as the sick souls, need the safe harbor of monism and an absolute deity. But there are those who rebel against both extremes, for they find that their experiences have tuned them into a pluralistic universe in which a moral deity is at work.[34]

James's overbeliefs fitted the last-mentioned type.

> The whole drift of my education goes to persuade me that the world of our present consciousness is only one out of many worlds of consciousness that exist, and that those other worlds must contain experiences which have a meaning for our life also; and that although in the main their experiences and those of this world keep discrete, yet the two become continuous at certain points, and higher energies filter in.[35]

Was he talking of panpsychism or of the "wider self" which has been emphatically established as a result of his studies? It is hard to tell.

When he spoke of a "piecemeal supernaturalism" to account for specific and concrete experiences, showing himself open even to a

---

[32] Perry, *The Thought and Character of William James*, vol. 2, p. 592.
[33] James, *Pragmatism*, p. 286.
[34] See ibid., p. 301.
[35] James, *The Varieties of Religious Experience*, p. 519.

42

possible polytheism in a pluralistic world, he was exhibiting a creative and magnanimous mind at work. It was this aspect of his contribution that Ralph Barton Perry emphasized in *In the Spirit of William James*. It is evident that a mind as sympathetic, open, and wide-ranging as James's fell into traps of incoherence and inconsistency. He believed in a loose-jointed universe, and his philosophy reflected this. But Perry also thought of James as having a spiritual statesmanship of which only great minds are capable. It was the fertility of James's thought that is significant, for many theologians and philosophers have found in him seminal ideas for their own development. It is in this sense that James is the American philosopher par excellence.[36]

Evaluation

James, as biologist, medical doctor, psychologist, and philosopher, saw religion as central to his interests. Although a member of no church and a critic of traditional Christian doctrines, James did attend the Harvard Chapel regularly. He saw religion as man's most significant function, and more and more his philosophy became a philosophy of religion.[37]

James saw his views as closely allied with those of Peirce, Frederick Schiller, and Dewey (among others), and yet his own position was highly personal and he belonged to no school of thought. His pragmatism, especially as applied to religion, placed an emphasis on beliefs that are satisfactory to ourselves. Just as his own philosophy spelled out what was satisfactory to him, so he saw this personal factor as part of any knowledge. As Dewey pointed out, philosophers are always sure that personal factors corrupt their opponents' views, but they usually assume that their own views are suitably objective. James was honest enough to include the personal factor, and therefore we are able to judge him more fairly. Dewey thought that perhaps James carried this too far in "The Will to Believe," so that such belief became a matter of personal privilege rather than responsibility for active participation.[38]

The catholicity of James's mind, essential to his genius, was also a

---

[36] See Perry, *In the Spirit of William James*, pp. 206-8; John E. Smith, *The Spirit of American Philosophy* (New York: Oxford University Press, 1963), p. 78.
[37] See Bixler, op. cit., p. 198.
[38] See Dewey, op. cit., pp. 325-29. See James, *A Pluralistic Universe*, p. 20: "A philosophy is the expression of a man's intimate character, and all definitions of the universe are but deliberately adopted reactions of human character upon it."

liability. He was more than generous to the views of his opponents, and sometimes admitted more than he should have concerning their beliefs. This broad-based approach, never very systematic, also led to misunderstanding of his position or at least to a vagueness of statement on his part. Many of his later writings and some of his letters were attempts to clarify his position.

At the center was his empiricism, his concern for experience of the concrete, and whatever could not be connected in some way with experience or possible experience was considered meaningless theorizing or vicious intellectualism. Abstract thinking was valuable only insofar as it affected the consequences of one's behavior. Thus, closely associated with his empiricism was his pragmatism as a way of testing—in a more complex way than readers usually realize—concepts, ideas, and objects of experience themselves. This led him to a view of the nature of chance which allowed for unpredictability in human behavior and in the universe, so that novelty was not something added from the outside but something that was essential to the totality of the process of reality. Ultimately, a pluralistic universe which is interrelated so that it does not result in chaos had to be the metaphysical result. When empiricism, pragmatism, tychism (chance or novelty), and a pluralistic universe provide a way of looking on the total picture, there is room for the reality of God, a MORE or divine consciousness who is in relation with man but who has limits and an environment. Ultimately, the idea of such a God, empirically experienced as an object, can be tested pragmatically and made, therefore, the center of one's life.

There are many ways to evaluate the significance of such a man, personally, philosophically, and religiously. This Ralph Barton Perry has done in his labor of love, the two volumes on *The Thought and Character of William James*, where we see the man, spots and all, in conversation with those who agreed with him and those who disagreed, but all of them friends.

There is a sense in which James is the father of empirical theology, but there is no school of Jamesians. His influence has been piecemeal, just as his philosophy was. It is hard to find a book by any American philosopher or theologian without discovering the name of James, often repeating one of his contributions, but without any footnote; for his ideas have been internalized in American thinking. The riches of his mind have been scattered on the American landscape, and the result has been what Perry calls "mixed Jamesians, who acknowledge their common relationship without feeling any bond with one another." [39]

The old mutual-admiration society of his own day is gone, but one thinks of Peirce, Flournoy, Shadsworth Hodgson, Schiller, the strange mystic Benjamin Paul Blood, German and French thinkers, including Bergson, and Dewey. Dewey's early career paralleled James's later years, and Dewey's instrumentalism was close enough to James's pragmatism to make it a next step in the development of the spirit of American thinking about both philosophy and religion.

---

[39] Perry, *The Thought and Character of William James*, vol. 2, p. 668. See, for example, the interpretation by William Clebsch of James's influence on H. Richard Niebuhr in *American Religious Thought: A History*, pp. 181-87.

CHAPTER 3

Instrumentalism and Religion

WILLIAM JAMES THOUGHT OF JOHN DEWEY AS A FELLOW EMPIRICIST and pragmatist, although he was aware of differences in some of their emphases. Dewey acknowledged this relationship. One difference was that of temperament. Whitehead commented that Dewey was "like Calvin Coolidge, a Vermonter who hesitates to 'let himself in,'—his philosophy is a tentativism, designed to avoid any final plunge; but James's philosophy is expressly designed to justify and embody an attitude of self-commitment." [1]

Particularly in the area of religion there were strong emphases in different directions. Dewey did not accept James's arguments for God because James had not derived them on pragmatic grounds but had only shown the effect of the results for one who accepted a prior definition, so that "the resulting consequences would serve to constitute the entire meaning." [2] Even as a working hypothesis, the idea of God as "eternal perpetuation" had no pragmatic significance.

However, Dewey thought that James's *Pragmatism* was likely to become a philosophic classic. There was a kinship of spirit in their empirical and pragmatic methodologies. Both men represented a

---

[1] Ralph Barton Perry, *In the Spirit of William James* (New Haven: Yale University Press, 1938), pp. 205-6.
[2] John Dewey, *Essays in Experimental Logic* (Chicago: University of Chicago Press, 1916), p. 315.

growing movement in American philosophy that reflected aspects of American culture. James was more individualistic than Dewey, who tended to be corporate in outlook and philosophic method, but both shared the interest in the immediate, concrete nature of experience as a basis for knowledge.

Dewey was born seventeen years after James and outlived him by forty-two years (he lived to be ninety-three). Unlike James, he did not have the advantages of a European exposure. He grew up in a small Vermont town in an atmosphere of New England Congregationalism. He rejected his mother's conservative piety but was active in liberal Congregational circles for some years. He studied under Charles Peirce at Johns Hopkins, but his philosophy at that time was informed by Hegelianism. What probably helped most in changing Dewey's approach from idealism to instrumentalism was a reading of James's *Psychology*; and later on the influence of George Herbert Mead matched that of James.[3]

Dewey was active in the Congregational Church in Ann Arbor, and it was only after he came to Chicago in 1894 that he dropped out of institutional church life. This did not lead to a lack of interest in religion, however. He was active at Hull House and was one of the charter members of the Religious Education Association in 1903; he was a speaker at the first convention.[4] He attacked traditional religion, but he never lost the crusading spirit of liberal Congregationalism as he moved into many kinds of social and political movements as an expression of his philosophy.

Dewey's Presuppositions

Underlying Dewey's philosophy was a faith in progress, although in his awareness of the tragic sense of life he recognized the resistance of reality to men's purposes.[5] He did not think that progress was automatic or due to divine Providence. Rather, he had faith in man and nature, and

[3] See George Dykhuizen, *The Life and Mind of John Dewey* (Carbondale, Ill.: Southern Illinois Press, 1973), pp. 68, 83.

[4] John Dewey, "Religious Education as Conditioned by Modern Psychology and Pedagogy," *Proceedings of the First Annual Convention of the Religious Education Association*, Chicago, 1903, pp. 60-66; reprinted in *Religious Education*, vol. 69 (Jan.-Feb. 1974), pp. 6-11.

[5] See Sidney Hook, "Pragmatism and the Tragic Sense of Life," in John E. Smith, ed., *Contemporary American Philosophy* (London: George Allen & Unwin, 1970), pp. 180-81.

this was synthesized in his expectation that man can ultimately control his environment. Man and his intelligence are united organically with the rest of reality, and therefore man can cope with his world.

He assumed the validity of evolutionary naturalism and saw biology, psychology, and physics as sciences which supported this view. The whole of reality, which is in constant flux, is an interrelated organism. Everything exists together in an interlaced naturalistic order. There is no such thing as "antecedent" reality; it is in immediate experience that we find our data; through our operational procedures we find ways of controlling nature; thus we can conclude that humanity is in organic unity with the processes of nature.

It is not difficult to reduce all the experiences of life to naturalistic categories. There is room in a naturalistic system for all the higher forms of living, such as art, logic, philosophy, and religion, provided that we are content that each shall remain a pure method. Thus there was no positive metaphysics in Dewey's thought, for this would imply confidence in intellectual certainties and antecedent realities that cannot be verified pragmatically.

Man has survived in the evolutionary process because he has had superb tools, and he will eventually gain control of all the aspects of reality which affect his destiny. Consciousness has emerged in this process, thus demonstrating survival value. Consciousness is interpreted in terms of functional psychology. Mind is defined in the light of what it does, just as anything else is. "The mind," he wrote,

> is within the world as part of the latter's own on-going process. It is marked off as mind by the fact that wherever it is found, changes take place in a *directed* way, so that a movement in a definite one-way sense—from the doubtful to the clear, resolved and settled—takes place.[6]

At this point individuals always seem to be absorbed into the process and lose their identity. What really is transformed, said Dewey, is the process of knowing, for the mind is no longer considered a spectator lost in self-contemplation but an active participant in a world that it can to some degree control.

---

[6] John Dewey, *The Quest for Certainty* (New York: Minton, Balch & Co., 1929), p. 291. Used by permission of G. P. Putnam's Sons.

Dewey's concept of the individual seemed at times to be conceived behavioristically, but Dewey was too much of an empiricist to deny man's freedom. The natural processes assisted by social pressure, necessity, and law bear upon the individual, but these processes are not rigid. There is always room for chance or indeterminacy. In the "use of desire, deliberation and choice, freedom is actualized." He wrote that "we use the foresight of the future to refine and expand present activity." [7] He did not see this process as a conflict within the self, however, for the sense of inner dialogue is lacking. He saw it in the interpersonal relations in a social context.

This may have been because he saw habit as the key to understanding outer behavior. One may bring intellectual analysis to bear upon habits and change them, or the intellect may take over when habits are inadequate. Habits assist us in achieving goals which we have proposed as well as in the means by which we seek them. Habits mediate between impulse and reason. This is important for Dewey, "for if man is primarily a creature of habit and habits are accessible to human intelligence, many of the most pervasive ills of human history *can* be attacked, and they *should* be, in principle at least, subject to elimination." [8]

Dewey had more confidence in science than did James, especially in biology. In his response to the volume in his honor he wrote that "the key to a philosophic theory of experience must proceed from initially linking it with the processes and functions of life as the latter are disclosed in biological science." [9] James also had moved from biology as a starting point and used it in developing his psychology, but he did not limit himself in the way that Dewey did.

Instrumental Knowledge

Dewey started with experience, as any good empiricist would. He began, however, with sense data and not with experienced objects. The data are selected by the senses for the purpose in question, which may

---

[7] John Dewey, *Human Nature and Conduct* (New York: Henry Holt & Co., 1922), p. 313.

[8] John E. Smith, *The Spirit of American Philosophy* (New York: Oxford University Press, 1963), p. 132. Used by permission.

[9] In Paul Arthur Schilpp, ed., *The Philosophy of John Dewey* (Evanston: Northwestern University Press, 1959), p. 530.

be the testing of a hypothesis which has been evoked by a previous experience upon which one has reflected. The purpose is to control selected data and their relations so that purposive human ends may be achieved.

Experience is of two kinds: there is the manifold of experience in flux, and there is directed and regulated change. In the former case, the experience is brought under control by understanding the relationships of the data through either modifying the data or manipulating the experiment. The model for such procedures is experimental science. One inserts change into the process to find out what other change results, and the correlation between these changes is the object of knowledge. This means that overt doing is central to the working out of consequences.

Sense qualities do not give knowledge. Dewey's empiricism leads to knowledge about what is experienced through elaborate operations. We reduce objects directly perceived to data. Then the thought of an operation is evoked, which may result in a solution to the problem, which in turn may suggest another problem. An idea or concept is always identified with the operational method. Dewey quoted with approval P. W. Bridgman's statement that "we mean by any concept nothing more than a set of operations; *the concept is synonymous with the corresponding set of operations.*" [10] These operations are part of experience, and they are tested by the consequences, which make them true.

The manifold of experience, however, is chaotic and does not lend itself readily to controlled change. The selection of data must, therefore, be intentional. The data are "taken" or "had"; they are not "given." The manipulation of selected data, followed by the use of operational concepts, leads to objects of thought about reality. This scientific object is not the "real" object, for the "real" object is "just what it is experienced as being," [11] but nothing is known until a problem is resolved by operational procedures. Dewey called this naïve realism, for his sophisticated experimentalism or instrumentalism always returns to experience as controlled in order to solve a problem.

Dewey's theory of the place of ideas in the search for knowledge may

---

[10] P. W. Bridgman, *The Logic of Modern Physics* (New York: Macmillan, 1927), p. 5. The italics are Bridgman's.

[11] Dewey, *The Quest for Certainty*, p. 131.

be summarized as follows: (1) Ideas have an active and productive character. An idea "is a mode of directed overt action. Ideas are anticipatory plans and designs which take effect in concrete reconstructions and antecedent conditions of existence. . . . Their worth has to be tested by the specific consequences of their operation." (2) Ideas are to be considered as hypotheses, evoked by prior experiences and tested by consequent operations. Ideas constantly give rise to new ideas through the process of creative imagination. They are always tools for directed action. (3) In this experimental view, "action is at the heart of ideas." There is no separation between theory and practice. "Knowing itself is a kind of action, the only one which progressively and securely clothes natural existence with recognized meaning." [12] There is no fixed or final certainty, but there is security in controlling operations through the use of ideas as tools.

Dewey's faith in scientific method was evident in his treatment of values. There is always a problem of valuing when one has to choose between courses of action. If this is carried out simply in terms of desire, the choice is not adequate to the situation. Unless knowledge and reflection are inserted into the process, the desire will be uninformed. The norm is not what is satisfying but what is satisfactory, a distinction which Dewey does not make entirely clear, but which is related to one's intention and anticipation of consequences. There are enjoyments of radically different sorts, and their relationships need to be distinguished. A past event may have been enjoyed and therefore valued, but a predicted event must meet specifiable conditions in order to be anticipated as being valuable. Value emerges when we decide to bring a fact into existence by our acts. Dewey's main proposition was: *"Judgments about values are judgments about the conditions and the results of experienced objects; judgments about that which should regulate the formation of our desires, affections and enjoyments."* [13] Means and ends belong together in the process of value judgments and are of equal importance. Intelligence informing action is the guide.

We cannot say in advance what these values are, for they emerge from experimentation and from the insights of modern science, but they

[12] Ibid., pp. 166-68.
[13] Ibid., p. 265; see John Dewey, *Experience and Nature* (La Salle, Ill.: Open Court Publishing Co., 1925), p. 96.

will occur in the process of living when intelligence and reflection are brought to bear on it.

In at least three ways, Dewey's philosophy reflected the American character.

> First, action and practical intelligence take precedence over all forms of contemplation and speculation; secondly, ideal goals are not "starry-eyed" projections of human desire but rather visions of improvement rooted in the actual possibilities of situations; and thirdly, value comes to be taken out of the sphere of the individual and personal and relocated in social progress and in the struggle to eliminate the ills of political, economic, and social life. A common theme runs through each of these characteristics; all thought and concern must be focused by the problems arising from the contemporary social situation.[14]

A Common Faith

Dewey's religious outlook was already clear in *The Quest for Certainty*. He discussed the relation of the possible to the actual and asserted that nature not only is the source of the potential for the realizing of ideals but that it responds to man's search for the idealizable. The religious attitude is to be found in this relation of the possible to the actual and not in any beliefs about matters of fact. One does not worship nature but has "piety toward the actual."[15] This involves a sense of dependence similar to that of Schleiermacher, said Dewey, but there is no sense of certainty.

Conventional religious beliefs have not been the outcome of experimental methods. Rather, said Dewey, "religions have been saturated with the supernatural—and the supernatural signified precisely that which lies beyond experience."[16] Furthermore, organized religion has supported the status quo. But primitive Christianity "demanded a change of heart that entailed a revolutionary change in human relationships."[17] We need to work toward a solidarity of human interests that is vital and growing.

Dewey did not discover a common empirical object underneath all the "supernatural encumbrances" of the historical religions. The study

[14] Smith, *The Spirit of American Philosophy*, pp. 156-57. Used by permission.
[15] Dewey, *The Quest for Certainty*, p. 306.
[16] In H. G. Leach, ed., *Living Philosophies* (New York: Simon & Schuster, 1931), p. 23.
[17] Ibid., p. 29.

of religion can only lead to confusion and contradiction as far as consequences are the basis for judgment. Historic religions are relative to the social cultures in which they arose, reflecting an outmoded society and cosmology.

Dewey distinguished between *religion* and the *religious*. Instead of a body of beliefs and practices found in a religious institution, "the adjective 'religious' denotes nothing in the way of a specifiable entity, either institutional or as a system of beliefs. . . . It denotes attitudes that may be taken toward every object and every proposed end or ideal." [18] It must mean devotion to those ends which serve and promote the actualization of human ideals. "The actual religious quality in the experience described is the *effect* produced, the better adjustment in life and its conditions, not the manner and cause of its production." [19]

It is obvious, according to Dewey, that persons have religious experiences, and the conditions that produce such an experience might be called "God," but this does not make it possible to claim the existence of God as a being or person as in some of the major religions. Religious experience has no knowledge value. Dewey disagreed with James at this point, for James took seriously the hypothesis that religious experience could be interpreted as continuity with a wider consciousness, a MORE that affected man's thinking and action. "Any activity," said Dewey, "pursued in behalf of an ideal end against obstacles and in spite of threats of personal loss because of conviction of its general and enduring value is religious in quality." [20]

Dewey, however, was willing to go further than this. He reasserted his operational procedures as being "the road of patient, coöperative inquiry operating by means of observation, experiment, record and controlled reflection." [21] Such an approach places religious faith clearly in the realm of the human imagination and sees the result as the "unification of the self through allegiance to inclusive ideal ends." [22] Man's many ideal ends are brought into unity through the use of imagination. This is the traditional God's real power.

There is something in experience which we can call God, said

---

[18] John Dewey, *A Common Faith* (New Haven: Yale University Press, 1934), pp. 9-10.
[19] Ibid., p. 14.
[20] Ibid., p. 27.
[21] Ibid., p. 32.
[22] Ibid., p. 33.

Dewey. "There are forces in nature and society that generate and support ideals. They are further unified by the action that gives them coherence and solidity. It is this *active* relation between ideal and actual to which I would give the name 'God.' " [23] Our response is in terms of "passionate intelligence," but we rarely see it in action that matches the appeal of traditional religious concepts. Almost wistfully, Dewey wrote, "Were men and women actuated throughout the length and breadth of human relations with the faith and ardor that have at times marked historic religions, the consequences would be incalculable." [24]

Finally, whatever God is, his actual unification takes place in the human imagination, without cosmic reference. God is not a conscious, unitary process or substance or being. He is a symbol of the general functions and trends toward the actualizing of value. The only *conscious* power bringing into actuality the ideal ends which exist as possibilities is the *human* mind.

For this kind of religious faith to operate, we need to get rid of supernatural views of revelation and truth and move toward an operational methodology of experimentalism. Ideals do tend toward actualization through human participation and action. The universe, as formulated by human imagination but never fully grasped, is "the matrix within which our ideal aspirations are born and bred. It is the source of the values that the moral imagination projects as directive criteria and as shaping purposes." [25] Such a view will open our religious faith to a "creed" that "will change and grow, because it cannot be shaken." [26]

Interpretations of Dewey

When Wieman reviewed *A Common Faith*, he welcomed Dewey into the camp of the theists, interpreting Dewey's concept of God as the "growing good." [27] But as Edwin E. Aubrey pointed out,

the integrative power binding actual and ideal is still restricted . . . to human imaginative intelligence. . . . Mr. Dewey is not yet talking of a

---

[23] Ibid., p. 51.
[24] Ibid., pp. 80-81.
[25] Ibid., p. 85.
[26] Ibid.
[27] See *The Christian Century*, vol. 51, no. 46 (Nov. 14, 1934), pp. 1450-52.

God who is a trans-human power or principle of integration . . . , but rather a divinely creative human intelligence.[28]

Dewey clarified his position:

What I said was that the union of ideals and with *some* natural forces that generate and sustain them, accomplished in human imagination and to be realized through human choice and action, is that to which the name of God might be applied, with of course the understanding that this is just what is meant by the word. . . . A . . . polytheist, using Mr. Wieman's logic, might attribute to me a belief in polytheism.[29]

There are many forces that generate and sustain human values, but the unification is definitely performed by the human mind.

Wieman criticized Dewey for isolating man from nature, for Wieman insisted on "a total system of interacting activities." However, Dewey's point was that "a humanistic religion, if it excludes our relation to nature, is pale and thin, as it is presumptuous, when it takes humanity as an object of worship." [30] In Dewey's mind, man was the product of nature who had survived in the evolutionary process just because he was capable of making conscious adjustments and through imagination could seek ways of relating ideals to the actual. Wieman believed that these forces operate without human choice, as in the early development of value in an infant, but Dewey even here would insist that purpose and conscious striving are part of the process. Of course, Dewey admitted that there are forces in nature which tend toward value whether men cooperate or not, but as such they do not participate in what Dewey called the religious. The difference was that Wieman was insisting on devotion to a cosmic force and Dewey on devotion to ideal ends.

Wieman and Meland criticized Dewey for not including the nonideal elements in his definition of the religious, for there are nonideal or neutral elements in life which move toward the ideal. Such an emphasis, they wrote, "would turn religious devotion in two directions, rather than one as in Dewey's philosophy: first, toward such existent reality as sustains and promotes value; and second, toward ideal possibilities, as

[28] Ibid., vol. 51, no. 49 (Dec. 5, 1934), p. 1550.
[29] Ibid., p. 1551.
[30] Dewey, *A Common Faith*, p. 54.

Dewey has said." [31] This indicates how close Wieman and Dewey were at that time, and Dewey's influence on Wieman has continued to the present day.

Dewey's optimism about man and progress permeated his position. He assumed, said Joseph Wood Krutch, "that if things are only given the opportunity to work themselves out completely, they must inevitably work themselves out well." [32] This can be contrasted with James's meliorism and the element of risk, which was a more dynamic religious attitude but had less security to offer. Dewey believed that his position provided security but not certainty, but even the security offered was based on a method and not on any metaphysical proposition. From a pragmatic view, Dewey believed that metaphysical beliefs did not work, as contrasted with James's conclusion that pragmatism ultimately required beliefs about the nature of the universe.

Dewey tended to take experience in its retail form, paying attention to particulars, but he refused to take the overall or wholesale look; this marked him off from both James and Whitehead. The knower became simply an agency of doing, rather than a subject; experience was truncated, and metaphysics was reduced to a biological picture of a naturalistic description. "The difference between James and Dewey at this point," said Bernard Meland,

> is that Dewey is oriented toward the positivistic view of experience, while James moves into a more radical empiricism, presaging the philosophy of emergence. In Dewey's view human consciousness will be defined as the summit of existence. . . . In James' radical empiricism, the knowing mind, the seeking mind, moves in a world of pure experience which continually confronts the human consciousness with intimations of a good not its own. [33]

This does not deny the importance of method. The instrumental pragmatism of Dewey, like the radical empiricism and pragmatism of

[31] Henry Nelson Wieman and Bernard E. Meland, *American Philosophies of Religion* (Chicago: Willett, Clark & Co., 1936), p. 283; see Henry Nelson Wieman, *Intellectual Foundation of Faith* (New York: Philosophical Library, 1961), pp. 30-57.
[32] *New York Herald-Tribune Book Review*, Oct. 20, 1929.
[33] Bernard E. Meland, *Higher Education and the Human Spirit* (Chicago: University of Chicago Press, 1953), p. 45. Meland goes on to claim that because Dewey's view dominated that of James in educational theory, the deeper aspects of James's philosophy have been lost to the educational experience.

James, has influenced modern American theology, as we will see. But Dewey, unlike James, refused to ask serious epistemological and metaphysical questions and therefore remained locked in his methodology.

Dewey refused to be limited in his thinking to atheism, or to humanism without God. As Charles Hartshorne wrote, there seems to be "nothing but a choice of words to distinguish Dewey's position from ordinary atheism. But Dewey feels there is a difference." [34] This feeling was expressed by Dewey in his writing on art:

> We are, as it were, introduced into a world beyond this world which is nevertheless the deeper reality of the world in which we live in our ordinary experiences. We are carried beyond ourselves to find ourselves. I can see no psychological ground for such properties of an experience save that, somehow, the work of art operates to deepen and to raise to greater clarity that sense of an enveloping undefined whole that accompanies every normal experience. This whole is felt as an expansion of ourselves. . . . Where egotism is not the measure of reality and value, we are citizens of this vast world beyond ourselves, and any intense realization of its presence with and in us brings a peculiarly satisfying sense of unity in itself and with ourselves. . . . It explains also the religious feeling that accompanies intense esthetic perception. [35]

Dewey did not expand this statement in terms of religion and tended to ignore it in his discussion in *A Common Faith*. But surely here is a suggestion of the other pole of religious experience, as developed, for example, by James and Whitehead. It is this failure to recognize the fullness of the aesthetic in Dewey's religious outlook that led to the lack of ardor in his devotion to a connection between value and actuality. Dewey's expression of religion in his own life was moral, political, and social. It was the pragmatic application of the fruits of devotion to values, rather than an appreciation of the aesthetic in religious worship.

Dewey's deep insights into the nature of aesthetic experience did not point to the God of theism, but they do supply us with data that may be used for this purpose. His statement can be correlated with what James

---

[34] Charles Hartshorne, *Beyond Humanism* (Chicago: Willett, Clark & Co., 1937), p. 40.

[35] John Dewey, *Art as Experience* (New York: Minton, Balch & Co., 1935), p. 195. Used by permission of G. P. Putnam's Sons.

wrote about appreciation of the wider world and the wider consciousness that implies a divine MORE. Dewey was not saying the same thing as James. Both men were properly critical of the historical accretions of traditional theological concepts.[36] Both were cautious in drawing theological conclusions from the data of experience. James seemed to reach out in a way that Dewey did not toward the cosmos as a framework for deity. When James spoke of polytheism as a possibility, however, he may have been close to Dewey's response to Wieman's logic, yet Dewey would never admit any acquaintance with God through religious experience as did James.

Dewey's antimetaphysical and antitheological stance led to a scientific positivism. His faith in science helped him to criticize many unsupportable metaphysical and theological claims, but it tended to glamorize science and to paralyze attempts at metaphysical and theological reconstruction. It was easy for those who had caught the enthusiasm of James's empiricism and pragmatism to move on to Dewey's more negative religious position.

The Christian theologian has difficulty with both James and Dewey, for neither of them had much use for the standard teachings of Christianity. Certainly they provided no basis for a Christology or a trinitarian view of God, as far as their own philosophies were concerned. But others thought they saw in the methodologies of James and Dewey new approaches to apologetics, so that even Christian teachings could be made respectable, often by distorting both the empirical and pragmatic methodologies and the historic teachings of the church.

But there was something more to be said, for the convinced Christian lives in a world where he needs to use all the tools of operational thinking, he needs to interpret experience, and he must make use of the latest and best knowledge. If the methods and attitudes so typical of the American mind that emerged from the American culture have validity for seeking any and all kinds of truth, American theologians need to perfect such methods for their own purposes.

James was a pluralistic theist whose radical empiricism and open-mindedness enabled him to examine morbid psychological reports,

---

[36] See Paul van Buren, *Theological Explorations* (New York: Macmillan, 1968), p. 147; Dewey, *A Common Faith*, p. 10.

spiritualistic séances, mystical experiences, prayer, and many aspects of healthy religious living. He could be sympathetic with the records of religious experience in other religions and throughout history, without for a moment relaxing his capacity for penetrating insight, analysis, and criticism.

Dewey, on the other hand, was, to coin a word, no more than a semitheist, who had hold of many important elements of living in such a way that man could work to bring potential values into the realm of actual experience. He was not as open as James, although, as we have indicated, he had deep aesthetic awareness that was akin to religious feelings. His operational theory of knowledge helped to place scientific procedures at the disposal of theological thinking, but he thought of the unlimited scope of scientific experimentation rather than of its limitations.

Both men, in their ways, have contributed to theological reconstruction both before and after World War II.[37] Their immediate effect was on the Chicago school of empirical theology. For example, after Dewey's *How We Think* was published in 1910, it became required reading for all students at the Divinity School of the University of Chicago, just as Whitehead's *Process and Reality* was in later years. Dewey's influence can be seen in the thought of Gerald Birney Smith, Edward Scribner Ames, and Shailer Mathews, as well as in that of Henry Nelson Wieman.

---

[37] See Eugene Fontinell, *Toward a Reconstruction of Religion* (New York: Doubleday, 1970). He utilizes insights from both James and Dewey in developing a Catholic theology.

CHAPTER 4

Theism
in Transition

THERE WERE SOME INTIMATIONS OF EMPIRICISM IN THEOLOGY AS FAR back as 1910. Before that there were a few efforts to apply religious experience to a received theology and some attempts to take seriously the pragmatic effects of James's *Will to Believe*.[1] By the time of James's death in 1910, however, his philosophic approach to religious truth through the application of radical empiricism and pragmatism was well known, owing to his widespread lecturing and popular style of writing. Dewey, on the other hand, was developing his operational theory of truth without reference to religious thinking,[2] and his legacy was being established at the University of Chicago, where a new approach to Christian theology developed along historical, empirical, and pragmatic lines, thus turning inquiry toward human behavior as the basis for theology.

If James and Dewey represented a dominant note in the spirit of

---

[1] For example: Lewis F. Stearns, *The Evidence of Christian Experience* (New York: Charles Scribner's Sons, 1890); William N. Clarke, *What Shall We Think of Christianity?* (New York: Charles Scribner's Sons, 1899); Eleanor H. Rowland, *The Right to Believe* (Boston: Houghton Mifflin Co., 1909); John E. Boodin, *Truth and Reality* (New York: Macmillan, 1911); Eugene W. Lyman, *Theology and Human Problems* (New York: Charles Scribner's Sons, 1910).

[2] But see John Dewey, "Religious Education as Conditioned by Modern Psychology and Pedagogy," *Proceedings of the First Annual Convention of the Religious Education Association*, 1903, pp. 60-66; reprinted in *Religious Education*, vol. 69 (Jan.-Feb. 1974), pp. 6-11.

American philosophy, as many would claim, it soon became evident that they had much to contribute to a similar spirit in American theology, especially as it was represented in the Chicago school in a variety of thinkers including Gerald Birney Smith, Edward Scribner Ames, and Shailer Mathews.

Is Theism Essential to Religion?

In 1925, Gerald Birney Smith posed the question, "Is Theism Essential to Religion?" His answer was that we must redefine theism if we are to defend it successfully. The theology of the future would employ empirical methods and would be based on the evidence and interpretation of a great mystical experiment. This had been foreshadowed in his Taylor Lectures at Yale, when he said, "The supreme question for theology is to discover how this environment may be so correlated to the needy life that the fullest possible use may be made of the divine power." [3]

He saw that the problem of religious belief is its static quality. If the perfect form of religion has already been established, all we need to do is call people to believe, and of course more and more people are unable to respond in the age of science and technology. Once the authority of received teaching has been demeaned, religious beliefs must be maintained on some other basis. What is needed is a platform for nonauthoritative belief. [4]

He approved the basic thesis of Douglas Clyde Macintosh's *Theology as an Empirical Science*, but he objected to its metaphysical reconstruction: "Is it not religiously as well as scientifically more satisfactory," he asked, "to set forth the *meaning* of religious beliefs in the total organization of our experiences rather than to try to reinstate realism?" It was Macintosh's testing of "the standard doctrines which were worked out in the Christianity of past centuries, and were formulated with a type of metaphysics which modern empirical science repudiates," which brought forth the objection. [5]

Religious humanism, at the time Smith wrote, was at the height of its

---

[3] *Social Idealism and Changing Theology* (New York: Macmillan, 1912), p. 243.

[4] "What Is the Matter with Religion?" *Religious Education*, vol. 23 (June 1928), pp. 507-8.

[5] Gerald Birney Smith, "Is Theism Essential to Religion?" *American Journal of Theology*, vol. 24 (Jan. 1920), pp. 153-54.

glory. It was, furthermore, the period in the middle of the post-World War I decade, when a false optimism spoke of the glory and power of man, who therefore asked how he could use God. Intelligent devotion to ideals was enough to bring in a new civilization.

"Is Theism Essential to Religion?" was a significant article for the times. Smith could see the older views breaking down in the areas of the cosmos, society, and personal relations, and he believed that the time was ripe for a revival of religion on a grand scale. Within the year there appeared Henry Nelson Wieman's *Religious Experience and Scientific Method*, which impressed Smith with its interpretation of religion as adjustment to that part of the environment upon which man is "most dependent for his security, welfare, and increasing abundance." In his review of the book, Smith indicated his willingness to approve this approach, although he doubted the wisdom of reducing it to a purely scientific concept. He wrote:

> Apparently the creative power of religion depends fundamentally on the possibility of feeling the reality of what has not been precisely formulated by science. . . . Must not religion, in order to remain religious at all, aim at symbolic expression rather than at scientific formulation? . . . The harmonization of religion and science is not quite as simple as the author makes it out to be.[6]

Religious beliefs must be consistent with the findings of science, but we have the right to employ symbols and poetry and pageantry and music as well.[7] This may lead to the development of new ways of expressing religious aspirations that fit the modern world, and this will take expert scientific analysis. We cannot escape the need for technical scholarship.

> When once confidence is established in scientific method in the study of religion, the old dread of science will disappear. Men . . . will rather wish to set religion free to modify existing doctrines or to create new doctrines in order to enable man to realize the best possibilities by relating himself to all the resources of the actual environment from which life must be nourished.[8]

[6] Gerald Birney Smith in *Journal of Religion*, vol. 6, no. 6 (Nov. 1926), pp. 638-40.
[7] See *Religious Education*, vol. 23 (June 1928), pp. 508-9.
[8] Smith, "An Overlooked Factor in the Adjustment Between Religion and Science," *Journal of Religion*, vol. 7, no. 4 (July 1927), pp. 356, 358.

There is a "vast cosmic mystery" that stands at the center of all religious living, and there is evidence that "points to a real reciprocity." [9] Smith was convinced that the current theology in 1925 could not be convincing, partly because it was so complete and self-assured. Perhaps a conception of a finite God who could preserve the quality of love without being responsible for the whole cosmos would be acceptable. This was a view similar to that of William James.

It is likely, Smith believed, that the theologian of the future will be partial to the methods of empiricism and induction, but he will be sensitive to the aesthetic and the need for symbols that speak to the emotions as well as the intellect. A careful examination of the mystical aspects of experience will provide new data. Religion will be seen as "an aspect of this life-process" of "adjustment between organism and environment," and "the character of God will be found in the experienced reciprocity between man and his environment." [10]

A revival of theology along these lines, said Smith, was already evident in 1925.

> The most evident results of twenty-five years of theological thinking in this country are the progressive development of a liberal movement which is committed to the use of scientific and historical method in the study of Christianity, and a sharp reaction against this tendency.[11]

Today, as then, we could say almost the same thing, with emphasis both on the development and on the reaction against it.

Smith called his position a "mystical naturalism." He did not believe that mystical experiences provided any esoteric knowledge, but that a naturalistic mystic, like the poet, "is sensitive to the full impact of the event rather than the detailed meanings involved." [12] He thought of such an approach as a theological experiment and did not live to de-

---

[9] Smith, *Current Christian Thinking* (Chicago: University of Chicago Press, 1928), p. 167; from *Journal of Religion*, vol. 5, no. 4 (July 1925), p. 374.

[10] Smith, *Current Christian Thinking*, p. 165; *Journal of Religion*, vol. 5, no. 4 (July 1925), p. 373.

[11] Gerald Birney Smith, ed., *Religious Thought in the Last Quarter Century* (Chicago: University of Chicago Press, 1927), p. 114; from *Journal of Religion*, vol. 5, no. 6 (Nov. 1925), pp. 593-94.

[12] Henry Nelson Wieman and Bernard E. Meland, *American Philosophies of Religion* (Chicago: Willett, Clark & Co., 1936), p. 292.

velop its implications. But he was convinced that such an experiment would

> express the experience of kinship between man and that quality in the environment which supports and enriches humanity in its spiritual quest. God will be very real to the religious man, but his reality will be interpreted in terms of social reciprocity with an as yet inadequately defined cosmic support of human values, rather than in terms of theistic creatorship and control.[13]

One cannot help but feel that Smith had his finger on the pulse of one group within the nation, the same group that had responded to the more loose-jointed and tentative conclusions of the radical empiricism and pragmatism of James and the instrumentalism of Dewey. Some of the developments since then have helped to fulfill Smith's prophecy for a minority. The lack of an adequate epistemology has been worked out by some thinkers, most notably D. C. Macintosh. Smith's lack of concern for metaphysics was overcome within the Chicago school itself by Charles Hartshorne.

Smith himself anticipated new interpretations of religious experience. He saw it as operating within a naturalistic framework, as adapting to changing circumstances, and as having moral consequences.[14] He thought that this would result in resistance from those who still relied on the old securities of fixed beliefs, but he was calling religious people to recognize that they were facing a new universe that had outgrown the old theology, as well as a new social order that no longer fitted the old morality. If this new world view seems more real to thoughtful people, he said, then they need to adapt their religious beliefs and practices to the new ways. Religion is vital only when it assists persons to adapt to the world in which they live. At the same time, he claimed, we need to recognize the nonrational factors in religion, so that we don't get caught in a dry intellectualism. Attitudes of reverence, awe, and wonder are part of the total picture. Furthermore, we need to remember that we express religious aspirations through the folkways of our subculture, but these need to be consistent with the total culture in which we live.[15]

---

[13] Smith, *Current Christian Thinking*, pp. 169-70; *Journal of Religion*, vol. 5, no. 4 (July 1925), pp. 376-77.

[14] *Religious Education*, vol. 20 (Aug. 1925), pp. 270-71.

[15] Ibid., p. 272.

The successor to Smith's tradition at Chicago was Bernard Eugene
Meland. He sought to extend Smith's view within the framework of a
process metaphysics and a broader empiricism, but still he kept a
mystical naturalism as basic to his approach. In Meland's view there was
no separation between man and the cosmos, so that man feels at home in
the universe. Man is sustained by the creative order at work in the
universe and in man. Man is increasingly devoted to this creative order
and therefore comes to know God progressively, thus fulfilling the hope
of Smith's mystical experiment.[16] Meland has gone beyond this position
because of his insights into the nature of culture, especially American
and secularized culture, so that he has been able to protest against a
theology that is subject to a culture while at the same time he has
insisted that theology be relevant to its culture.[17]

In 1925, Smith had caught hold of a condition in theology and of a
way out through empirical and pragmatic procedures.[18] What he
predicted came about most nearly in the theology of Meland, but others
took up some aspects of the same approach, most notably Wieman.
Macintosh had started talking about theology as an "empirical science"
as early as 1914. Within the Chicago school, however, approaches
through history and social science had been dominant for a long time,
especially in the thought of Shirley Jackson Case, George B. Foster,
Shailer Mathews, and Edward Scribner Ames.[19] We turn now to Ames.

God and Uncle Sam

One pragmatic test of theology is found in preaching. If theology as
applied to parish life in its preaching and teaching activities has
satisfactory outcomes, this can be one element in the verification

[16] See Wieman and Meland, *American Philosophies of Religion*, pp. 294-95.

[17] See, by Bernard E. Meland, *Modern Man's Worship* (New York: Harper & Row,
1934); *Faith and Culture* (New York: Oxford University Press, 1953); *The Realities of
Faith* (New York: Oxford University Press, 1962); *The Secularization of Modern Cultures*
(New York: Oxford University Press, 1966). See also below, chapter 12.

[18] See my article, "Theology in Transition," *Journal of Religion*, vol. 20, no. 2 (Apr.
1940), pp. 160-68.

[19] Meland writes that Mathews and Case were the real forerunners of Chicago-style
empiricism, although they applied empirical method historically. George B. Foster had
some influence on a few younger thinkers, particularly Macintosh. Smith moved from
Ritschlianism to empiricism and was instrumental in getting Wieman to Chicago, and
thus served as something of a bridge between the older and newer empiricisms. See
Bernard E. Meland, ed., *The Future of Empirical Theology* (Chicago: University of
Chicago Press, 1969), p. 14 note and pp. 16-17.

process. Edward Scribner Ames was primarily a parish minister who also taught at the University of Chicago. His interests centered in the psychology and philosophy of religion. His approach was primarily through social psychology, and he thought of God as a "generalized other," as "Reality idealized and personified." He used such analogies as "Alma Mater" and "Uncle Sam" to indicate that the idea of "God" referred to an objective social reality.[20]

Ames's pragmatism showed its indebtedness to both James and Dewey. He approved James's statement that religion does not refer to any specific thing. Religion, said Ames, draws on many emotions and is based on social experience that grows out of biological needs. Religion is a form of adaptation to the evolutionary process. It can best be understood through psychology, "the science which in its developed forms becomes theology or the philosophy of religion." [21]

Ames's approach was genetic, and he spent a good deal of effort explaining the origins of religion in various cultures. Religious ideas arise out of the social context, from "instinctive and habitual types of activity." [22] They retain their dynamic character only as long as they perform their expected functions. "The idea of God," said Ames, "like any other general idea, signifies a system of habits, and in this case, as elsewhere, the presence of the idea has for its normal effect the initiation of those habitual attitudes and endeavors." [23] He quoted and agreed with the well-known statement of James H. Leuba that *"God is not known, He is not understood; He is used*—used a good deal and with an admirable disregard of logical consistency, sometimes as meat purveyor, sometimes as moral support, sometimes as friend, sometimes as an object of love." [24] Of course, said Ames, this is true of every idea pragmatically conceived, and he quoted James to the effect that "when we cease to admire or approve what the definition of a deity implies we end by deeming that deity incredible." [25] Ames backed up this thesis by appealing to the

---

[20] See Ames's chapter in Wieman and Meland, *American Philosophies of Religion*, p. 334.

[21] Edward Scribner Ames, *The Psychology of Religious Experience* (Boston: Houghton Mifflin Co., 1910), p. 26.

[22] Ibid., p. 304.

[23] Ibid., p. 313.

[24] Ibid., p. 314; quoted from Leuba, "Contents of the Religious Consciousness," *Monist*, vol. 11, p. 571.

[25] Ibid., p. 316; quoted from William James, *The Varieties of Religious Experience* (New York: Longmans, Green & Co., 1902), p. 329.

history of religions, especially when the concept of God is removed from its social environment and becomes a false abstraction.

In 1910, Ames was still restricted to a psychobiological approach. His concept of God contained the highest ideals of the human race, signifying human purposes and values, including beauty and art. It was rooted in "the deep instinctive historical and social consciousness of the race." [26] This was the limit of empirical knowledge. It reduced religion to devotion to human values perceived by the social consciousness.

By 1929, Ames had restated his position. He wrote that there is an "order, power, and beauty" which is "an evident and significant characteristic of the world and of life itself." [27] He claimed that God is more than a projection of social ideals, but he still insisted that God is wholly natural. Reality was conceived as friendly, and God stands, like Alma Mater, as a symbol of reality's support of man's values.

He examined such specifically religious practices as prayer and mysticism, both of which he saw as natural aspects of "zestful living," but he did not see either experience as communion with a personal deity, but rather with an "idealized other." This "reality" which is God "includes at least human intelligence, and in the sphere of that intelligence, hears and responds." [28]

But had Ames's empiricism helped as far as knowledge of God's existence is concerned? At times he seemed close to Dewey's view of God as a relation between ideal and actual, and at other times he seemed nearer to James's view of God as a MORE. He identified God with value, including love as found in daily living, but this empiricism stopped short of any cosmic or metaphysical claims. It provided some satisfaction when tested pragmatically, for it pointed to activities among men which supported an optimistic view of a friendly universe.

Ames's emphasis was on the practical, and he developed a view of the "practical absolute." He used the illustration of a suit of clothes which is purchased after considering many possibilities, but when the transaction is completed it has all the finality that an absolute decision would have. So God, as a perfect person, can become more perfect, just as a stove called "New Perfection, No. 62" has moved beyond the "practically perfect" original model.[29]

To the "practical absolute" Ames added the "honorific absolute" as a

---

[26] Ibid., p. 318.
[27] *Religion* (New York: Henry Holt & Co., 1929), p. 152.
[28] Ibid., p. 215.
[29] See ibid., pp. 159-62.

variation. "The objects of our devotion appear as wholly satisfying. . . . We ascribe perfections to objects of appreciation." [30] Thus we take tentative attributes and make them absolute when applied to God, for *practical* purposes. Because the evidence is never complete, as James said, we still must act as if there is an absolute for which or whom we decide. This is a pragmatic rather than an empirical test, as James pointed out.

Ames saw salvation as an experience within the limits of this life, and not as an escape from original sin.

> It is won as the soul ripens in knowledge of the sciences, in appreciation of the arts, but above all in faithfulness to the elemental and instinctive relationships of life. Salvation is ethical. It means developed character. It is a life process and signifies the realization of the natural powers of the soul. [31]

This view is pragmatic and empirical and lacks the dogmatism of traditional views.

Ames's position demonstrated the value of social psychology for the understanding of religious behavior. He clarified some aspects of the origin of religion and its primitive nature. His insistence on the study of origins perhaps colored his interpretations of more sophisticated religious behavior. He saw the concept of God within this development of the social consciousness, like Alma Mater or Uncle Sam, the reality of which designates an actual organization of living people who stand for something particular. "So the word God," he wrote, "is not properly taken to mean a particular person, or single factual existence, but the order of nature including man and all the processes of an aspiring social life." [32] This view of God can point to a high moral idealism, for "the goal of religion is the fulfillment of the normal duties and opportunities of life as we experience it, with sympathy and idealism and passionately unselfish devotion." [33] It can lead to a church that practices union, has no creed, takes science as a guide, makes religion as vital as the day's work, and yearns for an ideal society. [34]

---

[30] Ames, in Wieman and Meland, *American Philosophies of Religion*, p. 335.

[31] *Beyond Theology: The Autobiography of Edward Scribner Ames*, ed. Van Meter Ames (Chicago: University of Chicago Press, 1959), p. 76.

[32] Ames, *Religion*, p. 177.

[33] Edward Scribner Ames, *The New Orthodoxy* (Chicago: University of Chicago Press, 1925), pp. 101-2.

[34] See Ames, "Theory in Practice," in Vergilius Ferm, ed., *Contemporary American Theology: Second Series* (New York: Round Table Press, 1933), pp. 11-28.

Ames did not follow the lead of G. B. Smith's mystical naturalism. He was sympathetic with James's "Will to Believe" but did not build on James's radical empiricism. He was closer to Dewey and made even more use of the social consciousness as a tool. As a result, Ames directed the interest of psychology of religion and its resulting theology to empirical results based on what occurs among persons who illustrate by their behavior that they can be called religious, and he provided a warning to those who move too easily to epistemological and metaphysical claims about the knowledge of God based on empirical and pragmatic testing.[35]

Just as empirical methods in theology did not stop at the point where James, Dewey, and Smith left them, so they did not stop with Ames. Ames enriched the scenario with empirical findings in social psychology. As we move on to study Shailer Mathews, we see how empiricism can be used for the understanding of history from a religious perspective.

Conceptual Theism

Shailer Mathews thought of a theologian as a member of a group, rather than as an individual investigator, and as one who operated within the confines of the Christian community. In his hands theology became church centered and moved from the individualism of James and the social psychology of Ames toward a view of history that recorded the experiences of the Christian tradition. Therefore, Mathews was able to bring into the picture a view of God who was in some sense cosmic and of Jesus as a crucial historical figure. In his hands, as in those of Shirley Jackson Case, empirical methods were brought to bear on the historical study of a social movement and on those who participated in it. The pragmatic element was found in the resulting moral and social life of the individuals who participated.[36]

As all theology is functional, thought Mathews, it is the purpose of theology to use terms intelligible to the present age. The analogies used must reflect the background of the group experience, and thus there is a

---

[35] See Darnell Rucker, *The Chicago Pragmatists* (Minneapolis: University of Minnesota Press, 1969), pp. 107-31 and 165, for a description of how Ames fitted into the Chicago school of philosophy rather than theology.

[36] See Meland, *The Future of Empirical Theology*, pp. 18-24.

constant need for theological reconstruction. Furthermore, analogies are symbolic, and the chief danger is that some people will take them literally. Due to the fact that change is localized in certain groups, tensions are sure to arise between groups. The theologian, therefore, is the perennial modernist: a heretic to those who are not aware of changes, a savior to those who have lost their old formulas, and a thinker with tentative conclusions even to himself.

A distinction must be made between an analogy and a pattern, said Mathews. Whenever a fact is to be understood, it must be tied in directly with some unquestioned concept. This process is a form of analogy. Conscious analogy, however, is insufficient. There is a tendency to include the analogy as part of the religious concept itself. Thus it becomes a pattern,

> a social institution or practice used to give content and intelligibility to otherwise unrationalized beliefs. What the axiom is to mathematics, a pattern is to thought. . . . An analogy becomes a pattern when it is so generally used as to become a presupposition of thought and action.[37]

Our theologies are the expressions of the social minds. A social mind is the total complex of patterns in any given period. The task of theology today is to meet the demands of a scientific-democratic social mind. For example, as Ray O. Miller wrote, for many centuries the message of Jesus

> has been wrapped up with such terms as Messiah (Christ), Lord, King, Saviour, Logos, Son of God—all of which are, after all, local and historical expressions growing out of the soil of language and experience. If socialism should mould into the language of the world the word "comrade," would it not be possible for us to say "Jesus, the Comrade," as we now say Jesus the Christ? Why not? [38]

Doctrines, said Mathews, arise from the tensions in group life, and we can evaluate them in terms of whether the tensions are still present. It is not a question of either epistemology or metaphysics but of social

---

[37] Shailer Mathews, *Atonement and the Social Process* (New York: Macmillan, 1930), p. 31; *The Growth of the Idea of God* (New York: Macmillan, 1931), p. 9.
[38] Ray O. Miller, *Modernist Studies in the Life of Jesus* (Boston: Sherman, French & Co., 1917), p. 36.

tensions and the analogies or patterns that provide satisfaction. The patterns evolve from the social mind and help organize human behavior toward the cosmos. The test is pragmatic, and yet man is related to the cosmos. Religiously, man is related to those forces which brought him into being, so "there must be personality-evolving activities in the cosmos." Otherwise men would perish. "We can no more escape the influence of these personality-evolving activities than we can escape the influence of those impersonal forces with which chemistry and physics deal." [39]

We need to think of God as unitary and personal, and this leads us to conceptual theism. Mathews defined God as "our conception, born of social experience, of the personality evolving and personally responsive elements of our cosmic environment with which we are organically related." [40] Such conceptions are pragmatic and change with the times, but the underlying reality is experienced by man as prior to any man's experience and is thus cosmic in nature. But Mathews refused to do any metaphysical speculating as to whether the universe was pluralistic or monistic, whether God was finite or infinite, transcendent or immanent. Such problems point to the abstract, and Christianity is concrete.

He insisted that "religion is the reciprocal personal relationship of humanity with those personality-producing activities of its cosmic environment with which it is organically related." [41] Our thoughts about God are in terms of meaningful patterns, such as we use when we select symbols: John Bull, Uncle Sam, Alma Mater. Here we see a connection with the thought of Ames, except that Mathews went further in his cosmic claims. Thus Mathews could speak meaningfully of prayer and the spiritual life as resources for creative living.

Because of his concern with history and the Bible, his treatment of the church and of Jesus was from a Christian point of view. As in his discussion of God, Mathews steered away from any ontological approach and sought to discover the ways in which Jesus could be understood as a "rallying point" who points human beings toward meaningful living, with the church as a supportive and cooperative community for the same purpose.[42]

---

[39] Mathews, *The Growth of the Idea of God*, p. 214.
[40] Ibid., p. 226; see Mathews, *Atonement and the Social Process*, pp. 182-94.
[41] Shailer Mathews, *Is God Emeritus?* (New York: Macmillan, 1940), p. 32.
[42] See Mathews' *Jesus on Social Institutions* (New York: Macmillan, 1928); *Christianity and Social Process* (New York: Harper & Row, 1934); *Creative Christianity* (Nashville: Cokesbury Press, 1935).

Mathews moved empirical theology somewhat beyond the findings of Ames and Dewey, but he ignored the kind of empirical evidence sought by James and Smith. Mathews placed the emphasis on identifying what was going on in the social process and deriving patterns that would express those Christian convictions that had come down through the historic social process, keeping those that helped one's relationship to the personality-producing activities of the cosmos.

Mathews distinguished his position from humanistic or atheistic interpretations. "It is the neglect of this personal adjustment with personality-producing forces," he wrote, "that separates humanism from religion." [43] It is this point, also, that distinguished Mathews from Dewey. Dewey recognized tendencies toward value in the universe, which might be called polytheism, but Mathews' plural forces that produce personality were conceived as unitary, and one could have reciprocal personal relations with God. This same distinction marked Mathews' position off from that of Ames and brought him closer to James.

However, because Mathews' empirical analysis of the social process lacked epistemological and metaphysical curiosity, one cannot be sure just how to treat his position in terms of truth claims, although he usually talked of experience as a realist and seemed to assume an organismic metaphysics. But these were not in his field of interests. Edwin Aubrey's article on Mathews was entitled "Theology and the Social Process," and this shows how concepts, analogies, and patterns originate and can be tested pragmatically.[44] But Mathews kept his balance at this point and not only said that we could go beyond such a position as held by Ames and Dewey but that we must do so. God, conceived as a unitary person, points to the experienced personality-producing processes in the cosmos. This has always been the empirical claim, whether located through religious experience with James or in the later empiricism of Wieman, who sought a unitary process as the basis for theological reconstruction.

In spite of Mathews' disavowal of liberal theology in favor of what he called modernism, he was caught in the liberal dilemma of trying to

[43] Mathews, in William P. King, ed., *Humanism: Another Battle Line* (Nashville: Cokesbury Press, 1931), p. 144.
[44] Edwin E. Aubrey, in Miles Krumbine, ed., *The Process of Religion* (New York: Macmillan, 1933), pp. 17-52.

harmonize an inherited Christian world view with that of modern science. There remained two competing world views. Mathews could start with his studies of Jesus and come to one conclusion, and with science and come to another. Meland recalls that he never got away from the feeling that Mathews "held two sources of theology in juxtaposition which could never fuse or give rise to one, integrated scheme of thought." [45] Thus, as Smith put it, there was "the last ditch of receding orthodoxy" rather than the establishment of "Christian thinking on an empirical basis," which is what Meland thinks Smith might have achieved had he lived longer. This would lead to a different kind of approach, one that would seek to establish the empirical meanings of what Christianity has been doing and thinking without the otherworldly and supernatural trimmings.[46]

But Mathews was significant in the movement known as empirical theology because he expanded the method to a concern with history and with the patterns of social thought. He was not caught up in a consideration of mysticism or the religious consciousness, and he did not identify morality with the personality-producing forces, but he expected results in terms of both social and personal morality. In these ways his contribution was important.

Empirical method in theology has not been one thing, although in all its variety it has come down on testing concepts in some kind of experience. Usually the concepts have been derived from reflection on experience by a process of induction and the use of imagination. In some cases there has been an assertion of some kind of knowledge by acquaintance through immediate experience, and in others it has been a more pragmatic kind of testing through the values that ideas have in experience.

Religious experience was considered central by James and Smith, who had room in their interpretations for a wide variety of approaches, including on the one hand the extremes of psychical visions and on the other the appreciative consciousness that includes deep feelings and the aesthetic use of symbols and art in religious expression. Both James and Smith saw their emphasis on mysticism as consistent with all other kinds

---

[45] Bernard E. Meland, "Some Unresolved Issues in Theology," *Journal of Religion*, vol. 24, no. 4 (Oct. 1944), p. 236.

[46] See ibid., pp. 234-37.

of experience. They tended, however, to stress the experience of the individual, even in his solitude, as being more important than group experience.

Dewey and Ames made no use of specifically religious experience, but they interpreted experience as having religious qualities under certain circumstances, especially when connected with moral ardor or (at least with Ames) with a sense of dependence on the universe. At the end of his life, Ames was more open to cosmic elements in religion, but both he and Dewey placed the major emphasis on man's capacity to respond to values perceived as potentially real. With both Dewey and Ames, the stress was on the social aspects and not on the individual.

Ames was a Disciples minister, and Mathews and Smith were Christian theologians. Dewey and James did not count themselves as Christians. But Ames wrote strictly as a psychologist and philosopher and made little attempt to align himself with Christian theology. Smith wrote a good deal about the current scene, but his own partly formulated theological position was not identified with Christian thinking in a direct way. Mathews, however, spoke from within the Christian community, and he dealt not only with the question of the concept of God but also with beliefs about Jesus and the church from the standpoint of the social process in history and today.

Yet there was a feeling among many readers that James spoke more directly to the religious community and even to Christians than did the other writers. This was partly because of his sympathetic recounting of religious experiences, many of them in language familiar to Christians, but also because his empirical method and pragmatism helped to relate the American spirit to an enlightened Christian tradition.

These writers are obviously within the spirit of American thinking as we have defined it. But still they have only represented a small minority among Christians in this country. This was probably because, as Ames pointed out, the analogies and patterns of thought that were still operative in most Christian churches were different from the empirical and pragmatic approaches of the culture to all other aspects of life. Smith saw clearly that the conservatives were still able to communicate, at least with each other, but he agreed with the others that the scientific and technological mentality would soon take over in every aspect of life, and unless theology could come to terms with new ways of thinking its ancient patterns would become obsolete. Yet there was an unexpected (for this group) revival of supernaturalism, traditionalism, and fundamentalism in some of the churches during the crisis of World War II, and in some cases there was a divorce of the scientific mentality from biblical thinking.

Throughout this period, however, empiricism continued to thrive in smaller portions of the population, kept alive in one sense by Wieman's continued activity, for his career has spanned the time from 1926 to the present writing. All the others are dead, and in many cases their writings are unavailable. Yet they provided the impetus not only for the development of Wieman's thought but for a post-World War II generation of empirical theologians with a process metaphysics. We need to look carefully at Wieman's thought and compare it with that of Macintosh, and then make a critical analysis of the story up to 1940.

Theocentric Empiricism

THE ONLY EMPIRICIST WHO WAS WRITING IN 1926 AND WHO CONTINUED to be active throughout World War II and after was Henry Nelson Wieman. He came to the University of Chicago while Gerald Birney Smith, Shirley Jackson Case, Edward Scribner Ames, and Shailer Mathews were at the height of their powers, and he had a large influence on such younger theologians as Schubert Ogden and Daniel Day Williams. At the same time, Bernard Eugene Meland emerged as a constructive theologian influenced primarily by Smith and Wieman. Through Wieman, also, the attention of the entire group was focused on the religious interpretation of Alfred North Whitehead, which was developed most fully by Charles Hartshorne and later by John B. Cobb, Jr. At first, Smith and Mathews tended to see their views as aligned with Wieman's, but soon the differences became obvious.

Wieman's background included many influences. He has written with deep appreciation of William Ernest Hocking's interpretation of God in experience and of Ralph Barton Perry's theory of value. At times Wieman's writings have seemed to reflect the thoughts of William James, but he never developed similar overbeliefs. However, the passive side of James's view of God acting on man rather than man as doing it all was essential to Wieman, so that man is never guilty of "using" God. In methodology, Wieman was close to John Dewey, but religiously he was closer to James.

Wieman's empiricism had a realistic base, so that concepts derived from experience had an objective reference. He stressed experience of process and of value, but sometimes the distinction between them was not clear. He examined the particular experiences of individuals, and yet he always wanted to have an experience of structure that pointed to the unity of God. Because he was suspicious of subjective interpretations, he came to reject the examination of the contents of the religious consciousness, but he never lost sight of the religious significance of experience. The brilliant analysis of mysticism in *Religious Experience and Scientific Method* is reiterated in *Man's Ultimate Commitment*, and as late as 1971 he said that he still retained the mystical element. Mystical experience may point beyond what we can comprehend about God, but it still points to the natural world which is known as a result of empirical methods of interpretation.

Wieman has recommended that readers begin with *The Source of Human Good* and ignore his earlier writings. This gives the impression that there is an "early" and a "later" Wieman, but such a view is at least partly false. There is development in Wieman's thought between 1926 and today, and he has changed his manner of presentation, but his seminal thought is evident from the beginning.

Wieman's Presuppositions

Wieman distinguished between theology and philosophy of religion. Theology, building on the tradition of a specific religion, seeks to present truth in such a way that a person will respond with belief and commitment; it uses a "religious vocabulary" that is suited for worship. On the other hand, philosophy of religion, even when operating within the Western Christian tradition, uses linguistic tools that assist in analysis of experiences that may take one beyond any tradition; it does not provide a language for belief and worship. At one point, he suggested that the philosopher of religion is like the dietitian who knows what reality consists of, while the theologian is like the cook who provides a tasty meal.

Religion is described in functional terms as a relationship in which one gives one's self in ultimate commitment to whatever will transform the self by enabling one to overcome sin, guilt, loneliness, and meaninglessness. He has expressed this in many ways in his various books: the word God designates "that Something upon which human life is most dependent for its security, welfare and increasing abundance." [1]

Man is capable of radical transformation but he cannot do it himself; he needs to be transformed in a creative way. He can be aware of the potential to be his "real self," but conventional experiences do not provide the opportunity, nor will conventional religion or belief in God. It is a question of a relationship with a real process which does actually transform a person.

This provides the focus for Wieman's investigation, behind which were several important presuppositions. Like Dewey, Wieman indicated a debt to biology, especially in his treatment of the relation of the organism to the environment. The social psychology which emerges from this biological approach was evident in Wieman's treatment of personality as applied to man and not to God. God may be something greater than personality, with whom or which man may have personal relations, but we cannot say that God is personal, for he is greater than personality.

Metaphysically, Wieman presupposed a naturalism which includes organic interrelatedness in an evolving world. This limitation of God's work to a naturalistic world view does not restrict God's operations, for empirically this is where God is to be discovered. It is within this framework that there are possibilities of growth.

Wieman's evolutionary naturalism was something like Dewey's, but Wieman rejected the idea of progress in favor of growth. Growth involves the destroying of some values to make room for others. It involves change and the increase of mutual enhancement and meaning, but this is no guarantee of progress. "Growth," he wrote, "simply means that in some quarter there is a development by which the connections of mutual support and mutual meaning are extended and made closer." [2]

Growth or change takes place in the time continuum, as we move from the past to the present and anticipate the future. It is within this process of duration that we have experience of creativity at work.

---

[1] Henry Nelson Wieman, *Religious Experience and Scientific Method* (New York: Macmillan, 1926), p. 9.

[2] Henry Nelson Wieman and Regina Westcott Wieman, *Normative Psychology of Religion* (New York: Thomas Y. Crowell Co., 1935), p. 51.

Within this matrix is the experience both of value coming into existence and of creative transformation of ourselves. Within this temporal process is a structure that does not change but which is the "constitutive character of the universe"; it corresponds to the "constitutive structure of the mind," and man's knowledge is restricted to this area of correspondence.[3]

> From all this, we conclude that the ultimate constitutive structure of reality is creativity itself because the order of creativity is the only order necessarily present in all knowledge and in all forms of experience and changelessly present through all changes which human experience can undergo. It is the only order which is logically prior to every other order. No other can be ultimate because every other order may be supplanted by creative transformation of the mind with corresponding transformation of the world as experienced by the mind.[4]

It is "changelessly present." [5]

If this is what is "logically prior" to any religious investigation, it is a presupposition on a grand scale. It sets up a metaphysical as well as an axiological framework for Wieman's empirical analysis and reconstruction. This is where we find ultimate reality, but it is temporal and not timeless, although it "commands the ultimate commitment of man." [6]

Wieman's main focus was on establishing the existence and nature of what transforms man, so that religion has been conceived as ultimate commitment to this reality. But Wieman never thought of this relationship as something pedestrian. He wrote:

> A man must not only be certain that this Object exists; he must have vision of it. This means he must have such appreciation of this Object that it transforms his life, glorifies his world and fills him with a great enthusiasm for life. He must be not only intellectually persuaded but emotionally stirred, not only cognize the fact but discern its value and catch its significance. He must so realize it that it wins his devotion and shapes his will. To have this appreciation of the divine Object, and thus to

---

[3] Henry Nelson Wieman, *Man's Ultimate Commitment* (Carbondale, Ill.: Southern Illinois Press, 1958), pp. 81-82; see Bernard E. Meland, in Robert W. Bretall, ed., *The Empirical Theology of Henry Nelson Wieman* (New York: Macmillan, 1963), pp. 56-57.
[4] Wieman, *Man's Ultimate Commitment*, p. 91.
[5] Ibid., p. 92.
[6] Ibid., p. 97.

feel the stimulus of it, is to have what we call vision of it. Vision involves emotion, imagination and conversion of the will in devoted self-surrender.[7]

The source of religious knowledge is not only found in empiricism, however, for it depends on who the empiricist is. Otherwise, we will find ourselves with all kinds of distorted experiences being reported. A hypothesis to be tested is derived from the imagination and from intuition, and much depends on who has the intuition. So it comes down to a healthy personality in a healthy body and responsible intuitions and hypotheses. Thus Wieman was not drawn to James's "method of extreme cases" but to the normal experiences of wholesome personalities. James, of course, used the same procedure to modify his interpretation of extreme cases. The way to eliminate illusions and fantasy from theology based on experience is to have a community of mutual support as part of the operation, as Charles Peirce suggested. Then the testing can be in terms of anticipated consequences that promote the values of mutual support and enhancement.[8]

Empiricism and Verification

Epistemology governs to some extent the conclusions of any philosophical method. Wieman had a realistic view of knowledge, close to that of Dewey. On this basis he built his empirical method of observation and reason. He insisted that what we claim as religious knowledge be restricted to what can be verified here and now. The only adequate method can be summarized under three headings: (1) sensory observation, (2) experimental behavior, and (3) rational inference. This method means the repudiation of what Wieman called "pure rationalism, pure behaviorism, and pure observation." [9] We can deal only with the nature of God as he can be verified on empirical grounds.

God, for Wieman, was an object of immediate sensory experience. "God *is* and *moves* in our midst in discernible ways." [10] Although

[7] Henry Nelson Wieman, *The Wrestle of Religion with Truth* (New York: Macmillan, 1927), p. 125.
[8] Michael Jackson, "Transcript of a Conversation with Henry Nelson Wieman, April 18-19, 1971."
[9] Henry Nelson Wieman, "God Is More Than We Can Think," *Christendom*, vol. 1, no. 3 (Spring 1936), p. 433.
[10] Bernard E. Meland, in *American Philosophies of Religion* (Chicago: Willett, Clark & Co., 1936), p. 296.

Wieman's method was similar to that of Dewey, at this point he claimed something about God that would separate his thinking from Dewey, and from Ames and Mathews as well. For Wieman, God is not a name for some activities or relationships but is a name that points to a process of creativity that operates to transform human beings.

Such a God can be perceived, claimed Wieman. Perception is a continuous flow of sense experience. It is only as we make our attention discontinuous that we note separate qualities. Perception is not like a motion picture, where films project a series of discontinuous images on the screen, giving an illusion of continuity by the rapidity of changing scenes. Whenever one notes his total experience of anything, he sees it "as a vast, panoramic, kaleidoscopic, massive experience reaching [him] in wide regions of space and time, with innumerable qualities interfused but all flowing together to make one continuous total datum." [11] It is only rarely that one explores the riches and complexity of an experience. It is forgotten that beyond the immediate experience and involved in it is the whole gravitational field, the stars, the sun, and one's own organism which enter the total event.

This complexity of perception includes relationships and the structure of interrelated events; it is physical, physiological, psychological, and social. We can control perceptual events in terms of relating previous and future perceptual events to the present "according to a certain structure of interrelatedness." [12] Within this framework, we can ask:

Are there certain happenings occurring to us and in us which, when proper meanings have been developed, assume the form of perceptual events found to have that structure of interrelatedness which can be identified as the structure of creativity which generates all value? If so, God is a perceived object. [13]

But this does not happen to just anyone. There are conditions to be met, willingness to open one's awareness, and finally an experience of being transformed, so that the hiddenness of God comes into one's consciousness. [14] Of course, this is true of every kind of empirical

[11] Wieman, *The Wrestle of Religion with Truth*, pp. 88-89.
[12] Henry Nelson Wieman, "Can God Be Perceived?" *Journal of Religion*, vol. 23, no. 1 (Jan. 1943), p. 26.
[13] Ibid., p. 27.
[14] Ibid., pp. 28-29.

knowledge, for persons need to be able to read the experience properly and then to interpret it in order to predict any event. Only then does verification take place, and the results are tentative.

Truth is something to be discovered, but it is the product of the creative event and is antecedent to all inquiry. It is a structure of events and of what they may become. Yet this structure may change when we interpose the knowledge process, so that it is abstract and partial rather than all-inclusive and unchanging.

So we begin the search for knowledge about truth with observation, which "is a series of perceptual events." [15] At this point, Wieman moved from an insistence on sense data as such to the phrase "perception involving sense experience." [16] For metaphysics or theology, we need more sophisticated interpretations of awareness and more sophisticated inferences and testing, but all knowledge comes in the same manner. Because "all experience is the experience of something, . . . in hallucinations we plainly are mistaken concerning the object experienced. But that does not belie the fact of some object. . . . There can be no question about the reality of religious experience." [17]

Wieman spoke of intuition as a way into knowledge. It is focused in the mind, as "the creative integration of diverse meanings to form a new, more ample meaning." [18] Sometimes it is like a hypothesis emerging from the creative imagination, and at other times it seems to be a form of knowledge by acquaintance, as in mystical experience. But it still needs to be tested empirically before any resulting concepts can be called knowledge.

On one level Wieman had seemed to reject the data of religious experience, or at least of the religious consciousness, but even in his latest writings, including *Man's Ultimate Commitment* and *Intellectual Foundation of Faith*, he referred to mysticism, and in 1971 he mentioned that he still retained the mystical element but did not talk about it so much because it was so easily misunderstood. [19] In *The Source of Human Good* he related mysticism and intuition, and later he referred to

---

[15] Henry Nelson Wieman, *The Source of Human Good* (Chicago: University of Chicago Press, 1946), p. 181.

[16] In Bretall, op. cit., p. 42; but see p. 5.

[17] Wieman, *Religious Experience and Scientific Method*, pp. 29-30.

[18] *The Source of Human Good*, p. 184.

[19] See Jackson, "Conversation with Henry Nelson Wieman, April 18-19, 1971."

intuition as knowledge by acquaintance, although still needing verification.

There was a brilliant treatment of religious experience in *Religious Experience and Scientific Method* which still stands as an authoritative statement. He approached the analysis through references to art and love as forms of open awareness. Both art and love feature the wholeness of the experience, and yet they must be selective so that nothing can break the unity of the awareness.

Religious experience arouses similar emotions but is aware of a more inclusive event, with less exclusion, if any. The object is so diffuse that it can be only partly experienced, and even that partial experience tends to extend the powers of human awareness, no matter how narrowly developed. The range of awareness depends upon the capacities of the person who has the experience. In ordinary religious experience this awareness is narrower, because it takes a more or less concrete form and loses some of the feeling of the flux of undifferentiated experience. Thus symbols, ceremonies, dogmas, traditions, art, moral laws, and beliefs are considered indispensable for normal religious experiences. These limitations, said Wieman, are arbitrary although of practical value, but the greatest developments of religious experience extend to a much wider awareness of creativity without the limiting concepts.

There is always a danger of either taking the contents of the religious consciousness as objective or of dismissing the whole experience as purely subjective. Wieman did neither. In religious experience, he said, the awareness is inclined to be dim, vague, and fluctuating with no discrimination of particulars. As a result, as one reflects on the experience the emotional response is the most vivid element, and there is no distinct concept adequate to symbolize its meaning.

What we actually experience is not the fantasies or illusions but what causes them. "This uprush from the subconscious is an incidental by-product. What we experience is not primarily the subconscious, but it is that which produces this response of the subconscious." [20] The cause is thought of as external, literal, and objective. This experience is not just an inner experience. It is a "stimulation of the sensorium affecting consciousness." [21] Out of such an experience, new energies are given

---

[20] Wieman, *Religious Experience and Scientific Method*, p. 208.
[21] Wieman, *The Wrestle of Religion with Truth*, p. 155.

which may be turned toward value or disvalue, for religious fanaticism often results in outright evil in the name of God. This is part of the risk one takes, for only through the working of creativity can one seek the good.

In recent years, Wieman placed less and less emphasis on religious experience and mysticism, but he has never lost sight of its centrality. In *The Source of Human Good*, he wrote that "our lives, our plans, and our persons must be broken to gain access to the depth of creative power where alone hope can securely take its stand, because our plans and purposes and organization of personality are too restricted." [22]

This point offers a transition to Wieman's view of values and qualitative meaning. After consideration of many theories of value, Wieman interpreted value as

> appreciable activity. Activity is objective. It can be observed, computed, foreseen. It can be controlled, redirected, elaborated. Activities can be connected in meaningful and supporting ways. Through activity all practical problems are solved. Above all, activity turns us outward. What we experience through activity is the nature of objective reality. [23]

He distinguished between "appreciated" and "appreciable." We can appreciate what is not appreciable, and often we fail to appreciate what is appreciable. We cannot let emotional response be our guide. "To be appreciable means that some living consciousness sometime, somewhere, some way, may be affected by it with joy or suffering." [24] Meaning is the connection that brings all this together. The value, then, is found in the meaning or the connection and not in the enjoyment. The growth of these connections is God.

Whenever Wieman was pushed far enough, he gave priority to value as the most real. This becomes clear in his discussion of "qualitative meaning" as the connection between events which interrelates past, present, and future. Here one finds not only appreciable activities but also future possibilities. Quality is seen as pervasive of every experience and every event, so that "all energy is quality." This led Wieman to

[22] Wieman, *The Source of Human Good*, p. 115.
[23] Henry Nelson Wieman, "Values: Primary Data for Religious Inquiry," *Journal of Religion*, vol. 16, no. 4 (Oct. 1936), pp. 385-86.
[24] Ibid., p. 388.

claim that quality "is ultimate reality. It is the substance of which all is made," as human experience sees it.[25]

These findings are consistent with Wieman's empirical method of observation, agreement, and coherence. They come from the discovery that all experience of energy is also the appreciation of quality. This quality is "apprehended by way of feeling." [26] As we perceive the structure running through all events, we have an empirical base for testing. This leads to agreement among observers, who observe the same thing, who have similar powers of observation, and who have the same kind of training. Consensus is of value only when it is found among competent persons. Then their findings need to be interpreted in a way that is coherent with other agreed-upon knowledge.

This seems to leave out revelation, but Wieman interpreted revelation not as knowledge but as a releasing of creative power for the transformation of persons and to save them from various evils. It provides data that need to be tested in the same way as the findings of other kinds of experience. Faith also is not a form of knowledge but is an act of self-giving which may be guided by knowledge. Other data come from the Bible and the teachings of Jesus, and they have value in so far as they assist in bringing a person into that relationship with creativity that will transform him.[27]

All such knowledge is limited in its scope, but it is all we have. This applies to our knowledge of God, although we can distinguish him from other forms of being, so that we cannot call him "being as such." The structure that we know is not the all.[28]

Bernard Meland suggests that in order to understand the development of Wieman's empiricism we have to go back to his original sketching out of the program based on religious experience in *Religious Experience and Scientific Method*. But although this is the distinctive note in Wieman, Wieman tended to disregard it as he developed a more rational conceptual apparatus which would help to distinguish the work of God from the totality of experience.[29] Wieman moved away from the

---

[25] Wieman, *The Source of Human Good*, pp. 302-3; see pp. 16-23.

[26] Ibid., p. 304.

[27] See ibid., pp. 209-17; *Journal of Religion*, vol. 23, no. 1 (Jan. 1943), p. 28.

[28] Wieman, *Man's Ultimate Commitment*, p. 103.

[29] Meland, "The Root and Form of Wieman's Thought," in Bretall, *The Empirical Theology of Henry Nelson Wieman*, p. 61.

instrumentalism of John Dewey and the process metaphysics of Whitehead; he measured his position against those of Tillich and Barth, among others; and at one point he called himself an "existentialist" as he identified God with creative interaction in interpersonal relationships, but his ruling commitment remained a religious one.[30] It is the implication of this commitment for his concept of God that now needs our attention.

God

One of Wieman's strongest statements about criteria for determining the categories in the structure of experience for understanding the reality we call God was in an article written in 1943. We need to examine the evidence from what he called "magnificent religious living," such as the record of the life of Paul. Paul's beliefs were obviously based on the kind of thinking available in the first century, but we can discover what these beliefs pointed to. This particular report was limited to the Christian tradition. Wieman's criteria for God were as follows:

I. In the world generally
   1. Creative of human personality and of all genuine good
   2. Creative of the world as appreciable to the human mind
   3. Is the only *absolute* good in human life
   4. Exercises power that is noncompetitive and incommensurable with any other
   5. Demands sovereignty over human life
II. In human living particularly
   1. Commands absolute commitment of faith
   2. Demands radical and continuous reconstruction of human living
   3. Engenders worship when human self-will is broken and the divine sovereignty accepted
   4. Receives and answers prayer
   5. Speaks in prophecy and appears in revelation
   6. Responds to commitment of faith by
      a) Giving triumph over every disaster
      b) Giving us our ultimate freedom
      c) Saving from spiritual death

---

[30] See Henry Nelson Wieman, *Religious Inquiry* (Boston: Beacon Press, 1968), pp. 202-18.

7. Imposes sanction and obligation carried by moral directives

III. In Christian living especially

1. Revealed in Christ
2. Identical with Christ crucified yet living
3. Determines the nature of sin
4. Engenders sense of sin when one becomes aware of it
5. Through Christ crucified "forgives" sin, i.e., is reconciled with sinner
6. Saves [salvation includes, above, II, 6a, b, c, and below, IV, 1, 2, 3, 4] on condition of repentance and faith in Christ
7. Generates the church and takes headship of church in Christ
8. Gives to the church its evangel
9. Rules the Kingdom of God
10. Reveals itself in the Bible

IV. In society and history generally

1. Is the basic requirement for solution of every social problem
2. Is directive for the social process and for history
3. Judges history and the social process
4. Through Christ reveals how history may be consummated in the Kingdom of God[31]

In spite of its strange mixture of philosophical and Christian words, this is probably the best single summary of what God does, according to Wieman. It is the kind of experience persons have in "magnificent religious living." It points to "a structure of human experience which distinguishes the reality of God from other realities." [32] Wieman used the word "creativity."

Creativity is an ongoing process and can be treated in terms of creative communication, creative interchange, creative transformation, or creative event. It is the source of all values, all of life's richness, all possibility for the future. But once it comes into existence in terms of its fruits, it is no longer creative but is created good or qualitative meaning. Although something we can appreciate, it is not the reality of God at work. Creativity "*creates* the human mind and personality . . . *sustains* life at the human level . . . *saves* man from the worst which can happen

---

[31] Henry Nelson Wieman, "Power and Goodness of God," *Journal of Religion*, vol. 23, no. 4 (Oct. 1943), p. 268. Used by permission of the University of Chicago Press.
[32] Ibid., p. 269.

to him on condition of faith . . . transforms, that is to say, *saves unto* the best that man can ever attain." [33] But it does this only when man fulfills the proper conditions.

Wieman broke down the creative event into four subevents, which he described in various ways. First, it gives man a new perspective whereby, through interrelations with other individuals and groups, there is increased awareness of qualitative meaning, an expanded range of knowing and valuing. Second, there is an integration of various perspectives, an expanding range and depth of mutually sustaining activities as one's values are modified and integrated into what one already has. This may be a lonely experience resulting in painful working through of alternatives. Third, there is an expansion of the appreciable world, as one seeks to carry on the evolutionary process at all levels. This expanding of the valuing consciousness is not a steady development but comes as the result of extraordinary experiences. Fourth, there is growth of community as interrelationships are transformed and deepened.[34]

It should be emphasized that these events are seen in the active mode, as "emergings, integratings, expandings, deepenings." [35] They are in process. "They are locked together in such an intimate manner as to make a single, total event continuously recurrent in human existence." [36] Thus Wieman was able to insist on the unity and universality of the creative event, while at the same time he made it clear that not all new developments could be applied to this working of the process of creativity.

Wieman often has been misunderstood for his claim that God is neither mind nor personality. The reason for this assertion from Wieman's point of view is clear enough. Both mind and personality are descriptive of human functions, and creativity is the *source* of such functions and therefore is neither identical with nor analogous to human mind or personality. Wieman put it this way: "Mind is just exactly what God is not. . . . God is greater than Mind. . . . Some things God

---

[33] Wieman, *Man's Ultimate Commitment*, pp. 29-30.
[34] See Henry Nelson Wieman, "Power and Goodness of God," p. 269; *Religious Inquiry*, pp. 23, 208; *The Source of Human Good*, pp. 58-69.
[35] Wieman, *The Source of Human Good*, p. 68.
[36] Ibid., p. 65.

could never do, apparently, if man with his intelligence did not do his part. But what God does is different from what man does." [37]

His objection to assuming that God is personal was based on this same kind of reasoning. "I deny personality to God," he wrote, "not by subtraction but by addition." [38] By this, he meant that because personality emerges from the social interaction of individuals, it is not something that can be applied to creativity. God is greater than personality, for he is to be thought of as the source of human mind and personality and therefore different categories must be applied.

As a result of this insistence, Wieman has been accused of thinking of God as less than mental or personal, or as nonmental or nonpersonal. But Wieman would prefer to speak of God as supramental or suprapersonal. God does what man cannot do, but God does many things through what men can do. As has been indicated, this can be spelled out in terms of the four subevents which, taken together, make up the creative event, which is the concrete working of God in our midst.

This creativity is at work in history, provided we see history as the past impinging on the present. This creativity has produced the mind of man, although there is no overall pattern of progress. Development has taken place wherever there has been creative transformation of men so that they act in commitment to creativity. "History can be defined as the creation, accumulation, and integration of meanings in all their dimensions." [39] Man has emerged from the world of animals, has created a civilization, has developed the capacity to live according to values, has learned to use technology, and now faces the problem that each of these developments has led to both evil and good. Unless man also is able to find ways to commit himself to creative interchange, further steps cannot be taken. "History is the supreme achievement of the creative event," [40] and this creative power can save us. But this creative good is not all-powerful, and the results are not guaranteed. What we have is a view similar to the meliorism of James, and how man commits himself and what he does with his responsibility makes a difference.

---

[37] From a review of Robert L. Calhoun's *God and the Common Life* in *The Christian Century*, vol. 52, no. 40 (Oct. 2, 1935), p. 1242.
[38] Henry Nelson Wieman, Max C. Otto, and Douglas Clyde Macintosh, *Is There a God?* (Chicago: Willett, Clark & Co., 1932), p. 48.
[39] Wieman, *Man's Ultimate Commitment*, p. 299.
[40] Wieman, *The Source of Human Good*, p. 307.

Such a view does not bypass the existence of evil in history and in the world. Evil is that which is opposed to God. It is equally real and can be specified. Evil can destroy goods that are created. It can obstruct the working of creative good but cannot destroy it. "Creativity carries the hope and potency of all the highest good that ever will be." [41] But there are many kinds of evil, some of which are caused by man's willful ignorance of creativity and some by disobedience.

Wieman made a distinction between creativity, which is an abstraction, and creative event, which is concrete reality. Creativity is the knowable aspect of the creative event, selected from the data of experience and thought of in abstract terms. The concrete event is constantly changing, but creativity is changeless. The creative event is experienced in a multitude of ways, pluralistically, but creativity is a unity.

It is not surprising that these distinctions remind one of Whitehead's primordial and consequent natures of God, but Wieman was quite clear (after an earlier flirtation with the primordial nature of God in *The Wrestle of Religion with Truth*) that he rejected Whitehead's basic approach. Wieman's primordial order is the structure of creative energy, which "is coercive, determinate, and antecedent to all that man may do or seek or know, setting limits to knowledge, to truth, and to all that may happen." [42]

God, then, is quite obviously something beyond man, to which man is related and on which he is dependent. This is different from Dewey's creativity of the human mind. God is what forgives, transforms, and sustains man, and there is a "grace" by which God makes possible man's capacity to participate in appreciable activities. When man is under the control of creativity, he has freedom because he is no longer under other dominations. He has the capacity to select options by the use of adequate criteria for choosing the best possible action, and he receives the power to attain what he has decided. This is a partial freedom, and it makes possible the growth of meaning and value in his life. [43]

Such a God who gives men freedom also transcends man. God is more than we can think, is beyond our control, and is ultimately a mystery only partly known. But to speak of God as transcending the

---

[41] Ibid., p. 87.
[42] Ibid., p. 195; see pp. 192-95, 299.
[43] See ibid., pp. 300-301.

natural order or transcending reason is to speak meaninglessly, for such supernatural transcendence cannot in any meaningful way be known.

Over the years between 1926 and 1968, the period of Wieman's major publications, he used many different ways of speaking in order to communicate his basic ideas about God. We may summarize the overall view as follows: God is a fact, empirically verified as existing independently of man's perception of him. He is unitary, being the process which brings all values into mutual support. He is superhuman, but not supernatural. He transcends man, but does not transcend nature. He is present to man as a potent and observable entity. He is more worthy of devotion than any other existent or possible structure. Men pray to God and he answers. He has transforming power which is creative. He has organizing power, but depends on man's cooperation in providing conditions for growth.

Frequently God acts in opposition to man's purposes. Sometimes he seems definitely to oppose intelligent human action. He is not mind, but is the source of human minds. He is not personal, but is beyond personality. "He is the *growth of connections between activities* which are appreciable." [44] He is "the growth of meaning and value in the world." [45] He is creativity and the creative event.

This empirical concept of God is derived from observation of the lives of men, especially those who have developed their religious living to a magnificent degree, of the processes of nature, and of the developments of the social order and of history. God is to be seen in the increasing interdependence of all mankind. "The superhuman power of God is shown shaping the lives of men into oneness that they never intended and which is, more often than not, contrary to their purposes." [46]

Finally, "to know God is to know love." [47] Men always love interactions, and as God is an interaction, they love him. Love itself is "a kind of interaction." [48] Thus man responds to this vision with passion, imagination, and utter devotion, for love has taken possession of him.[49]

There are two levels of commitment. The religious person is

---

[44] Wieman, *The Growth of Religion*, p. 353.
[45] Wieman, *Normative Psychology of Religion*, p. 137.
[46] Ibid., p. 532.
[47] Wieman, *Is There a God?*, p. 11; see *The Wrestle of Religion with Truth*, pp. 138-39.
[48] Wieman, *Is There a God?*, p. 18.
[49] See my essay, "Wieman's Theological Empiricism," in Bretall, *The Empirical Theology of Henry Nelson Wieman*, pp. 24-25, for a similar summary.

committed to the reality of God before he knows what it is. He gives himself to the reality of creativity and not to his ideas about it. This is the element of risk in all acts of faith. Whatever sustains and transforms the life that has been created is worthy of our absolute devotion, for this is the source of man's greater good.

But this does not justify stupidity, ignorance, or superstition. It does not justify the projecting of man's wishes onto the universe. There is a second level of commitment, which is to seek whatever evidence can come from man's experience and intelligence about the nature of creativity and the guidance and direction that is given as a result. This commitment has an openness and tentativeness about it, because all the evidence and interpretation are still in process and man is always liable to error. So man's ultimate commitment is to the transforming power active in his life, and his secondary commitment is to the processes by which he seeks better understanding. We can seek this understanding within the cultural heritage of the Christian faith, provided we recognize that the creative source of every great faith is identical, for God operates in many diverse ways.[50]

Wieman and Christianity

Wieman's writings were in the realm of philosophy of religion rather than theology, although it is proper enough to refer to him as an empirical theologian. He saw his work within the cultural heritage of Christianity, and as Daniel Day Williams wrote, "Wieman's thought arises within the Christian community as an expression of the essential truth of the Christian faith." [51] In the search for deeper knowledge and devotion, the advantage "in being a Christian is that one has access to certain insights, clues and suggestions that may help in the search." [52]

Another important aspect is that within the Christian heritage we have the nonprofessional responsibility of living in devotion to creativity rather than simply developing new techniques for thinking accurately about religious concepts. In a helpful analogy, Wieman wrote that

religion, in one sense, is like baseball or any other form of play or art. The professionals who play in the big leagues render a great service to

---

[50] Wieman, *Religious Inquiry*, pp. 79-84.

[51] Williams, "Wieman as a Christian Theologian," in Bretall, *The Empirical Theology of Henry Nelson Wieman*, p. 73.

[52] Henry Nelson Wieman, *The Issues of Life* (New York: Abingdon Press, 1930), p. 40.

baseball. Baseball would certainly not pervade our national life as it does, if it were not for these big leagues. But if you want to find out the true spirit of baseball in all the glory of a passion you must not go to the big leagues. You must go to the back yard, the sand-lot, the side street, and the school ground. There it is not a profession, it is a passion. When a passion becomes a profession, it often ceases to be a passion. That is as true of religion as it is of baseball. Among the professionals you find a superb mastery and a great technique, but not too frequently the pure devotion. Perhaps in baseball the passion is not too important, but in religion it is all important. A religion that is not passionate simply is not worth considering. Therefore, I say, we need more sand-lot religion. The professional, whether White Sox or Methodist, controls inordinately our baseball and our religion.[53]

Thus, Wieman was concerned about the Christian use of words, with full awareness of the significance of the traditional vocabulary. Of the three uses of words for religious communication, the emotive one is essential, for this is how words have power over personalities, where passion is expressed, and where responses are evoked. But such uses need to be related to the designative ones, where we are able to correct the errors of past and present. Then there are words which have formal and technical uses and do not have any emotional effect. Emotive words change their meanings, however, as they are related to designative and formal uses and as the latter are refined by proper technical methods.

Wieman would not repudiate traditional words or operate by selection of a few of the most effective ones or use words for emotive power only. Traditional words have been used to designate the reality which saves mankind and to arouse loyalty and sensitivity to God. Such words have power because they have emerged from use in a community that responds emotively. The Christian community owns the Christian symbols, which have ancient and current power. We cannot dispense with them or invent new ones, although new technical terms can be used to illuminate them. An adequate empirical methodology gives us entry into the capacity for determining their current meaning, and this entails a development of creative communication. This forces the

---

[53] Henry Nelson Wieman, "How I Got My Religion," *Religious Education*, vol. 26 (Dec. 1931), p. 844; reprinted in *Religious Education*, vol. 69 (Jan.-Feb. 1974), p. 33. Used by permission.

theologian and philosopher back to the sand lot, where religion is lived passionately and where we can translate back and forth from the old to the new forms of words and symbols and their meanings.[54]

Wieman treated myth, symbols, and art as noncognitive, yet he qualified this by saying that they awaken "some concrete fullness of individual existence" and "are not entirely noncognitive." [55] They help people to see reality as "one unitary movement." But symbols lose their power as cultures develop, and this poses the challenge of education to help people reinterpret them. This includes a process of demythologizing in terms of a naturalistic metaphysics.

But when it comes to the use of myth, Wieman made a sharp turn in terms of the psychological needs of worshipers. After making clear that God is not a person, he concluded

> that the mythical symbol of person or personality may be indispensable for the practice of worship and personal devotion to the creative power, this need arising out of the very nature of creative interaction and so demonstrating that the creative event is the actual reality when this symbol is used most effectively in personal commitment of faith.[56]

It can even be used effectively by those who know better, for we address God by his name and not in terms of philosophical analysis.

"Christianity is a continuing social movement shaped by a certain historic past in which Jesus Christ is the central figure." [57] This past guides us both unconsciously and consciously as we live in the present. Wieman saw Jesus as the key figure in the creative interchange that brought a sense of unity and mutual support to his followers. But this creative event centered in the fellowship and the interaction and not in Jesus as an individual. The resurrection shattered the disciples' fixation on rules and ideals and freed them to accept the dominance of the creative event.

Because sin is whatever obstructs the work of the creative event, it

[54] Henry Nelson Wieman, "On Using Christian Words," *Journal of Religion*, vol. 20, no. 3 (July 1940), pp. 257-69.

[55] William S. Minor, ed., *Charles Hartshorne and Henry Nelson Wieman* (Carbondale, Ill.: Foundation for Creative Philosophy, 1969), p. 102.

[56] Wieman, *The Source of Human Good*, pp. 267-68; see Wieman et al., *Is There a God?* p. 125.

[57] Wieman, *The Growth of Religion*, p. 280.

94

can be the work of good people as well as bad, if they are limited to the peak of current human goodness. God acts to forgive sin as he overcomes the alienation due to sin, and thus releases God's victory in our midst. God can do what men cannot do. Out of this process that centered in Jesus came the church, which is a historic community in which God's creative working is to some degree evident, and which is open to God through its prayer and worship.[58]

Such religious living looks to the future, but we cannot predict what we do not know. Yet there is a place for hope, even if not for life after death. "Empirical theology," said Wieman,

> opens the way for hope, because it can show that if creativity and its demands are studied and searched, and if its demands are accepted, it can and will transform human life toward the greater and deeper satisfactions of life, and save man from self-destruction and from the mechanization of life which occurs when action is not inspired and guided by appreciation of individuality.[59]

Conclusions

Of the empiricists studied so far, Wieman made the most consistent use of the method, refined it, and applied it to every aspect of life. The personal element came out most strongly in *Methods of Private Religious Living* and the social in *Now We Must Choose*, where he was concerned over the future of democracy and the threat of dictatorship. The same issues run through the latter chapters of *Man's Ultimate Commitment*. In spite of empiricism's concern with what can be experienced now, he wrote *The Directive in History*. He saw God at work in history as well as in interpersonal and social and political relationships.

But his empiricism has been challenged in a number of ways. At times, it seems too precise in its empirical claims, limiting the characteristics of God as he is known. But he also tended to include within his empiricism certain unstated presuppositions. He never escaped completely from Hocking's idealism, and Meland suggests that there is a "veiled absolute" in his total outlook that led Ames and Dewey to disagree with him. The claim, for example, that evil may be plural while the good is always one is a form of neoplatonism; experience

[58] See Wieman, *The Source of Human Good*, pp. 39-44, 268-93.
[59] Wieman, in Bretall, op. cit., p. 102.

shows a plural experience of both evils and goods unless some form of idealism creeps in.[60] This protected Wieman from an empirical positivism at the expense of his rigid empiricism.

At the same time, Wieman rejected metaphysical speculation. He was attracted at first by Whitehead's process metaphysics, but he turned against the whole movement, keeping only a rather simplistic materialism with spiritual overtones. He specifically rejected the organic wholeness of the cosmos as he saw it in Charles Hartshorne, the unconditioned transcendent as he saw it in Paul Tillich, and the biblical orientation of Karl Barth, and spoke of being an existentialist without identifying this with existentialism.[61]

Many of Wieman's critics objected to his use of faith as commitment to what is already known. Like William James, his critics saw faith as commitment prior to having enough evidence and as contributing to the accumulated data that assist in gaining knowledge, all within the empiricist orbit.

Wieman's empiricism leads one to talk of the structure of creativity in terms of an abstraction and the creative event as an object of experience. Is the structure a metaphysical proposition, a phenomenological category, or an object of experience? Wieman would claim the last, but this is difficult to point to as something observable. Also, although obviously there are experiences of values, how does one experience something as general or vague as "felt quality" or "qualitative meaning?" Are the criteria for judging derived from previous experience or rational concepts?

A classic debate between Wieman and Robert L. Calhoun took place in the pages of *Christendom* during 1936-37. It was probably stimulated by a review of Calhoun's *God and the Common Life*, in which Wieman stated that on Calhoun's terms mind is what God is not. Calhoun picked this up as a starting point. He argued that when empiricism is properly interpreted by analogical inference we can say that God is mind. Wieman responded in terms of mind and personality as "summit" terms applying to human beings. Calhoun argued that in order for there to be some connection between structure and the creative event, some factor

---

[60] See Bernard E. Meland, *The Future of Empirical Theology* (Chicago: University of Chicago Press, 1969), p. 36; Robert L. Calhoun, "God As More Than Mind," *Christendom*, vol. 1, no. 2 (Winter 1936), p. 341.

[61] Wieman, *Religious Inquiry*, pp. 202-5.

must oversee and guide the process. There is evidence, said Calhoun, of conscious and purposive action. We may not fully understand or predict such action, but it gives no evidence of being nonconscious and nonpurposive. Furthermore, the interaction between the creative event and man seems to be intelligent and personal.[62]

Charles Hartshorne made a similar criticism but added memory and purpose to consciousness as characteristics of deity. Hartshorne argued on rational rather than empirical grounds, but in terms of empirical consequences. Can God experience anything? Can he communicate? Can he intend? If not, he may be just a characteristic found in many experiences. If not, how do facts or values become intelligible to human minds, which are the product of this creativity? If not, does God have the capacity to change his actions when events he has not foreseen occur? If not, the pluralistic experiences of creative goods cannot be seen as a unity, and God lacks integrity.[63]

Both Calhoun and Hartshorne wrote that Wieman's rigid empiricism needed to be expanded by the use of analogical inference. Wieman intended to eliminate this kind of thinking, but Calhoun thought he did not succeed. By starting with the admitted limitations of knowledge derived from empirical procedures and then making assertions about everything that exists, said Calhoun, Wieman was making "a very bold use of analogy indeed." Most of what Wieman said about interaction, even between trees and the wind, is a projection based on a limited observation. When this conclusion is applied to all that is, it is no longer simple abstraction or rigorous deduction but analogical inference.[64]

There is always the question for the empiricist that he assumes that his verified knowledge can be appropriated by anyone. If God is a perceptual reality and the empiricist can point to God's activity in creative transformation, why are there many people who disagree with this conclusion? There is a mystery of disclosure as part of the process, and this Wieman has failed to take account of. When one shares Wieman's presuppositions and commitments, it is possible to agree with

---

[62] Robert L. Calhoun, "The Power of God and the Wisdom of God," *Christendom*, vol. 2, no. 1 (Winter 1937), pp. 44-47.

[63] Charles Hartshorne and William L. Reese, eds., *Philosophers Speak of God* (Chicago: University of Chicago Press, 1953), pp. 404-8.

[64] Robert L. Calhoun, "How Shall We Think of God?" *Christendom*, vol. 1, no. 4 (Summer 1936), pp. 595-96.

him, but his perspective is too expanded for some and too limited for others.

Part of the problem on the negative side is the limitation of his metaphysical outlook. Again, for some his naturalism claims too much and for others too little. Those most deeply influenced by Wieman, such as Daniel Williams, Schubert Ogden, Bernard Loomer, and Bernard Meland, have started with empiricism but have moved rapidly in the direction of the process philosophy which Wieman repudiated. Williams, for example, finds Wieman's emphasis in *Religious Experience and Scientific Method* more satisfactory than his later writings, because there was a greater awareness of the richness of a "total datum." [65]

Wieman tried to make room for a more specifically religious language, but he treated myths and symbols as almost completely noncognitive. This literalism as applied to his philosophical vocabulary, as contrasted with the figurative and emotive use of "Christian words" made it difficult to develop a methodology for examining the truth value of traditional religious language. There may need to be a more sophisticated understanding of what Wittgenstein called "language games" and the criteria for determining their truth value in terms of their use.[66]

Wieman's appreciation of history and of the Christian tradition is an important factor in his total outlook, and it is possible to read history within the framework of his naturalism and empiricism. But history is never simply the accounting for factual events, and an objective description, even when it is reasonably accurate, does not communicate its meaning and value. To see the working of creativity in the events surrounding the life of Jesus and the formation of the church is to go beyond the obvious.

The criticisms I have listed are from the standpoint of those who agree fundamentally with Wieman's approach. Criticisms from other points of view would be less sympathetic and less significant for our purpose. Wieman's insistence that we need an empirical objectivity and honesty in examining religious assertions is essential to any understanding of the American spirit in theology, especially when it is used to

[65] See Daniel Day Williams, in Bretall, op. cit., p. 65.
[66] See my *The Language Gap and God* (Philadelphia: United Church Press, 1970), pp. 40-61.

expose the many false claims made in the name of theology. Wieman's negative criticisms of theology were almost as important as his constructive contributions to our thinking.

Wieman never admitted that he would go beyond legitimate rational inferences, and so he restricted his assertions to what he considered proper empirical conclusions. Yet he cheerfully denied aspects of God that other theologians thought of as conclusions based on other than empirical evidence. Macintosh, for example, limited his so-called verified knowledge of God to the concept of a divine value-producing factor, and claimed that all concepts such as God's mind, personality, transcendence, and metaphysical attributes were a matter of reasonable beliefs or permissible surmises beyond the realm of empirical verification. He also focused his empiricism on an analysis of the right religious adjustment. Therefore, he was very close to the conclusions of Wieman in *Religious Experience and Scientific Method*, where Wieman was cautious about applying or denying categories of mind or personality to God. But within a few years, Wieman moved away from religious experience as a reliable source of knowledge and at the same time began to deny categorically that God could be mind or personality. Their discussions of these issues were sharply etched in *Is There a God?*, to which Max Otto contributed with humanistic criticisms of both Wieman and Macintosh.

Wieman still stands as a unique practitioner of empirical theology, hewing a methodology within a naturalistic framework that harks back to James and Dewey and that represents the American spirit in theology. Williams has argued

> that while Wieman's position stands apart from obvious trends, he has actually stated what has become the practice of people in wide areas of our culture, including much of the practice in the established religious institutions. When we ask what men actually put their trust in as revealed by their actions, we see that we may require something like "creative interchange" to describe the operative process to which we give our attention and even our devotion.[67]

This statement by Williams has a significance today because of the new theological situation. As we moved into a post-Barthian age, we came

---

[67] Daniel Day Williams, in Minor, *Charles Hartshorne and Henry Nelson Wieman*, p. 56.

upon the slogan that God was dead. This bothered many people, but it did not upset Wieman because the God who was dead had never been Wieman's God. The demand for some kind of verification for beliefs about God was exactly where Wieman's empirical theology stood, and therefore it was relevant to the new demand that we need evidence before we can have faith.

This did not mark the end of developments in empirical theology for the Chicago school, as we shall see when we look at the post-World War II developments. But along with Wieman was Yale's Macintosh, who also represented the American spirit in theology as based on empiricism, and to him we now turn.

Empiricism and Religious Experience

CHAPTER 6

In 1932, for twenty-five weeks there appeared in *The Christian Century* a series of exciting articles. Henry Nelson Wieman, Douglas Clyde Macintosh, and Max C. Otto exchanged ideas, criticisms, and constructive arguments about God, along with some body blows to the others' positions. Most of it was good, relatively nontechnical defense of their positions. Otto cheerfully affirmed the nonexistence of God, Wieman reasserted the position outlined in the last chapter, and Macintosh, while making skirmishes to criticize the others, doggedly developed an argument for God which was a reverse of his usual order.

What is important for us is that these articles show how Macintosh differed from Wieman. In their empirical methods, especially when Wieman's first book appeared, they seemed to share their approach to knowledge of God, but even at this point they differed in their interpretations of the evidence. Macintosh accused Wieman of being like "a tight-rope walker at a circus. At one time it almost seemed as if he were going to come down on the side of theism." [1] Because Wieman refused to interpret God as having mind, will, or personality, Macintosh thought that his position was "strongly reminiscent of behaviorism in psychology," [2] and we should not study deity as we study animal

---

[1] Henry Nelson Wieman, Max C. Otto, and Douglas Clyde Macintosh, *Is There a God?* (Chicago: Willett, Clark & Co., 1932), p. 24.

[2] Ibid.

behavior. A behavioristic theology leads to an analysis of God's behavior as "interaction" or "process of integration" or "system of patterns," but not a superhuman cosmic spirit. So Wieman was devoted to "The Wonderful What-Is-It?" [3] He was so concerned with establishing the fact that God exists that he drastically reduced what God means. Wieman returned the compliment by saying that Macintosh was trying to verify beliefs about God because men need such beliefs and ought to have them, justifying his preconceptions rather than searching for reality.

However, their agreements were equally important. They agreed that empirical method was essential, although Macintosh concentrated on religious experience and Wieman on experience in general. They agreed that God exists independently of being perceived as objective reality, "working for man *in spite of himself*." [4] They agreed that God works for man's good when man cooperates, is devoted to the common good, perseveres in moral achievement, and uses the best scientific knowledge. Macintosh's resulting concept, the divine value-producing factor, was not much different from Wieman's growth of meaning and value at the strictly empirical level of investigation. Most of their disagreements came at the secondary level that Macintosh called reasonable faith, where he could talk about God as mind and person.

Macintosh, like Wieman, grew up in a Protestant evangelical home. In both cases, this background was never lost, although Macintosh stayed more in his Baptist tradition. Macintosh had a conversion experience which led to a relationship with the divine that he later called "the right religious adjustment." When he was in college, his mother died, and he wrote about it: "I experienced a profound inner certitude of immortality and of the goodness and sufficiency of God." [5] Already we can see the roots of his empiricism, his emphasis on conversion, and his moral optimism.

Among the influences that brought him from a traditional to a nontraditional orthodoxy, as he styled it, was William James, whose pragmatic "will to believe" and emphasis on the strength of value were

---

[3] Ibid., p. 95.
[4] Ibid., p. 295.
[5] Douglas Clyde Macintosh, "Toward a New Untraditional Orthodoxy," in Vergilius Ferm, ed., *Contemporary American Theology*, vol. 1 (New York: Round Table Press, 1932), p. 290.

later to become part of Macintosh's theology.[6] He read the writings of William Newton Clarke, who used empiricism to verify his Christian beliefs.

When Macintosh studied at Chicago, he was influenced primarily by George B. Foster, but also by Gerald Birney Smith, Edward Scribner Ames, and Shailer Mathews. He was exposed to the theology derived from value judgments of Albrecht Ritschl, especially through Foster and Smith, and in response to Ritschlianism he wrote his dissertation on *The Reaction Against Metaphysics in Theology*.

At this time, Macintosh's interests were closer to Wieman's sand-lot religion with its passion than were others at Chicago. The empiricism at Chicago was to stay in the realm of social process rather than religious experience until the arrival of Wieman in 1927. In 1909, however, when Shailer Mathews was asked if Macintosh should be invited to join the Yale faculty, he wrote, "If you don't hire him, we probably will." [7] Away from the Chicago influences, Macintosh developed his own distinctive empirical theology. He became interested in a realistic theory of knowledge that would account for all knowledge, including religious, which included a balanced view of the place of pragmatism, resulting in a mammoth book on *The Problem of Knowledge* (1915). But chiefly Macintosh became known for asserting that theology can be an "empirical science," and his development as a theologian followed these lines, supported by what he called "moral optimism" and a continuing interest in metaphysics related to emergent evolution and process thinking.

Even the responses of infants to their new world, Macintosh thought, have within them the dawning of religious consciousness. Even if the response is only an inarticulate cry, there are expressions of awe and wonder, a sense of mystery, and reactions of fascination and fear which are also part of the experience of primitive man. This is a human response rather than an expression of infantile needs. It is the root of experiential religion. Combined with this is the appreciation of values as they come into existence. Even though values are relative, they make absolute claims upon mankind. "Rooted in our awareness of reality and

---

[6] Ibid., p. 292. See J. Seelye Bixler, Robert L. Calhoun, and H. Richard Niebuhr, *The Nature of Religious Experience* (New York: Harper & Row, 1937), pp. 72-74.

[7] Bernard E. Meland, ed., *The Future of Empirical Theology* (Chicago: University of Chicago Press, 1969), p. 11.

in our quest for values, *the distinctively religious interest is an interest in the relation of reality to values.*" [8] As we become conscious of the relation between reality and value on increasingly higher levels, and respond by participating in this process, we become religious.

We can observe such processes in all religions, but except for rare excursions into other religions, Macintosh was concerned to draw his evidence from Christian experience, especially in the Protestant evangelical tradition as interpreted by his own brand of liberalism. Thus, most of what he wrote, and most notably in *The Reasonableness of Christianity*, was apologetic rather than creative theology.

The Problem of Religious Knowledge

Macintosh, more than any other of the empiricists and pragmatists who exhibit the American spirit in theology, was concerned with the way in which we gain knowledge. Two of his books, *The Problem of Knowledge* and *The Problem of Religious Knowledge*, evidenced his broad and deep understanding of epistemology, in which he measured other theories against his own critical monistic realism. In any empirical investigation leading to knowledge, there needs to be a theory to support the objective existence of what is known, and this can be established by some kind of immediate experience. We cannot achieve this, he thought, with the various forms of idealism or with dualistic realism, both of which are defective for a wide variety of reasons. Furthermore, any naïve realism is too simpleminded to account for error or psychological factors. What we need is a view that allows for direct experience of the object and sufficient correctives to account for error, hallucination, psychological overtones, and the like. It needs to be critical enough to provide criteria for adequate discrimination.

Macintosh taught that

the object perceived is existentially, or numerically, identical with the real object at the moment of perception, although the real object may have qualities that are not perceived at that moment; and also that this same object may exist when unperceived, *although not necessarily with all the qualities which it possesses when perceived.*[9]

---

[8] "Experimental Realism in Religion," in Douglas Clyde Macintosh, ed., *Religious Realism* (New York: Macmillan, 1931), p. 312.

[9] Douglas Clyde Macintosh, *The Problem of Knowledge* (New York: Macmillan, 1915), p. 311.

Macintosh developed this theory with great sophistication—for example, under twenty points in *Religious Realism*—but the main purpose was to apply it to the field of religion. In religious experience, there may be many aspects of the experience which do not necessarily belong to the object, what is experienced does not exhaust divine reality, and there is some overlapping between experience and the reality as it is.

In many instances our awareness depends on sense perception, but in others there is a wider basis of awareness. Macintosh referred to this broader awareness as "perception in a complex" or intuition, by which he meant

> that in the midst of a complex of colors, sounds, and other sense-qualities, subjectively produced but objectively located, we are able to intuit or perceive the presence of a physical reality with qualities such as direction, distance, extent, shape, duration, motion, energy, and the like, none of which are sense-qualities, but none of which can be discerned except in and through sense-qualities to which the stimulations they originate give rise.[10]

Such intuitions may be rational, appreciative, imaginal, and perceptual; they are also fallible without further empirical testing.[11] The obvious danger of this theory is that by extending the meaning of perception to such a broad area, it may lose its empirical base entirely. It becomes very easy to make intuition the final court of appeal rather than empirical observation.[12]

One way of guarding against this danger is the use of pragmatism as a form of testing, but after an earlier flirtation with pragmatism, although even then a cautious one, Macintosh cut loose from this emphasis except to describe a representational pragmatism that was virtually synonymous with religious faith at work. He tied it in with the statement that a Christian would become a moral optimist,[13] which is not truly a

---

[10] Douglas Clyde Macintosh, *The Pilgrimage of Faith* (Calcutta: University of Calcutta Press, 1931), pp. 214-15.

[11] See "Empirical Theology and Some of Its Misunderstanders," *Review of Religion*, vol. 3 (May 1939), p. 396.

[12] See James Alfred Martin, Jr., *Empirical Philosophies of Religion* (New York: King's Crown Press, 1945), p. 69.

[13] Douglas Clyde Macintosh, *The Problem of Religious Knowledge* (New York: Harper & Row, 1940), pp. 322-23.

pragmatic test. In his earlier statement, however, he had insisted that truth was a representation of reality that could "mediate satisfactorily the purpose for which a judgment is made," [14] which was nearer to the intellectualist point of view than to either the pragmatic or empirical. But he dropped this approach in his later writings, although he still thought that judgments needed to be evaluated for their practical working value, so that the notion of truth and the criterion of truth are brought together. Then the final test can occur by the use of immediate experience. [15]

Because of Macintosh's critical monistic realism, he claimed that in immediate experience there could be verification of concepts because of the overlapping of percept and reality. This theory can be applied to every kind of knowledge, including the knowledge of God. But, as we shall see, such knowledge is extremely limited, and we need to speculate beyond the area of what can be immediately verified in experience. Such reasonable beliefs are less certain than verified ones, but they are rationally and logically necessary. Lower on the scale of certainty are permissible surmises and ideas that have symbolic or poetic value only. With an overall view like this, Macintosh had a catch-all method for defending his Protestant evangelical liberal theology. But always he made clear the distinctions on the levels of certainty between verification and the lesser levels, although it was evident that he expected his readers to buy the whole package. There was a cumulative power to this carefully constructed argument that commanded respect.

Religious Experience

The center of Macintosh's theology was his interpretation of religious experience or, as he liked to call it, the "right religious adjustment." His position was close to Wieman's, for Wieman insisted that God is known when the right conditions are met. It was also close to that of James, although James provided a great deal of case-study-type evidence that Macintosh ignored. Macintosh already had his description of the right religious adjustment at hand, probably drawn from his own experience over a long period of time. The religious data would include the sense data that Wieman insisted on, but also the renewing changes

---

[14] Macintosh, *The Problem of Knowledge*, p. 444.
[15] Macintosh, *Religious Realism*, pp. 330-34.

in the will, "even as introspectively cognized," and the effects of such a change which can be observed externally.[16]

When Macintosh turned to mystical experience, he was suspicious of it because of its connection with idealism and with the insistence of some mystics that nothing else is real except a pantheistic deity. He saw in such interpretations a high degree of hallucination and self-hypnosis, and distinguished such experiences from the right religious adjustment.

The primary element in the right religious adjustment is devotion to values, with the sense of wonder or awe or the numinous as secondary. "It begins," he wrote, "in aspiration toward an ideal of higher moral and spiritual attainment, not only as an ultimate end in itself but also as instrumental to the redemption and regeneration of society." [17] There is no exact predictable result, although with greater intensity and persistence it becomes satisfactorily dependable. Many elements in the environment or background can get in the way of such an experience, but when successful it results in an increase of energy and insight in activity toward the higher good. In this experience we find the criterion for the divine "where the numinous reality and the production of values overlap or coincide." [18]

Macintosh, however, was never clear about this concept of values, simply listing them under traditional terms such as beauty and goodness. But he immediately moved on to talk about "divine" values on the basis of the expectations of spiritual religion. These values seem to be those of Western Christian civilization. The divine, as Macintosh admitted, is affected by human behavior.

The result of such experience in human life is that of conversion. In this experience one presupposes the activity of God, and as an outcome one can observe a conversion of the moral will. To keep this conversion experience alive, one must continue in the right religious adjustment. This position led Macintosh to insist that the churches include a program of personal evangelism in their religious education and other activities.[19]

Religiously, the importance of this approach is that men can do

---

[16] See *Review of Religion*, vol. 3 (May 1939), p. 395.
[17] Macintosh, *Religious Realism*, p. 323.
[18] Ibid., p. 375.
[19] See Wieman et al., *Is There a God?* pp. 253-55; see Douglas Clyde Macintosh, *Personal Religion* (New York: Charles Scribner's Sons, 1942), pp. 315-32.

something about it. One does not have to wait and hope, with nothing happening. In a law-abiding universe, which men can know by empirical testing, whatever is the object of religious experience is consistently present and available. There is a permanent possibility of finding God through the avenues that have always been open to mankind.

The Concept of God

Although empirical theology cannot be called an exact science, it has its laws just as science has. In *Theology as an Empirical Science*, Macintosh formulated a number of such laws which were as much psychological as theological, for they described what happens to persons as a result of religious experience. He reformulated these laws in *The Problem of Religious Knowledge*. Chiefly, they all asserted that a divinely functioning reality would bring certain expected results on occasion of the right religious adjustment.

On the basis of all the evidence from an analysis of religious experience and the laws derived therefrom, Macintosh came to his verified concept of God:

> There is in the universe a divine-value-producing factor (which we may call God) which works more effectively toward the production of divine values on condition of appreciation of spiritual values, scientific adjustment to the world, and intelligent and friendly coöperation on the part of human persons. But the divine-value-producing factor in the universe (God) works *most* effectively for the production of divine values, other things being equal, on condition of the right specifically religious adjustment.[20]

Obviously everyone does not know God in terms of this definition, because the evidence by which one reaches this conclusion comes from experience as defined by Macintosh. Wieman's earlier position was very close to Macintosh's, and it may reflect something of James's divine MORE. But Macintosh insisted that his concept of God was not giving the name of God to some process which already exists for many people by some other name. One could not move from atheist to theist simply

---

[20] Macintosh, *Religious Realism*, p. 378.

by changing the name of a process. It is a question of "proving the existence of God in essentially that specifically religious sense in which the term has been used throughout history . . . and proving this by a new and regenerating experience." [21]

It is to be noted how little Macintosh claimed for his verified knowledge of God. He labored to establish a critical monistic realism, an analysis of the right religious adjustment, and the laws of empirical theology, and then came up with an immanent process which produces values and a sense of awe in men. More than this is beyond our verification processes. The reason that this empirical venture is worth the effort is that this is what, in Macintosh's system, established the objective reality of God working beyond man and yet known to man. Like James and Wieman, Macintosh was able to place God within the immanent processes of the cosmos; unlike Dewey, Ames, and Mathews, Macintosh did not think of God as simply a concept to describe the relation between the possible and the actual, or as a concept to describe the social consciousness, or as a concept to unify in the mind the personality-producing processes of the universe.

But Macintosh would not stop at this level, and this is where he and Wieman differed. Macintosh, like James, had a system of overbeliefs which he called reasonable faith, permissible surmise, and symbols. At these levels, also carefully marked off, he was able to discuss God as both immanent and transcendent, as mind and person, and as within some metaphysical scheme. He believed that what he brought into the picture at these levels was consistent with his empirical findings, but even if consistent, such concepts seem to have been limited to his own Christian tradition.

It is reasonable to believe in the conservation of values, and, if the divine factor conserves values, to that extent it is a transcendent power. Furthermore, in the light of our observations we judge this reality to behave as if intelligent and good, so we may surmise that God is intelligent and good. Because our relationship with this factor is personal on our side and God responds, we may surmise that God is personal, although he may also be superpersonal in some sense unintelligible to us. Thus a normative theology can be built on empirical foundations.[22]

---

[21] Ibid., p. 401.
[22] See my "Professor Macintosh and Empirical Theology," *The Personalist*, vol. 21 (Jan. 1940), p. 39.

Macintosh saw empirical theology as a natural theology, expressing what it is possible for any man to know if he is willing to meet the conditions. Therefore, knowledge about God was prior to any thought about the place of Jesus in the Christian scheme of things. This has been the logical order in theology throughout history, with the exception of Karl Barth and others who begin with Jesus Christ. Macintosh was acquainted with scholarship surrounding the historic Jesus as well as theories about the nature of Christ.[23] The theological significance of Jesus, thought Macintosh, was that he provided a clue to the character of God. There is a Christlike norm for interpreting theocentric religion. We can say that, in the historic situation the New Testament describes, Jesus exercised a divine function, that "God was in Christ reconciling the world to himself" (2 Cor: 5:19). There was, then, a special immanence of deity in Jesus. As Macintosh worked this out, he formulated a doctrine of the Trinity by thinking of "the one God of our faith as the perfect and all-powerful Father revealed in the Spirit of Jesus of Nazareth, the divine Son, and immanent in the spiritual life of man and active in the religious experience of moral salvation as the Holy Spirit." [24]

At various points in his thinking, Macintosh inserted the doctrine of moral optimism. It became the basis for right thinking prior to his argument for God in *The Reasonableness of Christianity*. It became a step between belief in God as immanent and God as transcendent in *Religious Realism*. In *The Problem of Religious Knowledge* it was interpreted as a religious intuition based on subjective certitude after a normative theology had been established. Then, and only then, "we may morally will to believe and to keep on believing as we must in order to be at our spiritual best." [25] This is the intuitional and pragmatic result of belief in God as Macintosh conceived him.

Macintosh kept reaching out toward a metaphysics, but he spent so much time backtracking and refining his empirical approach that he never came to terms with metaphysical issues. But metaphysics was a major concern, and he was influenced by Bergson, Lloyd Morgan,

---

[23] See Douglas Clyde Macintosh, *Social Religion* (New York: Charles Scribner's Sons, 1939), pp. 6-38, 114-27; *Theology as an Empirical Science*, pp. 52-67, 160-64; *The Reasonableness of Christianity* (New York: Charles Scribner's Sons, 1925), pp. 134-60.

[24] Macintosh, *The Reasonableness of Christianity*, p. 155.

[25] Macintosh, *The Problem of Religious Knowledge*, p. 368.

Whitehead, and others. He leaned toward an emergent-evolution, process-thinking position. He was impressed by Whitehead's thought and agreed with Whitehead's view that we should not bifurcate nature, but then asked why Whitehead should bifurcate God? Macintosh thought that if Whitehead's primordial nature of God has consciousness it would be possible to bring it into unity with the consequent nature.[26]

Macintosh, however, would have run into difficulty if he sought to relate the transcendent and immanent natures of deity in a metaphysics, for the connection cannot be empirically verified if transcendent is by definition that which is beyond experience. Wieman had some trouble relating the structure of creativity to the creative event, which are the two elements in his concept of God. Perhaps there is some hope in the dipolar concept advocated by empirical theologians who have taken process metaphysics seriously. In due time, we will need to examine this position as developed by Schubert Ogden and Daniel Day Williams. But when Macintosh stopped writing in 1942, he had no firm solution to his metaphysical query.[27]

Criticisms of Macintosh

Macintosh's influence almost vanished after his retirement from Yale in 1942. This was the period of the ascendency of neoorthodoxy, and all empirical theology went into an eclipse. Since World War II, Wieman's books have come back into print and are being widely read, but Macintosh's theology has not been taught even at Yale. Yet at the important point of agreement that an empirical approach can provide at least an inductive theory about the existence of God, Wieman and Macintosh were in agreement and were consistent with the conclusions of James and possibly Gerald Birney Smith. Bernard E. Meland, making use of empiricism and cultural and process thinking, also continued this manner of approach.

It seems to me that the basic appeal of empirical theology and its enduring significance lies in its interpretation of experience, including religious and mystical experience, in a realistic way. It therefore becomes possible to establish that there is a dual process toward both the

---

[26] See Macintosh, *Religious Realism*, pp. 390-91.
[27] See Wieman et al., *Is There a God?* pp. 61-66; Macintosh, *The Problem of Religious Knowledge*, pp. 370-82.

increase of value and toward the producing and releasing of energy, existing independently of man's experience of it. It combines, as Macintosh saw, the experience of the numinous as interpreted by Otto and the value process as described by Macintosh. The results in man's responses are in terms of creative transformation as described by Wieman, James, and Macintosh. Furthermore, it is possible to think of God in these terms within the developments of process theology.

Macintosh also served an apologetic function that is as important now as it was when he retired. In the light of our increasing sophistication about psychology, physics, technology, and new views of the nature of reality, Macintosh's defense of his Christian faith appealed to the common sense of those influenced by these new ways of thinking. The challenge that Gerald Birney Smith saw in 1925 not only remains but has become even more sharply etched on the American mind. William James spoke to these concerns in all his writings, which is why he remains a symbol of the American spirit in philosophy. What got Macintosh into trouble were two things: some of his assumptions that were not empirically verifiable in his empirical level and his input of a dated Christian evangelicalism into his overbeliefs and normative theology.

In 1937, when Macintosh's former students presented him with a volume of essays on his sixtieth birthday, their comments in *The Nature of Religious Experience* were both kind (to Macintosh as a teacher) and brutal (to Macintosh as a theologian). They asked, first of all, whether any theology can be scientific in the experimental sense. Certainly Macintosh's warnings throughout his writings would indicate that although psychology might assist in the understanding of the right religious adjustment, there are no controlled experiments and consistent results that can be measured. Certainly the laws of empirical theology are only helpful guidelines for understanding religious behavior, and they have no status as scientific descriptions of the actions of God. What Macintosh did was to make use of the scientific spirit in his interpretation of the data of experience, and this is a significant advance over noncritical common sense.

Some critics who would find Wieman's appeal to sense data too narrow say that Macintosh's appeal to perception was too broad. It seems that perception in a complex has much to commend it if there are proper limits. It can take care of our experiences of various kinds of relationships, as well as the wide variety of data from which we must choose in order to develop concepts from controllable data. But when this concept is broadened to include perception of psychical processes, or even to say that all cognition is perceptual, one wonders what has happened to the experiential data, unless the assertion is made that there can be only experience-based cognitions and all other claims are false.[28]

In narrowing the data for reflection, it may be that in one direction Macintosh went too far. If we are to consider religious experience as a source of empirical data, we cannot limit the search to one tradition within Christianity or even to Christianity itself, even if we are concerned to construct a natural theology as a basis for Christian theology. We need information from a variety of religious traditions, at least enough for the data to be representative, in order to draw conclusions from the empirical evidence. Philosophers such as White-head and Northrop have seen this, and in Macintosh's day James Bissett Pratt used other religions for his understanding of the religious consciousness. But Macintosh selectively narrowed his data until it was limited to one tradition within Western Protestantism. It may be that this kind of right religious adjustment is representative of all religious traditions in its essence, but Macintosh made no effort to indicate that this was so.[29]

Many critics have attacked Macintosh's concept of the right religious adjustment. What makes it "right?" Why is Jesus a model for all men as to his own adjustment? If one uncritically follows a "right" adjustment and gets "right" responses, what does this prove? [30] Peter Bertocci asked where the concept of God comes from that is used as the minimum idea in this adjustment. Is it inducted from the data or is it a circular argument? Is it confirmatory of something already revealed or in the tradition? If it is intuitively certain that there is a divine-value-producing factor, why do we need proof from the effect? [31]

Such questions cause one to look closely at Macintosh's argument. It seems to me that it is important that one take seriously Macintosh's

---

[28] See Macintosh, *The Problem of Knowledge*, p. 350.

[29] See James Alfred Martin, Jr., *Empirical Philosophies of Religion* (New York: King's Crown Press, 1945), p. 79.

[30] See James C. Livingston, *Modern Christian Thought* (New York: Macmillan, 1971), p. 428.

[31] See Peter A. Bertocci, "An Analysis of Macintosh's Theory of Religious Knowledge," *Journal of Religion*, vol. 24, no. 1 (Jan. 1944), p. 53.

critical monistic realism as a basis for establishing the objectivity of the data. If one then follows good empirical procedures, he will ask what hypotheses are suggested by the data from a wide variety of religious experiences (somewhat in the tradition of William James, but with representative evidence from other religions as well). If this hypothesis should be a value-producing factor other than man that causes a response that arouses wonder and awe and leads one to be transformed in his seeking to realize value in the world, one would have a straight inductive approach with some kind of evidence to back him up. At the heart of the empirical procedures of both Macintosh and Wieman, it seems to me, this is the empirical methodology. Note that the term divine (which is a value-loaded term) has not been used at this level, but we could say, with Wieman, that it is "the growth of meaning and value." Because such a concept is reached by induction from empirical evidence, of course, it would be only a highly likely yet tentative formulation. It would have the practical certitude of which Macintosh spoke, but not the theoretical certainty that he desired. This is not a serious defect if one takes seriously Wieman's view that the commitment to reality is where the certainty lies, rather than in the formulation of the concepts. As Ian T. Ramsey put it, "Being sure in religion does not entail being certain in theology." [32] It is this kind of being sure that is strengthened by persistence in the right religious adjustment.

By asserting that devotion to divine values is central to the right religious adjustment, Macintosh was in danger of recreating the old moral argument for God, as John Dewey said.[33] This becomes even more clear when Macintosh asserted the right to believe on the basis of moral optimism. But what makes this more difficult from the empiricist standpoint is the question of where one finds the criteria for identifying any value as absolute or divine. The only values one knows are those which are found in and through experience, and they may be objective but are always relative. This is the basis for H. Richard Niebuhr's criticism of both Macintosh and Wieman, although, as we will see, Niebuhr's solution does not resolve the problem.[34] We may see values

[32] Ian T. Ramsey, *On Being Sure in Religion* (London: Athlone Press, 1965), p. 47.
[33] See "Mr. Wieman and Mr. Macintosh Converse with John Dewey," *The Christian Century*, vol. 50 (Mar. 1, 1933), p. 301.
[34] See "Value Theory and Theology," in J. Seelye Bixler, Robert L. Calhoun, and H. Richard Niebuhr, eds., *The Nature of Religious Experience* (New York: Harper & Row, 1937), pp. 96, 107-8.

coming into existence in the events of daily experience, and we may have a view of the universe that allows for this potentiality becoming actual, but it remains a process that we observe and experience and about which we can reflect. Macintosh did not move in this direction, but tied in his view of value with a teleological interpretation of the process, thus introducing what amounts to a theistic assumption early in his argument by definition.[35]

Are Macintosh's value-producing processes any more unitary than Shailer Mathews' personality-producing activities or John Dewey's plurality of relations between ideal and actual? The demand for unity on Macintosh's part, at the empirical level, was an intellectual one. His dual approach, through the numinous and through values, had no necessary unity, and could be seen as at least dipolar if not pluralistic unless a metaphysical judgment were made. The similarity between Macintosh and James in their appeal to religious experience would indicate that Macintosh, like James, might have to consider a polytheism, unless panpsychism or some other metaphysical concept were brought to bear. Also, like James's God, there is no empirical evidence that Macintosh's God is not finite.

Even if we grant, as I would, that at the level of empirical theology, with the qualifications mentioned, one can speak of a dynamic deity that arouses wonder and brings values into existence, which is a modification of the views of Macintosh, Wieman, and James, we would still run into trouble if we follow Macintosh into his overbeliefs. For as he incorporated much of the liberal theological tradition into his reasonable beliefs and permissible surmises, he was faced with the problem of evil in a world which had an all-powerful, all-good, conscious, and personal deity. At this point, Macintosh made strenuous use of intellectual and moral arguments to account for evil and finally concluded that we need immortality as a belief to make up for the injustice of much of existence. We may reasonably believe that this is "the best possible kind of world for the present stage of man's development." [36] It could be the best possible world if all that man did was in line with the will of God, but Macintosh admitted we could not make that claim. Man has freedom and may use it in a hit-or-miss fashion and keep failing to improve the

---

[35] See Bertocci, *Journal of Religion*, vol. 24, no. 1 (Jan. 1944), p. 44.
[36] Macintosh, *The Reasonableness of Christianity*, p. 117.

world; or he may use his freedom to seek the right religious adjustment and then work to bring the world into what the Bible calls the kingdom of God. Evil and suffering that are due to sin can obviously be overcome by man's obedience to the will of God, but this does not account for the existence of a realm identified as demonic by some and as the opposite of God's work by others. Macintosh wrote very little about the problem of evil, however, just as he only touched upon the problems of metaphysics, and the two problems go together, as in current process thinking. Macintosh found so much that was good in his own experience that even when he was faced with the death of his wife and brother he experienced an upsurge of renewed faith and moral optimism which carried over into his theology. It is this faith, empirically grounded in Macintosh's own life, which speaks clearly through his cautious and careful explication of empirical theology.

An End of an Era

With the conclusion of Macintosh's contribution to empirical theology, only Henry Nelson Wieman and Bernard Eugene Meland remained from the pre-World War II thinkers, and they were joined later on by Schubert Ogden, Daniel Day Williams, and others who started their work with Wieman at Chicago. Out of Yale, however, came Macintosh's students, not sold on empirical theology but profoundly influenced by his realism, especially Reinhold Niebuhr and H. Richard Niebuhr. The latter saw clearly the significance of Macintosh and wrote, "The enduring contribution of empirical theology, from Schleiermacher to Macintosh, lies in its insistence on the fact that knowledge of God is available only in religious relation to him." [37]

What comes through most strongly was that Macintosh, the accomplished theologian, was a man of abiding and deep faith. The week after his first wife died, he happened to have the chapel assignment; he took his text from Habakkuk: "Although the fig tree shall not blossom, neither shall fruit be in the vines; the labour of the olive shall fail, and the fields shall yield no meat; the flock shall be cut off from the fold, and there shall be no herd in the stalls: Yet I will rejoice in the Lord, I will joy in the God of my salvation." [38]

---

[37] Bixler et al., *The Nature of Religious Experience*, p. 112.
[38] Hab. 3:17-18, KJ; quoted by Roland Bainton, *Yale and the Ministry* (New York: Harper & Row, 1957), p. 233; see pp. 227-33. See Herbert R. Reinelt, "D. C.

But theology was moving in a different direction, as could be seen in the response of his students in *The Nature of Religious Experience*. With the coming of Karl Barth, Macintosh saw on the horizon what he characterized as "reactionary irrationalism." Reinhold Niebuhr rapidly moved in a direction foreign to his old mentor as his realism led to the reassertion of Augustinian insights about man and a hard-nosed realism about politics. Except for Wieman and Meland, there was little discussion of empirical theology during and after World War II until the "death of God" theme of the early 1960s, which provided an opportunity for a new assessment of empiricism and a rebirth of the American spirit in theology.[39]

But even in 1940, empirical theology had its critics, and we need to see what questions were asked and how they could be defended at that time.

Macintosh," in Martin E. Marty and Dean G. Peerman, eds., *A Handbook of Christian Theologians* (New York: World Publishing Co., 1965), pp. 212-32; Kenneth Cauthen, *The Impact of American Religious Liberalism* (New York: Harper & Row, 1962), pp. 169-87.

[39] See Sydney E. Ahlstrom, "Theology in America: A Historical Survey," and Daniel Day Williams, "Tradition and Experience in American Theology," in James Ward Smith and A. Leland Jamison, eds., *The Shaping of American Religion* (Princeton: Princeton University Press, 1961), pp. 232-321 and 443-95.

CHAPTER 7

Empirical Method and Its Critics

EMPIRICAL METHOD AS A BASIS FOR RELIGIOUS KNOWLEDGE HAS BEEN variously criticized. Sometimes the whole enterprise has been questioned. Those sympathetic to the possibility of some appeal to empiricism have often been critical of specific efforts, because the empiricism is too restricted or too broad, or because its claims are mixed with presuppositions that are nonempirical assumptions.

Against the background of the varieties of empirical approach we have already discussed, with some help from others in the same field of endeavor, our task now is to restate the nature of empirical method and its proper extensions as a basis for examining the typical criticisms that have been made. These are representative criticisms, not exhaustive ones, but they help to clarify the claims that empiricists make.

A *rigorous* empiricism is the restricting of all knowledge to what can be observed and the inferences which may be made on the basis of the data. We experience "events" and we assume that we know an object by what it does. We can introduce elements of change into a process and see if this leads to a change of activity. We find this in the operationalism of John Dewey and in some of the procedures followed by Henry Nelson Wieman. Edwin R. Walker outlined an approach that attempted to avoid straying from this strict view of empiricism. "It is a method," he wrote, "of getting knowledge by developing a hypothetical proposition to explain a body of observed facts, then deducing the implications of the hypothesis, and then testing these implied propositions by means of further observation."[1] Even this method, however, was modified from a strictly scientific empiricism, so that Walker spoke of it as a rational or modified empiricism. It is difficult to restrict one's experiments to a pure empiricism, without presuppositions beyond the expectation that operations will work. But unless there are other assumptions about metaphysics as well as operations, one may not get further than the instrumentalism of Dewey, with the conclusion that a thing is how it works in practice, although, as we have seen, even Dewey did not stop at this point but included aesthetic appreciation in his interpretation of the data.

An *expanded* empiricism is nearer to common sense. Even Wieman expanded his view of sense perception to include that which affects the sensorium. Macintosh used the concept of perception in a complex. Furthermore, there are some who would expand empiricism to include what Whitehead called "nonsensuous" perception. In these cases, empiricism operates with both epistemological and metaphysical assumptions, preferably some variety of critical realism and the philosophy of organism. Empiricism becomes not an isolated methodology leading to some kind of positivism but is put into a framework of presuppositions about reality.

This type of empiricism finds its data first of all in sense experience, and this remains primary. However, experience may be vaguer than some exponents have claimed, even including a sense of the whole or an undifferentiated response of the subliminal realm. Thus man finds a place in his response to the environment for appreciation, intuition, imaginative insight, and personal relations, all of which are sources of data. This empiricism may be just as rigorous in its investigations, but in order to account for the meanings that actually are found in the universe it must be expanded to give an intelligent picture of the whole. Empiricism is still the appeal to experience, but it considers the richness of human experience and is not limited to the sense data of a positivistic outlook.

The *supplements* to empirical method must also be recognized. As long as we must return to experience for any kind of verification, our

---

[1] Edwin R. Walker, "Can Philosophy of Religion Be Empirical?" *Journal of Religion*, vol. 19, no. 4 (Oct. 1939), p. 316.

knowledge must be of finite processes. As applied to the knowledge of God, empirical method gives us only an interpretation of how God works in the world, and this concept of God is finite, possibly pluralistic, and relative to man's experience and values. It is the area of a probable literalness of interpretation, which is why it is essential for establishing the existence of God as the logical prior basis for any kind of constructive thinking. We may be able to move from a rigorous to an expanded empiricism to enrich our concept as we take account of the fullness of experience, but from the point of view of the religious devotee the conceptual results are insufficient.

While empirical method provides the most certain inductive knowledge that can be discovered by man (outside the abstract sciences, which are deductive), the results are tentative, providing practical absolutes but not theoretical certainties. When we move beyond empirically certified results, the certainty is less even if, perhaps, the concepts carry more meaning. But the supplements to empirical method can add to the total picture in a manner consistent with empirical findings. By the use of logical analysis, speculation, value judgments, analogy, myth, poetry, and symbols, we can develop additional meanings of the concept of God, can place the concept in a metaphysical perspective, can find a language suitable for both theology and worship, and can work out the implications of all this for religious living.

This method, as has been suggested, is suitable for all religions, and the evidence from experience of devotees of all religions should be taken into account. But chiefly this kind of thinking has emerged as part of an American tradition within a culture influenced by Christianity and specifically by Protestantism. Within this culture has emerged an experimentalism that has been applied to Christianity, so that we can talk of an empirically derived Christian theology. Wieman never got away from his Christian heritage. Macintosh's presuppositions about values and experience were derived from his own Christian background, and he was willing to use empiricism to defend his own evangelical theology. This is a development that makes it possible to speak of the American spirit in theology[2] rather than the spirit of American philosophy of religion.

---

[2] I attempted to do this in my *What We Can Believe* (New York: Charles Scribner's Sons, 1941).

122

The empiricism which is worth defending thus begins with the data of sense experience, is enriched with additional factors of human experience more broadly interpreted, and is supplemented by auxiliary methods deemed to be consistent with the empirical findings. Theology and philosophy meet, and the presuppositions of epistemology and metaphysics are used to put the concept of God in its proper place in the cosmos. Empiricism offers primarily a means of verification and reconstruction of Christian theology which is not necessarily the discovery of new truths, although a neoclassical theism may prove to be different in outlook and in many conclusions from traditional or classical theism. When new truths do come, they can be accounted for on empirical grounds. Let us look now at the criticisms.

All Empiricism Invalid

First and foremost is the claim that any natural theology is invalid, for God is only known through revelation. In America, this has been tied in with a view of biblical inspiration and with doctrines derived from scripture. In some cases, the emphasis has been simply on nonempirical sources of all belief, focused on the religious imagination or on faith as a willingness to believe on some basis of authority.

One of the strongest attacks on the empiricism of Macintosh and Wieman was presented by Richard Kroner. After making it clear that God as transcendent holy one is simply not available to human experience, because God is no force, or factor, or process, or entity, he asserted that God cannot be known by any process of interpretation of experience. Any such attempt reduces God to less than his majesty requires. "Measured by the standard of the Bible, most definitions of the empirical, realistic, critical school are blasphemous and betray a level of religious experience far below that reached by the level of revelation." [3] Furthermore, there is a danger that man will use this power of God for his own ends, he will experiment in order to know him, and he will tie faith to empirical knowledge.

It is hard for the empiricist to know where to begin to answer such criticisms, for Kroner assumed that knowledge of God comes through the religious imagination and revelation and is not open to any empirical checks. To the empiricist Kroner has no religious concepts that can be

[3] Richard Kroner, *How Do We Know God?* (New York: Harper & Row, 1943), p. 47.

called knowledge in any sense, and on the basis of the impossibility of verification he would be classed either as making unfounded claims about God or as a practical atheist whose God makes no difference in experience. The point is that the charge of blasphemy on Kroner's part comes from a fundamental assumption that empiricism in religious knowledge is impossible. As the assumption cannot be discussed on empirical grounds from Kroner's point of view, his criticism is simply meaningless.

Empiricism and the Common Man

A minor criticism stems from Kroner's comments. This is that most people accept their beliefs on the basis of what they assume to be supernatural authority, whether it be Bible or church, and that any discussion of empirical theology would bring in foreign assumptions that they could not grant. With the revival of conservative theology and biblical fundamentalism, for example, any such claims as those made by the empiricists would fall on deaf ears.

It is a fact that there has been an anti-intellectualism in American religion that has resisted scholarship of any kind, from the acceptance of the Revised Standard Version of the Bible to the teaching of evolution, on the one hand, and to a subculture of biblical thinking that remains unrelated to the ways of knowledge of the general culture, on the other. This strain has been present from the beginning of American Christianity, and there is no sign of its abatement. This is not a criticism of empiricism; it is a statement that for a great number of Christians empiricism or any other theological discipline that makes use of scholarship is irrelevant. But this does not touch the crucial issue, which is the question of the ways of seeking religious truth with the tools that we have as human beings.

A form of this argument is that we should not fool people with technical details. John Baillie wrote that

> no view of religion can possibly be correct which makes it depend on learned and scientific inquiry; for history shows that those members of our race who are accounted as having the surest insight into religious truth could boast of little learning and no science at all.[4]

---

[4] John Baillie, *The Interpretation of Religion* (New York: Charles Scribner's Sons, 1928), p. 105.

Coming from a man of Baillie's sophistication, this statement is surprising. It is obvious that religious insights may come to anyone, but the working out of the meaning of those insights in terms of the data and their interpretation is a problem for the trained theologian, and the history of Christian thought is the story of theologians and not of the occasions of insight. The common man, who in some cases will follow the fundamentalist preacher, will in other situations be looking for the grounding of his beliefs in the interpretation of experience. In both cases, he will follow the person whom he judges to be an expert.

Concrete Images and Abstractions

Religion is always a question of specific experiences and concrete images, but empirical theology deals with abstractions. It is like asking for a piece of bread and receiving a chemical formula.

Yet it was Wieman who insisted most emphatically that one's commitment should always be to the reality underlying the concept of God and never to the belief about him. It was Macintosh who said that we intuit deity in the concrete experience of the right religious adjustment, where we can find the data for any interpretation. It was James who started with the varieties of religious experience. The great plurality found in religious experience makes it difficult even to assume that God is unitary, as John Dewey pointed out. Shailer Mathews started with the personality-producing activities and then developed his conceptual theism.

However, the process of knowing necessarily involves abstraction of two kinds. First, it is necessary to select some experiences from the perceptual flux in order to have any data to interpret. If the reality we are to designate as God is at work in the midst of all our experience, we can discriminate between what is God and what is not God only by making a selection from the data for the human purpose of observing what changes this will make in the consequences.

Second, in the development of concepts we move from concrete to abstract imagery. Concepts, ideas, and principles are abstract generalities based on the critical evaluation of concrete data, however blurred they may be in perception. Thus, when Macintosh speaks of a value-producing factor or Wieman of creativity, we are dealing with abstract concepts. But we are not to treat an abstraction as if it is the concrete reality, which is the fallacy of theologians who insist that their particular concept is the religious object; nor are we to assume that the abstraction is an adequate definition of the total reality under consideration. Thus, as Wieman wrote, "God is more than we can think."

This is not a fault of empiricism but a necessary aspect of any method of thinking, including that of Kroner or Barth or the findings of the mystics. It is the only way out of a nominalism that has a name for every bit of experience and no way of tying anything together.[5] It is important that we develop the right sort of abstractions, for the data selected may point in a number of directions. This is why any empirical theology needs to have its assumptions reexamined and its speculations logically developed.

Empiricism Is Inconsistent

Empiricism has been accused of constantly shifting its base of operations. This criticism takes three major forms.

First, when empiricism is attacked on the basis of trying to justify tradition, the appeal is made to experience. The answer of the empiricist is that the final means of verification is always experience. The data to be interpreted, however, may be drawn from the experience of the race. Traditional doctrines, especially those founded on scripture and the official pronouncements of the various communions, remain open to empirical investigation. The empiricist assumes that traditional teachings arose from the attempt to explain experience, and therefore they reflect data which cannot be ignored. There is, also, a certain pragmatic appeal about any doctrine which has been useful through the ages.

Second, when empiricism is accused of contemporaneity, it points to the traditional doctrines which it has justified. It is true that Macintosh spoke of untraditional orthodoxy and Wieman was impatient with most historic doctrines, but they counted themselves within the Christian faith. The empiricist who is a Christian theologian may have a bias toward justifying historic beliefs. The data of historical records are difficult to recover, and it has proved particularly hard to get a consensus on the historical records of the life and teachings of Jesus. But the actual verification of beliefs and other information derived from the past must lie in present experience. What bothers the empiricist is that while he is

[5] Walker, *Journal of Religion*, vol. 19, no. 4 (Oct. 1939), pp. 317-20.

selective in evaluating beliefs taken on empirical grounds, he notices that other theologians pick and choose and it is difficult to discover the basis for their choices.

Third, when empiricism is criticized because of inadequate sense data, it is accused of shifting to value judgments. Some empiricists have been guilty of this shift; this may be due to early exposure to a false dualism inherited from Kant or Ritschl. We need to note that there are two kinds of value judgments in empirical theology. The first is made on the assumption that facts and values are part of the same order of reality and are experienced in the same way. This assumption is derived from a realistic theory of knowledge that includes secondary and tertiary qualities as well as sense data. This leads to the discovery of particular goods in the world of experience, and to the observation that these goods tend to emerge. The description of certain processes as "the growth of meaning and value" (Wieman) is a legitimate empirical procedure. A second use of value judgments does not depend on any theory of value, provided values are not considered as purely subjective. When a theologian begins to make use of the methods which supplement empiricism, he is justified in using the techniques of the value judgment that God *ought* to be such and such. He has no right to argue from the *ought* to the *is*, but once the existence of God is established on empirical grounds as producer of values, then value judgments about his nature are legitimate overbeliefs although less certain than strictly empirical judgments.

Value as a Criterion for the Divine

Many critics have accused empirical theologians of relying on the experience of value as part of the primary data of religious knowledge, of arguing from the *ought* to the *is* by a faulty use of value judgments, and of using logically prior relative values as a basis for treating the divine as absolute.

Values are an essential element in the achievement of religious knowledge. Macintosh spoke of a divine value-producing factor; Wieman's creative event is related to his earlier definition of God as the supreme value because he is the growth of all values; Mathews placed a high value on personality; Ames spoke of a practical absolute. One aspect of religious experience obviously seems to be value experience.

Those who refuse to accept a theory of values as being in some sense objective, or who see values as the product of human activity in their entirety, would reject the basic assumption of empiricism, which is that values are objective and part of the world of experience, whether found in relationships between events or in appreciable activities. All empiricists do not have the same theory of values; for values may be thought of in terms of objective relativism, of the externality of relations, or even as existing in a realm of essences. The important point is that values do not depend for their existence upon an evaluating agent. It is a denial of subjectivism in value theory. That this is a large assumption is obvious; but once the assumption is made, either the assumption can be flatly denied by critics or else the position should be criticized as it is developed from its presuppositions.

If values exist independently of an evaluating agent, the emergence of those values has obvious theological significance. Of this the empiricist is convinced, even though he assumes that God is a process out of which come values. On the basis of the assumption that a thing is what it does, this is a legitimate conclusion. If what a thing *does* tells us the nature of what it *is*, we can speak of God as the *source* of what he does, and therefore of God as a value-producing factor, process, or source.

A second criticism of the empiricist's use of values is that he argues from the *ought* to the *is*. When this is done at the level of empirical analysis, it is not valid. God is not necessarily what he ought to be; this inheritance from the Ritschlian tradition is rejected by most empiricists, although Ritschl's influence on Gerald Birney Smith and George B. Foster was very strong, and this carried over into Macintosh's reasoning at the level of reasonable faith.

There is, however, a valid use of the argument from value to God's attributes at the level of one's overbeliefs. In building the superstructure of theology which is consistent with empirical conclusions, one may argue that the God-who-is has attributes which we know through value judgments, and especially through the values that we can observe as moving from potentiality to actuality. Even John Dewey made use of this kind of evidence, although he did not start with an empirically based concept of God. It becomes a serious question in this use of value judgments whether one may speak even at this level of absolute values, as Macintosh did, but certainly some would claim that this is a possible conclusion.

This leads to a third type of criticism of the use of value by empiricists. H. Richard Niebuhr accused both Macintosh and Wieman of making use of logically prior relative values obtained from nonreligious sources as absolute criteria for theology. To claim that values which are admittedly relative, even for Macintosh and Wieman, are criteria for the divine because they are absolute for persons

> is either to assume that the divine must be personal or to regard persons as the one wholly worshipful reality and God as a means to personal ends. To proceed from the values of persons to an integrated system of values, which overarches and includes them, is to assume a harmony of values similar to that one which liberalism assumed in the case of individuals and society.[6]

Niebuhr then proceeded to develop his own position, in which he spelled out a view of values in terms of objective relativism, which meant that values are

> relative to structure and organic needs, rather than to desire and consciousness. . . . The important question for religion is not the question whether a god exists, but rather, what being or beings have the value of deity. . . . Man's need for God cannot be described in terms of his feeling of dependence or his sense of the numinous. . . . What is revealed in revelation is not a being as such, but rather its deity-value.

There is, then, "a primitive and original" valuing as man "is able to recognize himself as valued by something beyond him."[7]

Wieman welcomed this point of view. Niebuhr, he wrote,

> declares that deity stands starkly before us here in our experience of nature, only waiting for our evaluations and conscious appreciations to be so transformed that we can recognize the deity-value of what we already know with our natural powers of cognition.[8]

---

[6] H. Richard Niebuhr, "Value Theory and Theology," in J. Seelye Bixler, Robert L. Calhoun, and H. Richard Niebuhr, eds., *The Nature of Religious Experience* (New York: Harper & Row, 1937), p. 108.

[7] Ibid., pp. 113-15.

[8] Henry Nelson Wieman, from a review in *Christendom*, vol. 2, no. 3 (Summer 1937), pp. 499-500.

Macintosh, on the other hand, reasserted his position. "Value," he wrote, "may be defined as that special kind of quality which things, persons, or processes have by virtue of their relation to some end-directed process." [9] They may be positive or negative, instrumental or terminal, and they are "*formally* relative." The value-producing process in the world has a valid end, and we may assume, on the basis of appreciative intuition, that the end is the absolute will of God.

Furthermore, Niebuhr's own position did not do justice to the evidence, because he avoided the question of whether God exists and simply ascribed "deity value" to what is already in experience. Such a form of existentialism ends up with "agnosticism as to the existence of God." [10] But this was not his only difficulty, for was not Niebuhr's concept of deity value just as much a logically prior relative value as any other? Niebuhr, like Macintosh and Wieman, saw in religious living the possibility of reconstructing the ethical system, of revaluing values, and of transforming the religious person. And there is one other point: Niebuhr started with religious needs as the stimulus toward seeking the "supremely worthful being," which inserts an absolute value into a system of relative values.

Niebuhr's warning was important, but it did not resolve the problem. If we recognize that all experiences of value are relative, that religious values are not different from other values, that value judgments are secondary in developing a concept of God, and that in religious living at its best there is the experience of being valued as well as of creative transformation or renewed dedication, we may have an approach that makes possible the use of relative and objective values in relation to a process toward the emergence of values in our experience. The experience of reality is primary and the evaluation is secondary in the doing of theological analysis, however much they may be mixed in various kinds of experience. It is probable that values and other forms of reality are always experienced together, but analysis is still necessary. [11]

Tentativeness, Certitude, and Certainty

Empiricism has been criticized because its results are tentative. When empiricism is supplemented by reasonable beliefs and permissible

[9] Douglas Clyde Macintosh, *Review of Religion*, vol. 4 (Nov. 1939), p. 42.

[10] Ibid., p. 43.

[11] See *Review of Religion*, vol. 2 (Nov. 1938), pp. 472-77; *The Personalist*, vol. 21 (Winter 1940), pp. 29-30; my *What We Can Believe* (New York: Charles Scribner's Sons, 1941), pp. 214-16.

surmises, or other forms of overbelief and even myths and symbols, this accusation seems even more pointed.

The answer of the empiricist can only be the counterclaim that all methods of knowledge are tentative, and empiricism is the method most likely to lessen the degree of tentativeness. A consideration of the history of ideas will show that all ideas keep changing, being altered by cultural changes, new insights, and scientific formulations. Simply because the empiricist is never satisfied, and because of his concern to practice open awareness, he keeps refining his method, clarifying his concepts, increasing the variety of his data, and enlarging the scope of his procedures. His tentativeness is an approximation of certainty, however, and is not to be equated with uncertainty, agnosticism, or lack of faith and commitment.

Theoretical tentativeness is congenial with practical certitude. If one can be as certain of God as he is of the rising of the sun and the going down of the same, that is sufficient practical certitude for religious commitment. There is no reason why one cannot have the psychological and religious attitude of absolute commitment to God, about whom one has practical certitude. As long as the deity to whom one is committed gives every indication of being sovereign, just, and loving, there is an adequate basis for faith.

From the practical point of view, empiricism provides just as certain a foundation for religious living as any other theology. It is in the realm of *theory* that the empiricist admits that all the evidence is never in. And his claim is that any other theological methodology, in spite of its dogmatic statements, actually leads to less demonstrable certainty and lacks the capacity to decrease its degree of tentativeness except by use of empirical procedures. The empiricist has learned from interpersonal relations that even in the deepest relations of affection, love, and commitment, all the evidence is never in, so that one's commitment to spouse or friend is only on the basis of the evidence at hand.

If faith can be said to have any place in epistemology, it is a faith that what is perceived corresponds to reality. This is the faith behind the assumption that a critical realism is a workable method, but it is present to some extent in every theory of knowledge except solipsism. The empiricist trusts in a process of investigation and reflection that leads to assertions that to some degree correspond to reality. He is dealing with reality as it is, although his conclusions about it are necessarily tentative.

Because of this attitude, he is capable of trusting the reality for which the word God stands or toward which the word points, and by that act of trust he may discover additional data which will increase his knowledge.

Empiricism Has a Bias

Empiricism has been accused of having a hidden bias. It has been accused of assuming a faith in Christianity and of eliminating any data that get in the way. Empiricism, wrote George F. Thomas, "can yield religious conviction only to those who already possess religious faith or at least are conscious of a religious need." [12] There is a sense in which this is an obvious statement no matter what theological methodology is being considered. Learning does not lead to faith or commitment, unless other factors are operating outside the rational process. But Thomas was claiming that empiricism spoke only to the already or almost already convinced.

In the area where argument is valid, as in theological discussion, there can be no effective dialogue unless the presuppositions are recognized by the participants. The more unusual and hidden the presuppositions, the less chance there is of a genuine interchange of ideas. It seems to the empiricist that there is greater likelihood of dialogue in his case because the appeal is to our common human experiences, thus providing an interpretation of something already held in common, and to the tools of thinking which are acceptable to most people in a technological culture.

It is hard to find a bias toward Christianity in such empiricists as James and Dewey, and conservative Christians would probably doubt a favorable bias in the case of Smith, Ames, and Mathews, while Wieman has been castigated and Macintosh considered too liberal. But all except James and Dewey counted themselves as Christians and church members. They simply could not escape from their pro-Christian bias because they were professing Christians. Wieman claimed that he did not care whether he was considered a Christian, but he spent considerable space discussing the positions of Barth, Tillich, Hartshorne, Bertocci, and others in *Intellectual Foundation of Faith* and *Religious Inquiry*, his latest books.

When a person recognizes his bias he may be able to take account of

---

[12] Bixler-et al., *The Nature of Religious Experience*, p. 50.

it, but often this bias is hidden even from the creative thinker. The problem of the empiricist is to take account of his bias and compensate for it, without restricting his right to be a participant in his tradition even while he examines it.

It is important to recognize the place of bias in all knowledge. The fact that the empiricist is interested in establishing the truth of religious beliefs is a bias. He becomes an advocate rather than an objective evaluator of the evidence. But knowledge is always the result of interest and attention, and even which facts we are likely to select are determined by many factors in the observer, for even the distinction between subjective and objective in considering the data may be due to a hidden presupposition unknown to the observer. The empiricist, like any other scholar seeking to be objective, seeks to take account of his bias and compensate for it.

But bias is not always to be discounted. It may be that "this religious intensity of bias may heighten sensitivity to data and suggest lines of solution for problems which might otherwise be missed." [13] The power for a compulsion to seek for evidence in out-of-the-way places or unusual situations has led to both scientific and religious discoveries, and the solitary way of the adventurer may throw light on questions for which better answers are needed.

Empiricism and Revelation

It is sometimes claimed that empirical theology has no place for revelation. This criticism usually assumes that there is a distinction between natural and revealed theology, or that natural theology is invalid. But in Christianity, traditionally, there has at least been a continuity between natural and revealed theology, as in Thomism or the theology of William Temple.

For the empiricist, the problem is not one of turning to revelation after the empirical processes have been exhausted. Neither is it starting with an authoritative revelation which is to be verified by further empirical evidence. Revelation is seen within the scope of empiricism as a source of data, along with religious experience and experience in general. If revelation is thought of, in the terms of William Temple, as

---

[13] Edwin R. Walker, "Can Philosophy of Religion Be Empirical?" *Journal of Religion*, vol. 20, no. 3 (July 1940), p. 244.

"the coincidence of a particularly revealing event and a particularly appreciative mind," [14] it becomes a significant aspect of empirical theology, for often there is special evidence that can be interpreted by a mind with unusual sensitivity and insight, so that there may be breakthroughs in the interpretation of data. These moments of discernment or disclosure, which are unpredicted and unexpected, are open to further testing by others, so that we can continue to discriminate between illusion and reality.

When empiricism operates within the bias of the Christian tradition, it takes seriously the record of revelation found in the Bible. It assumes that all experiences are capable of contributing to our understanding of God at work and that there are unique experiences which may be interpreted as special revelations which can be further verified by empirical testing. However, there is much in the Bible that reflects the extensions of empiricism in terms of reasonable faith and permissible surmise, and the language is often that of poetry and myth, so that it is difficult if not impossible to get back to any original data. At this level, we discover that much that is contained in the Bible is consistent with the history of religious experience in the Christian tradition and with the life of Christians today. On the negative side, empiricism assists in the discarding of false claims.

The critical examination of the findings from revelation, religious experience, and the expectations of faith does not place them outside the empirical orbit. It keeps them within the framework of empirical procedure and builds a superstructure of beliefs which are not capable of empirical verification but are consistent with what has been verified. It is not a question of empiricism *or* revelation, for that impoverishes both. It is a problem of expanding empiricism so that the claims for revelation will be considered seriously and critically. The empirical theologian may not be able to discover new revelations (unless he is also a prophet or seer), but he should be able to develop the techniques for examining the revelations which come to others, however unique they may be.

Because the empiricist takes the theories of scientists, historians, and biblical scholars seriously, he is likely to take a critical approach to the Christian tradition as well as to the study of other religions. This reconstruction of the evidence may lead to new and helpful religious

---

[14] William Temple, *Nature, Man and God* (London: Macmillan & Co., 1934), p. 306.

concepts, with concern for the record of revelation in other religions as well as in Christianity.

Empiricism and Interpersonal Relations

Empiricism has been accused of supplying only impersonal relations between the divine and the human. The first answer is that it is to empiricism's credit that the nonpersonal working of God has been established in nature and history, for the understanding of God's work according to natural and social laws is essential to our understanding of theology. The weakness of much traditional theology has been its failure to see nature as in any real sense God's handiwork for which man has religious responsibility. The current ecological crisis, insofar as it has religious roots, is due to religion's failure to spell out man's relation to nature in terms of responsibility to God.

There has been a tendency, however, to interpret empiricism in terms of impersonal relations at every level, so that even the relations between human beings have been described in terms of nonhuman statistics. Much of the success of the empirical sciences has been due to their capacity to eliminate the personal equation to some extent. Continental theologians have sometimes dismissed empiricism because they have restricted it to an "I-it" relationship. If we can be empirical about such intimate relationships as friendship, marriage, the family, and the community, however, we can have a partial understanding of an interpersonal relationship between man and God. Theologians of all camps have either made God too personal, in the image of man, or they have made him so transcendental and unapproachable that he has seemed to be impersonal, or at least lacking in such personal qualities as feeling, suffering, and joy.

Such critics, suspicious of the religious consciousness because of the actual frustration and lack of dependability which are present in many searchings for God, and concluding also that any evidence from the religious consciousness is subjective as well as impersonal, turn to other sources of theology. What they do not see is that empiricism includes in its method an analysis of the kind of personal trust that comes from the right religious adjustment, as well as the frustration evident in any relationship.

The element of trust or faith or commitment which is involved in all interpersonal relationships is essential to the experience of God and is therefore part and parcel of the "I-Thou" relationship between man and God. All this is grist for the empirical mill. When faith operates as an integral part of the empirical method, it carries its own authority and certitude, although this is not theoretical certainty.

Empiricism and Literalism

Empiricism has been accused of insisting upon literal statements and avoiding other forms of language in the presentation of religious truth. Charles A. Bennett went so far as to say that it is impossible to take religious truth literally and it is disastrous to reduce it to poetry.[15] Others, such as Rudolf Otto, would agree to the empirical study of religious phenomena and literal descriptions of religious behavior but would not allow for any empirical statements about the activity of deity. Reinhold Niebuhr, in his essay "The Truth in Myths," claimed that myths stated religious truths that were distorted by any attempts at translation into literal language. He concluded that

> mythical terms are the most adequate symbols of reality because the reality which we experience constantly suggests a center and source of reality, which not only transcends immediate experience, but also finally transcends the rational forms and categories by which we seek to apprehend and describe it.[16]

Macintosh's response to this kind of criticism, as might be expected, was vigorous. One way of stating the main task of a theologian, he said, was to make "the distinction and separation of literal truth from all mere figure of speech in the language of religion." [17] Except for his vigorous moral concern, suggested Macintosh, he could not see anything in Niebuhr's theology except a fictional statement. If one accepts a realistic epistemology, which underlies all empiricism, then the claim that it is literally true that God is a person can be held.[18]

In the ongoing discussion, Niebuhr caricatured Macintosh's position

[15] Charles A. Bennett, *The Dilemma of Religious Knowledge* (New Haven: Yale University Press, 1931), pp. 67-70.
[16] Bixler et al., *The Nature of Religious Experience*, p. 135.
[17] Douglas Clyde Macintosh, *Review of Religion*, vol. 4 (Jan. 1940), p. 150.
[18] Ibid., p. 154.

by asking for literalism where it does not apply. Macintosh answered with a claim that God's consciousness could be thought of literally. If God is aware of something and knows what he is about, and there is a literal distinction between consciousness and unconsciousness, between knowledge and ignorance, we can say, "If then God knows what he is about, there is in religion significant literal truth." [19]

Macintosh left very little room for poetry and myth, unless somehow it could be reduced to his own terms. Wieman, on the other hand, agreed that we could move from technical terms, which included literal truth, to Christian words which had high emotive value for the purposes of worship and religious living. But neither Macintosh nor Wieman accepted Niebuhr's insistence that myth could provide access to truth that can be reached in no other way and that such truth was essential for the understanding of religion.

It needs to be remembered that Macintosh and Wieman were working in the field primarily of philosophy of religion, using the tools of empiricism and pragmatism to develop the basic truths of religious concepts. Therefore, they tended either to avoid traditional theological language or to translate such terms into their own frameworks. Yet the translation has to go the other way, so that the traditional concepts and symbols will be reinterpreted in order to be consistent with the concepts of empirical theology.[20]

One other attack on literal concepts which can be verified comes from overseas. In 1916, Ludwig Wittgenstein had written, "To believe in a God means to understand the question of the meaning of life." He spoke of "the feeling of being dependent on an alien will. . . . What we are dependent on we can call God." He qualified this by saying that God is "fate" or "the world," but he also said that "it is correct to say: Conscience is the voice of God." [21]

But this hint was not known or was ignored, and most logical empiricists moved toward the positivism of A. J. Ayer. The truth of synthetic statements depended on empirical verification, and here is where all religious and ethical statements were treated as emotive rather than descriptive. Ayer would admit that a private religious experience

[19] Ibid., vol. 4 (May 1940), p. 436.
[20] Walker, *Journal of Religion*, vol. 20, no. 3 (July 1940), p. 253.
[21] Ludwig Wittgenstein, *Notebooks 1914-1916*, ed. G. H. von Wright and G. E. M. Anscombe (New York: Harper & Row, 1961), pp. 74e-75e.

could exist and have meaning for the experiencer, but it could have no public significance. Furthermore, most claims made by those who have such experiences are too vague to be tested in terms of sense content. The same is true of value judgments, for there is no empirical reference which would settle any issue. Any argument from empirical data depends on the certainty of its premises, so no empirical proposition can ever have certainty. If we want certainty, and if only a priori propositions can be certain, we cannot have certainty about God. So Ayer concluded that "all utterances about God are nonsensical." [22]

This position was strengthened by what is called the principle of falsifiability. This means that an empirical statement must be open to negative testing. If nothing one can experience counts against the proposition that God exists, then the proposition has no status. As Antony Flew put it, belief in the power and goodness of God dies a "death by a thousand qualifications." [23] It was this kind of questioning concerning propositions about a wholly other deity of absolute power and goodness, similar to Calvin's God, that led to the death-of-God movement.

Wieman's response to such criticisms was that they did not touch his position. He claimed that the kind of evidence he was proposing was available in the experience of everyone, that he did not need to qualify his concepts owing to additional data of a negative sort because he was not arguing that all reality had to be consistent with his view of God. All the qualifications due to the experience of every kind of evil were already accounted for. Therefore, his position could stand both empirically and rationally against the logical positivists. He would have agreed with Wittgenstein's statement that "the problems are solved, not by giving new information, but by arranging what we have always known." [24]

This sensitivity to qualifications which do not destroy the concept of God runs throughout the theologians we have considered. Simply because they start with the immanent process which can be experienced rather than from a transcendent reality about which all claims are

---

[22] Alfred J. Ayer, *Language, Truth, and Logic*, 2d ed. (London: Gollancz, 1936), p. 115.
[23] Antony Flew and Alasdair MacIntyre, eds., *New Essays in Philosophical Theology* (London: SCM Press, 1955), p. 106.
[24] Ludwig Wittgenstein, *Philosophical Investigations*, 2d ed. (Oxford: Basil Blackwell, 1958), p. 47e.

absolute, they are in a position to take all the findings of experience seriously. The pluralism of James, the operational theory of Dewey, the limits placed on God's activity in mystical naturalism, the use of the social consciousness as a basis for the symbol of God, the plural personality-producing activities as a basis for conceptual theism, and the insistence on empiricism in both Macintosh and Wieman provide for limits on the concept of deity and on the possibility of evidence for other processes in the universe in competition with God. Ultimately, this approach admits the possibility of data which might negate the evidence for God. That these thinkers would consider the last possibility as unlikely is perfectly obvious, but to hold it even as the most unlikely possibility would answer the falsifiability principle and therefore make possible the use of the verifiability principle.

Metaphysics

A final criticism of empiricism is its lack of an adequate metaphysics. Either the empiricist has no metaphysics or he is a naturalist. Within empiricism itself there is no requirement for a specific interpretation. As John Bennett wrote,

> On the basis of sense experience and all the ideas and values which are related directly or indirectly to sense experience we are able to construct several possible systems of inferences. The choice between these systems of inferences depends upon the weight which we give to various elements in the mass of data, values, and the like, involved; and I doubt if that process of giving more weight to some elements than to others can itself be vindicated by an appeal to sense experience.[25]

Inferences take one rapidly away from empirical data, although one needs constantly to refer such inferences back to the data. Metaphysics obviously operates at two levels, first in terms of presuppositions about the nature of things which make empiricism possible and second in terms of the speculations to which our inferences lead. It is possible to start, as did Wieman, with a naturalistic materialism as a basis for his empirical methods and interpretations; some would claim that this definitely limits the kind of inferences he is willing to make. James

---

[25] John C. Bennett, *Journal of Religion*, vol. 20, no. 2 (Apr. 1940), p. 174.

found that his empirical and pragmatic findings pointed sharply toward a pluralistic universe, so that there was room for evil and still an accounting of intelligent good. Macintosh, because of his reasonable beliefs and permissible surmises, moved toward more absolute claims, that perhaps needed to be qualified, but they could be fitted into metaphysical schemes such as emergent evolutionism or process thought.

Empiricism is particularly congenial to the philosophy of organism. Whitehead's thinking was already making an impression in the period prior to World War II, but it remained for theologians of a later period to make full use of it, critically evaluate it, and adapt it to their own systems. Only Charles Hartshorne was operating at full speed at the end of the pre-World War II period, and he was instrumental in the new developments.

Conclusion

We have looked at some of the major criticisms of empirical theology and have attempted to show how some empiricists would reply. It is the thesis of this chapter that if empiricism is understood in both its rigorous and broader sense, it can meet the criticisms advanced by other theologians and philosophers. If these criticisms have actually been met with any degree of satisfaction, the spirit of American theology as we have described it can survive. It can develop into a complete theology which does justice to the general truths of religion and to the history of the Christian faith in terms which are vital enough and concrete enough to win the allegiance of men to the living God.[26]

---

[26] For a briefer and earlier survey of some of these topics, see my "Empirical Method and Its Critics," *Anglican Theological Review*, vol. 27 (Jan. 1945), pp. 27-34.

Empiricism and Process Philosophy

CHAPTER 8

AMERICAN THEOLOGY REFLECTED THE INSIGHTS OF EMPIRICISM UNTIL about the beginning of World War II, but already there was an upswing of interest in the continental theologies of Karl Barth and many others which swept empirical theology into the background. There were strong cultural and ethical reasons for this shift of emphasis. Empiricism had been associated, quite properly, with the liberal spirit of openness toward new ways of thinking; but it had also been related to a doctrinaire liberalism which overestimated the goodness of men and nations and the possibilities of moral progress, and it was this kind of optimism that was destroyed by the events of war, the rise of fascism and communism, and the general exposure of the sins of mankind. Perhaps, on the American scene, Reinhold Niebuhr's penetrating *The Nature and Destiny of Man*, which had some roots in what he had learned from Macintosh, was the most significant book.

Yet during this same period the books of Alfred North Whitehead were appearing. After a distinctive career in England as a mathematician and a philosopher of science, Whitehead came to Harvard University in 1924 at the age of sixty-three and started a new career in philosophy that reflected his scientific background and interest in general ideas about the nature of things, and later showed a genuine religious interest. In quick succession came *Science and the Modern World*, *Religion in the Making*, and *Process and Reality*. For a brief time, these writings made an impression on Henry Nelson Wieman, who explained them to his colleagues at the University of Chicago, but there was no lasting effect except for the impact on one of Whitehead's most renowned students, Charles Hartshorne. In England, William Temple made use of Whitehead's thought in his *Nature, Man and God*, although he was critical of some of the implications of Whitehead's concept of God; Lionel Thornton used process categories for his *The Incarnate Lord*. So it could be said that in the area of American theology and philosophy of religion, Whitehead's views lay dormant until after World War II, but there was a spectacular revival after that time, as we will see.[1]

Whitehead thought of himself as in the tradition of Plato, Aristotle, Locke, Leibniz, and William James. Of James he wrote that

> the essence of his greatness was his marvelous sensitivity to the ideas of the present. He knew the world in which he lived, by travel, by personal relations with its leading men, by the variety of his own studies. He systematized; but above all he assembled. His intellectual life was one protest against the dismissal of experience in the interest of system. He had discovered intuitively the great truth with which modern logic is now wrestling.[2]

John Dewey found himself close to Whitehead's thought in the emphasis on "activity, function, and interaction as the context of all theory."[3] Dewey especially liked *Adventures of Ideas*, with its emphasis on the living body as a whole which is continuous with the rest of the natural world. The expansion of the basis of empiricism beyond the sense organs to every possible variety of bodily response suited Dewey, so that artists, poets, and prophets may share such an approach. He quoted with approval the following passage:

---

[1] The best brief story of process thought is by Gene Reeves and Delwin Brown, "The Development of Process Theology," in *Process Philosophy and Christian Thought*, ed. Delwin Brown, Ralph E. James, Jr., and Gene Reeves (Indianapolis: Bobbs-Merrill, 1971), pp. 21-64. On Thornton, see Robert M. Cooper, "A Note on Lionel Thornton: An Early Process Theologian," *Anglican Theological Review*, vol. 55 (Apr. 1973), pp. 182-88, and Lewis S. Ford, in ibid., vol. 55 (Oct. 1973), pp. 479-83.

[2] Alfred North Whitehead, *Modes of Thought* (New York: Macmillan, 1938), p. 3. Copyright 1938 by Macmillan Publishing Co., Inc., renewed 1966 by T. North Whitehead. Used by permission.

[3] Daniel Day Williams, "How Does God Act?: An Essay in Whitehead's Metaphysics," in *Process and Divinity*, ed. William L. Reese and Eugene Freeman (La Salle, Ill.: Open Court Publishing Co., 1964), p. 164.

The world within experience is identical with the world beyond experience, the occasion of experience is within the world and the world is within the occasion. The categories have to elucidate this paradox of the connectedness of things:—the many things, the one world without and within.[4]

It is clear that at many points Dewey disagreed with Whitehead, but there was an area in which they agreed, which was on the empirical base for all knowledge.[5]

For Whitehead, however, empiricism could be valid only when supported by an adequate speculative theory, for otherwise evidence may be dismissed as irrelevant because the theory is not looking for such material. A theory is tested by whether it has adequate scope to make a useful application. Theory is therefore subject to revision, but it is prior to the evidence at the start, and it is subject to observation without being a slave to its necessary selectivity.

This leads to a method of "comparing the various schemes of abstraction which are well founded in our various types of experience." [6] One must have faith in reason, in order, and in something other than arbitrary mystery. This faith underlies the method and is not a matter of induction. "It springs from direct inspection of the nature of things as disclosed in our own immediate present experience." [7] Thus we are able to get at the depths of reality and fit them into a total scheme which is an aesthetic harmony.

Underlying this is the sense of worth, the realization that something matters and that individuals matter. "My importance is my emotional worth now, embodying in itself derivations from the whole, and from the other facts, and embodying in itself reference to future creativity." [8] As one approaches his environment, his development of the art of life is

---

[4] Alfred North Whitehead, *Adventures of Ideas* (New York: Macmillan, 1933), p. 293. Copyright 1933 by Macmillan Publishing Co., Inc., renewed 1961 by Evelyn Whitehead. Used by permission.

[5] John Dewey, "The Philosophy of Whitehead," in *The Philosophy of Alfred North Whitehead*, ed. Paul Arthur Schilpp (Evanston: Northwestern University Press, 1941), pp. 641-61.

[6] Alfred North Whitehead, *Science and the Modern World* (New York: Macmillan, 1925), p. 26; Mentor ed., p. 19. Copyright 1925 by Macmillan Publishing Co., Inc., renewed 1953 by Evelyn Whitehead. Used by permission.

[7] Ibid., p. 26; Mentor ed., p. 20.

[8] Whitehead, *Modes of Thought*, p. 117.

in terms of being alive, of being so in a satisfactory way, and of acquiring an increase in satisfaction. Reason functions to develop the art of living creatively and meaningfully.[9]

Dominant in Whitehead's thought was the idea of "relatedness" in process. "The becoming, the being, and the relatedness of 'actual entities' " leads to "the doctrine that the creative advance of the world is the becoming, the perishing, and the objective immortalities of those things which jointly constitute *stubborn fact*." [10] Therefore, the ultimate concept is creativity. The empirical base for such thinking is often obscured by the power of Whitehead's total vision of reality, but the empiricism is there, although with a difference. Not only concrete data but also the experience of the whole are part of the process. The principle of concretion is not discoverable by abstract reason but is the basis for empiricism, leading to the region of particular experiences for further knowledge.[11]

Religion was significant in Whitehead's thinking. One of his most eloquent and moving passages, so often quoted, is the following:

Religion is the vision of something which stands beyond, behind, and within, the passing flux of immediate things; something which is real, and yet waiting to be realized; something which is a remote possibility, and yet the greatest of present facts; something that gives meaning to all that passes, and yet eludes comprehension; something whose possession is the final good, and yet is beyond all reach; something which is the ultimate ideal, and the hopeless quest.[12]

Religion begins in solitariness, in the intuition that comes when one is separate in his individuality, and yet there is always the return to society, for one cannot be absolutely solitary and one needs the consensus of a community for both enjoyment and verification.[13] It is a complex and many-sided matter, and we need to harmonize our

[9] See Alfred North Whitehead, *The Function of Reason* (Princeton: Princeton University Press, 1929), p. 8.
[10] Alfred North Whitehead, *Process and Reality* (New York: Macmillan, 1929), pp. viii-ix. Copyright 1929 by Macmillan Publishing Co., Inc., renewed 1957 by Evelyn Whitehead. Used by permission.
[11] See Whitehead, *Science and the Modern World*, p. 250; Mentor ed., p. 179.
[12] Ibid., pp. 267-68; Mentor ed., p. 191.
[13] See Alfred North Whitehead, *Religion in the Making* (New York: Macmillan, 1926), pp. 16, 58, 137-38.

intuitions, emotional responses, decisions, and behavior, which is an exercise of reason.[14] It results in what might be called "world loyalty," involving both duty and reverence and centering on worship.

It should be noted that critics often claim that exercises in theology and philosophy of religion have to do only with the mind and that we need some other kind of devotion to inspire worship. But at all times, Whitehead was talking about a religious vision, and the immediate response is worship. The vision needs to be refined by reason in order to be effective, and this is a highly disciplined endeavor.

> The vision claims nothing but worship. . . . The power of God is the worship He inspires. That religion is strong which in its ritual and its mode of thought evokes an apprehension of the commanding vision. The worship of God is not a rule of safety—it is an adventure of the spirit, a flight after the unattainable. The death of religion comes with the repression of the high hope of adventure.[15]

The death of religion has been built into the tradition, as God has been placed outside the process of reality. Instead of a God of love acting by persuasion, we have had an absolute monarch and an ultimate metaphysical principle, who is the personification of ruthless moralism; God is more real than the world;[16] and, in extreme cases, the reality of God implies the unreality of the world. This religiously unsuitable deity cannot be proved by any appeal to either experience or reason but is the hangover of a culturally determined false dogmatism. Religion can recover its power only as it changes to meet the demands of current experience, science, and metaphysics.

Empiricism

As we turn to Whitehead's theological method, we will need to simplify his argument, for our understanding of his complex total system is the product of many books by and about him. Our task is to see how his thought fits into the American spirit in theology as we have outlined it in previous chapters. Mankind, he believed, is in the process of shifting

---

[14] See *Adventures of Ideas*, p. 207.
[15] Whitehead, *Science and the Modern World*, pp. 268-69; Mentor ed., p. 192.
[16] See Whitehead's *Process and Reality*, pp. 519-20, and *Religion in the Making*, pp. 68-70.

its outlook and is ready for a logical and coherent view based on a
necessary induction from experience. This can lead to beliefs of a
general character, which "show how the World is founded on
something beyond mere transient fact, and how it issues in something
beyond the perishing of occasions." [17]

Immediate experience, as analyzed for its components, is the
beginning point for thought. The datum is the world, including the
observers. Because we cannot develop an adequate analysis of experience, however, we need to work out a "method of difference," whereby
we both notice and do not notice objects. A rigid empiricism is
inadequate because we seek larger generalities. [18]

Every existent has feeling, purpose, and value, so that we can say that
experience means the "self-enjoyment of being one among many, and of
being one arising out of the composition of many." [19] The mutual and
reciprocal relation between environment and organism is directly felt
and provides significance; this is the empirical anchorage. [20] When
experience receives further analysis, we see the identity of the ego and
the experiencing. As Whitehead put it, "The ultimate momentary 'ego'
has as its datum 'the eye as experiencing such and such sights.' " [21]
Furthermore, whatever is experienced is already past and is recalled in
memory. Any experience includes a recognition of significance.
Particular experiences always involve selection of data from a broader
experience, and Whitehead insisted that the feeling tone of vagueness
was more important than the specific selection of data. Perception is
wider than sense perception, and we are justified in talking of
nonsensuous perception, by which, for example, we can know our own
immediate past, lying just a portion of a second ago. The present
moment includes what has momentarily preceded it. [22]

What is important in this approach is that Whitehead inverted the
usual order, making the vague affective tone of experience primary and
the specific selection of data secondary, and then brought them together.
This primary mode is unconscious or preconscious, and from it we

---

[17] Whitehead, *Adventures of Ideas*, p. 221.
[18] See Whitehead, *Process and Reality*, pp. 6-8.
[19] Ibid., p. 220.
[20] See Victor Lowe, "Whitehead's Philosophical Development," in Schilpp, *The
Philosophy of Alfred North Whitehead*, pp. 108-11.
[21] Whitehead, *Process and Reality*, p. 180.
[22] See Whitehead, *Adventures of Ideas*, pp. 232-33.

select data for the present moment. "The basis of experience is emotional." [23] A feeling is a "positive prehension" which has five factors: "(i) the 'subject' which feels, (ii) the 'initial data' which are to be felt, (iii) the 'elimination' in virtue of negative prehensions, (iv) the 'objective datum' which is felt, (v) the 'subjective form' which is how that subject feels that objective datum." [24] This feeling or concern or grasping is an activity of the whole body and not just the senses, for our body and soul are "fused together" in the same way that we sense our unity with our immediate past experience,[25] so we can say that "the living organ of experience is the living body as a whole." [26]

Whitehead distinguished between the modes of presentational immediacy and causal efficacy. The former is the immediate experience, which has a "temporal thickness 'spatialized' as the specious present of the percipient," such as scientific observations. The latter is "a direct perception of those antecedent actual occasions which are causally efficacious both for the percipient and for the relevant events in the presented locus." The locus of both modes provides the basis for symbolic reference, which brings together the two modes in a unity of feeling, and this brings in the possibility of error. Human experience is almost always in the mixed mode of symbolic reference.[27] Conceptual analysis can distinguish the data of both modes.

> Thus the result of symbolic reference is what the actual world is for us, as that datum in our experience productive of feelings, emotions, satisfactions, actions, and finally as the topic for conscious recognition when our mentality intervenes with its conceptual analysis.[28]

Such concepts, including religious concepts, are hypothetical and need to be checked by a return to experience, a test which is to some extent pragmatic.

Religion and philosophy have sources of evidence in human experi-

---

[23] Ibid., p. 226.
[24] Whitehead, *Process and Reality*, pp. 337-38; see Whitehead, *Adventures of Ideas*, pp. 226-27.
[25] See *Adventures of Ideas*, p. 243.
[26] Ibid., p. 289.
[27] Whitehead, *Process and Reality*, pp. 255-57.
[28] Alfred North Whitehead, *Symbolism, Its Meaning and Effect* (New York: Macmillan, 1927), p. 18. Copyright 1927 by Macmillan Publishing Co., Inc., renewed 1955 by Evelyn Whitehead. Used by permission.

ence as found in symbolism, language, social institutions, and action. But language has many weaknesses, and there is no common agreement on technical terms. Whitehead felt obliged to invent many new words for this reason. But at least we can get away from an exclusive reliance on sense data and introspection by an understanding of symbolic reference through the appeal to great literature, and we can begin to realize that there is a world transcending our own experience. Language tells of the way we live, in terms of choice and responsibility, and it points to both order and disorder in our lives and in the world.[29] The truth, however, is to be sought in the presuppositions of language, and philosophy is akin to poetry. Any claim of exactness is a "fake." [30]

Religious Experience

Whitehead was not willing to place religious experience in a special domain. He quoted Edward Scribner Ames on this point. Religious truth, he thought, must come from ordinary experience and mental powers, although there is room for special seers and their intuitions. Religious experience, however, is a fact that includes metaphysical presuppositions. Experience may operate on the fringes of consciousness, as William James suggested, but "it is our consciousness that flickers, and not the facts themselves." [31] There are "direct intuitions of special occasions" which are "a small selection from the common experience of the race." [32]

The origin of religion takes place in solitariness and intuition, but its expression "is the return from solitariness to society. There is no such thing as absolute solitariness. Each entity requires its environment." Furthermore, "what is known in secret must be enjoyed in common, and must be verified in common." [33] Although an appeal to the majority who are limited by lack of vision in their cultures will not lead to agreement, there is still a large consensus among those who seek a rational interpretation of the evidence. The problem is to get away from

---

[29] See Lyman T. Lundeen, *Risk and Rhetoric in Religion* (Philadelphia: Fortress Press, 1972), for a full treatment of Whitehead's view of language.

[30] Schilpp, *Philosophy of Alfred North Whitehead*, p. 700. See Whitehead, *Adventures of Ideas*, pp. 292-93, and *Modes of Thought*, pp. vii, 237.

[31] Whitehead, *Adventures of Ideas*, p. 209.

[32] Whitehead, *Religion in the Making*, pp. 31-32. Copyright 1926 by Macmillan Publishing Co., Inc., renewed 1954 by Evelyn Whitehead. Used by permission.

[33] Ibid., p. 137; see pp. 16, 47, 58.

a deity which is outside the metaphysical scheme or which is limited to the concepts of a single religion.

If the facts are to be discovered within the world of experience, obviously what will be discovered is a God who is immanent as well as transcendent, at work as a "permanent rightness" both as efficient and final cause. There is no evidence of a personal deity, especially if we examine the interpretations of Confucian, Buddhist, and Hindu thought, just as there is no consensus on the impersonal order of Eastern religion or the Semitic monarch or pantheism. Furthermore, such views cannot resolve the problem of evil.

There is a place in this scheme for novel intuitions, for a new way of looking at things, which adds something to the meaning of life for many of us. The intuitions are appropriated, analyzed, and fused with other experiences, but they still have their own unsurpassed significance in themselves. Religion finds its vitality "in the primary expressions of the intuitions of the finest types of religious lives."[34] Both the evidences and the concepts need to continue to grow and to be fitted into changing metaphysical systems; otherwise the result is idolatry. Science, metaphysics, and theology cannot be isolated from each other, and all three must be allowed to develop in conjunction with each other. Ultimately, religion needs to turn to metaphysics, and metaphysics must take the independent evidence of religious experience into its total picture.

Important as religious experience is, we must not forget that for Whitehead theory is important also. His metaphysical system serves as a theory for the interpretation of experience. Religious experiences are genuine facts, but they need to be incorporated into the system based on common and public facts.

Process

It is proper to approach Whitehead's metaphysics through an examination of his empirical methods, although in *Process and Reality* his categoreal scheme appears at the beginning. Whitehead did not approach his scheme deductively, however, and it is the result rather than the background of his method. Dorothy Emmet suggested that we have to read Whitehead both backward and forward in order to grasp the total picture. The result is a system of baffling complexity, and yet it

---

[34] Ibid., p. 144.

presents a picture that in a sophisticated way is consistent with our experience.[35]

Central to Whitehead's metaphysics is a concept of process with an emphasis on interconnectedness and interpenetration. Reality is a constant becoming and perishing, and yet it has a structure. The empirical anchorage is derived from the insistence that the relationship between environment and organism is directly felt in experience, a view which is very close to James's theory of the stream of consciousness. The resulting view is of a connected pluralistic universe.

Whitehead's vocabulary and concepts are difficult to master, but perhaps an overview can be obtained with a few references. He listed a number of key concepts which "correct each other." [36] One crucial concept is "creativity," which is the principle of novelty; it is not an actual entity, not a creator, but is the principle by which the many become one. This growing together ("concrescence") has no one meaning, but every meaning "is to be found in various stages of analysis of occasions of experience." [37]

The real world is made up of actual entities. "There is no going behind actual entities to find anything more real." They differ in importance and function, yet they are on the same level in the principle being exemplified. So we never get behind these final facts, which are "drops of experience, complex and interdependent." [38] Finite actual entities are termed actual occasions. Actual entities are linked together into societies which give historical continuity to the world, but they retain their individuality and novelty, differing in richness or degree of quality. Actual entities are affected by each other, but they also have what is called their "subjective aim," which means that there is an end in view of their activities. This "subjective aim" is not necessarily conscious or purposeful, although it may be at higher levels. Thus an organism determines its own end, its ultimate definiteness, although influenced by eternal objects and other actual entities. At the highest level this is freedom, "which is the whole point of moral responsibility."[39]

In this process eternal objects, which are potentials for actuality

[35] Dorothy M. Emmet, *Whitehead's Philosophy of Organism* (London: Macmillan & Co., 1932), pp. 37-38.
[36] Whitehead, *Adventures of Ideas*, p. 304.
[37] Ibid., p. 303.
[38] Whitehead, *Process and Reality*, pp. 27-28; see Victor Lowe, "Whitehead's Metaphysical System," in Brown et al., *Process Philosophy and Christian Thought*, pp. 10-11, 14-15.
[39] Whitehead, *Process and Reality*, p. 390.

(somewhat like Plato's forms), are "exemplified in everything that is actual, according to some proportion of relevance." [40] They are abstract entities. "An eternal object can be described only in terms of its potentiality for 'ingression' into the becoming of actual entities." [41] In the process of nature, eternal objects recur as forms of definiteness of the data and of the subjective forms of the prehensions which constitute actual occasions. For example, in the process of becoming an actual occasion, a novel possibility is prehended, and the process consists in the attainment of this subjective aim. [42]

Eternal objects are not actual, but they become possibilities for existence. They are pure potentials and have no existence except in process, where they are responded to by positive or negative feelings. "There is nothing in the world which is merely inert fact. Every reality is there for feeling; it promotes feeling; and it is felt." [43] These eternal objects affect what Whitehead called a "society of occasions," which changes as time goes on but retains an identifying characteristic until it is satisfied and perishes, and no two actual entities are alike.

There is a creative advance into novelty followed by perishing subjectively, but actual entities are "immortal objectively." It is thus that the past lives in the present through causation, memory, and perception of derivation of events. There is an emotional continuity of the past and present. "Thus perishing is the initiation of becoming. How the past perishes is how the future becomes." [44] When an actual entity has ceased to exist and therefore lacks living immediacy, it has attained "objective immortality," so that it does not now exist for itself but for other occasions. It is no longer actual but is to be used by future acts of experience. It is nonexistent and yet a fact for the future. [45]

If we try to explain Whitehead's philosophy of organism more simply, we distort it. If we take the model of the human organism, we recognize how complex a process it is. The interrelatedness of the psychophysical functions of the human body, in which one function affects all the rest, with its constant becoming and perishing, with its

[40] Whitehead, *Religion in the Making*, p. 90.
[41] Whitehead, *Process and Reality*, p. 34.
[42] See William A. Christian, *An Interpretation of Whitehead's Metaphysics* (New Haven: Yale University Press, 1959), pp. 210-11.
[43] Whitehead, *Process and Reality*, p. 472.
[44] Whitehead, *Adventures of Ideas*, p. 305.
[45] Ibid., p. 248; see Christian, *Whitehead's Metaphysics*, pp. 37-38.

drive toward life, with its seeking of meaning and value, with its self-determination and freedom in search of purpose, and with its capacity for feeling the harmony of harmonies, points to the direction of Whitehead's thinking about the nature of reality. It is a good model, but it cannot be looked at as an unconscious process of automatic movement. Essential to such a metaphysics is a concept of God as the chief "exemplification" of its basic categories.

Whitehead's Concept of a Dipolar God

There are a number of reasons why Whitehead placed the concept of God at the center of his metaphysical system. His own religious intuitions were very strong, in his person and in his thought. Because metaphysics consists of general ideas that interpret all possible experience, it must include whatever comes from religious experience. Whitehead was willing to consider what is suggested by existing religions, and then "we must investigate dispassionately what the metaphysical principles, here developed, require on these points [where religions conflict], as to the nature of God." [46]

Whitehead started with the statement that "God is not to be treated as an exception to all metaphysical principles, invoked to save their collapse. He is their chief exemplification." [47] Victor Lowe's comment at this point is significant:

> If you start to use its fundamental categories—creativity, actual entities, and eternal objects—in the manner prescribed by Whitehead's categoreal scheme, you cannot avoid introducing an actual entity which from eternity to eternity holds the entire multiplicity of eternal objects in its conceptual experience. And once you have this primordial nature of God, the completeness of the system in its own terms necessitates some doctrine of God's consequent nature. I think that the marvellous coherence of Whitehead's completed metaphysics constitutes the strongest argument for the theistic element in it—provided this general characterization of the universe has any considerable success as an interpretation of mundane experience, which to my mind it does. [48]

---

[46] Whitehead, *Process and Reality*, p. 521; see Christian, op. cit., p. 285.

[47] Whitehead, *Process and Reality*, p. 521.

[48] Victor Lowe, "The Approach to Metaphysics," in *The Relevance of Whitehead*, ed. Ivor Leclerc (New York: Macmillan; London: George Allen & Unwin, 1961), pp. 205-6.

Logically prior to thought about God is the principle of creativity, which requires an infinite and unordered realm of possibilities and an unending production of novel actualities; thus there is no exhaustion of eternal objects and there is a process by which the many become one, which is the principle of novelty. But there is no limitation, and therefore the result could be chaos.

There must, therefore, be a principle of limitation or concretion. It is a limitation of conforming logical relations, of relationships, and of particularity. No reason can be given for this limitation, for it is the basis of all reason.

> God is the ultimate limitation, and His existence is the ultimate irrationality. . . . The general principle of empiricism depends upon the doctrine that there is a principle of concretion which is not discoverable by abstract reason. What further can be known about God must be sought in the region of particular experiences, and therefore rests on an empirical basis.[49]

As the principle of limitation, God distinguishes between good and evil, which he cannot do if he is simple creativity.

Whitehead spoke of the primordial and consequent natures of God, a dipolar deity who is yet one actual entity. In his primordial nature he includes as data all eternal objects. In his consequent nature he prehends the actualities of the evolving universe. Thus he "is considered as the outcome of creativity, as the foundation of order, and as the goal towards novelty." [50]

God is "the primordial creature." As such, he is immanent and has an urge toward actuality and the future. "It is God in abstraction, alone with himself. As such it is a mere factor in God, deficient in actuality." [51] His feelings are conceptual only, and he lacks subjective consciousness. Yet he has vision of eternal objects and a wisdom that orders them in their ingression into actuality. He does not perish, but provides the basis for permanence. He is "not *before* all creation, but *with* all creation." [52] He has a conceptual realization of ideal forms or

[49] Whitehead, *Science and the Modern World*, pp. 249-50; Mentor ed., p. 179.
[50] Whitehead, *Process and Reality*, p. 134.
[51] Ibid., p. 50.
[52] Ibid., p. 521.

eternal objects. He operates by persuasion through the subjective aim in a new process of actuality. This, however, does not lead to specific finite aims at a particular possibility; it is more general than this and includes many possibilities.[53] God is never inconsistent, and he is limited by and in his goodness.[54] He has knowledge of evil, but seeks to overcome it with good. As an actual fact, he transcends the world.

This is one side of God's dipolar nature, and it is

> free, complete, primordial, eternal, actually deficient, and unconscious. The other side originates with physical experience derived from the temporal world, and then acquires integration with the primordial side. It is determined, incomplete, consequent, "everlasting," fully actual, and conscious. His necessary goodness expresses the determination of his consequent nature.[55]

As the order of eternal objects comes into the temporal order of events, we see the process which is called the consequent nature of God. It is the interweaving of the primordial nature with the course of events, as found in the order of immediate experience. God as consequent is fully actual, for he is the measure of order attained in the world. He is conscious in his relation to each actual entity, and each actuality contributes to the aesthetic harmony of God's experience of the world. The past of all actual entities is maintained in the immediacy of God's nature, which is what is known as objective immortality; this is tied in with the immanence of God in all actual occasions. "Thus God has objective immortality in respect to his primordial nature and his consequent nature."[56] This is his everlastingness. "He saves the world as it passes into the immediacy of his own life. It is the judgment of a tenderness which loses nothing that can be saved. It is also the judgment of a wisdom which uses what in the temporal world is mere wreckage."[57] He is conscious, personal, and patient. Values flow from him and provide a meaning in terms of values for our own existence.[58] "The purpose of God is the attainment of value in the temporal world."[59]

Whitehead rejected any claims of absolute transcendence or imma-

[53] Whitehead, *Adventures of Ideas*, p. 256.
[54] Whitehead, *Religion in the Making*, p. 153.
[55] Whitehead, *Process and Reality*, p. 524.
[56] Ibid., p. 47.
[57] Ibid., p. 525.
[58] See Whitehead, *Religion in the Making*, p. 124.
[59] Ibid., p. 100.

nence; he used the terms as relative. There is a sense in which the world both transcends and is immanent in God, as there is a sense in which God both transcends and is immanent in the world. God's transcendence is in terms of not being subject to the limitations of the world and in terms of his initiatory power. He preserves the achievements of the past and also has power over actual occasions. "God does what no temporal actuality can do." [60]

Christian summarized God's attributes as follows: He is a unity; he is beyond space and time; he is immutable in terms of character and the perfection of experience; his power is that of persuasion; he is good. Whitehead avoided speaking of God as a person, and yet he also rejected the concepts of infinity or impersonality. God has freedom and achieves satisfaction. Whitehead spoke symbolically and nonsystematically of God's patience, wisdom, love, and tender care, but these images do not necessarily imply personality. So while Whitehead's concept approached what we mean by personality, we cannot say that God is a person.[61]

If God is both good and persuasive but not in coercive control, this gives a new perspective on both the existence and the overcoming of evil. Destruction is evil, violence is evil, triviality is evil, and God is the one who transforms the world. God cannot prevent the occurrence of evil because he is not omnipotent power and because there is genuine freedom among actual entities. Evil is a "brute motive force" which is unstable and moves toward its own elimination. There can be a constructive outcome to evil through the working of God. "The fact of the instability of evil is the moral order of the world." [62] God's goodness is not the equivalent of man's moral goodness, but points to a constructive outcome for every situation. God has knowledge of evil, but sees it as overcome in his own nature as good. This is "the kingdom of heaven." [63] "All order is therefore aesthetic order, and the moral order is merely certain aspects of aesthetic order, and the aesthetic order is derived from the immanence of God." [64]

---

[60] Christian, op. cit., p. 380; see pp. 364-81.
[61] See ibid., pp. 390-411; see Donald W. Sherburne, "Whitehead Without God," in Brown et al., *Process Philosophy and Christian Thought*, pp. 305-26, for an interpretation of Whitehead's system without God.
[62] Whitehead, *Religion in the Making*, p. 95.
[63] Ibid., p. 155.
[64] Ibid., p. 105.

Whitehead was able to move from philosophical language to poetic and symbolic language from time to time, and such concepts are helpful. He spoke of God as love, "a little oblivious as to morals," as "tenderly saving the turmoil of the intermediate world by the completion of his own nature." "He is the lure for feeling, the eternal urge of desire." "He does not create the world, he saves it; or, more accurately, he is the poet of the world, with tender patience leading it by his vision of truth, beauty, and goodness." "He is the binding element of the world. The consciousness which is individual in us, is universal in him: the love which is partial in us is all-embracing in him." "He is not the world, but the valuation of the world." "The power of God is the worship He inspires." We never get rid of wonder.[65]

Whitehead's position is religiously viable, but, as he would have expected, others took his basic position and developed in many directions. Is his position pantheism? Almost surely not. Is it panentheism? Many thinkers, most notably Charles Hartshorne, have interpreted Whitehead's position as panentheism. Christian has suggested a slightly more complex conclusion that puts Whitehead closer to traditional theism:

(a) God is not the cosmos, nor does he include [in Hartshorne's sense] the cosmos; and (b) his activity is always conditioned though never determined by the cosmos. This view agrees with traditional theism, against traditional pantheism and panentheism, in asserting that God is neither identical with nor inclusive of the world. It agrees with panentheism and traditional theism, against traditional pantheism, in asserting that God transcends the world. And it agrees with traditional pantheism and panentheism, against traditional theism, in asserting that God is conditioned by the world.[66]

Conclusions

Although today Whitehead has become a significant source for theology, the impact of his work was slight and delayed. Wieman was excited about the primordial nature of God and a process metaphysics, but he rejected the concept of the consequent nature of God, and later

---

[65] Whitehead, *Process and Reality*, pp. 520, 525, 522, 526; *Religion in the Making*, pp. 158-59; *Science and the Modern World*, p. 268; Mentor ed., p. 192.
[66] Christian, op. cit., p. 407.

he turned away from process metaphysics as well. However, as time went on, Charles Hartshorne became prominent as an outstanding philosopher who built his own distinctive system from Whitehead and others. From both Whitehead and Hartshorne, with some other influences, came the current interest in process theology.

But there were negative reactions as well. Langdon Gilkey spoke for many of them when he criticized the basic assumptions of rationalism and empiricism. Current philosophy, as Gilkey saw it, rejects any rationalistic assumptions, and therefore it is invalid to seek a philosophically and metaphysically intelligible theology. Furthermore, the modern secular mind finds such claims equally unsuitable on rational and empirical grounds. A shift from a traditional to a neoclassical language game fails to solve any problems, for both are equally anachronistic.[67]

Others criticized Whitehead's position on the grounds of its religious unsuitability. Whitehead's God is not the God of religion, and therefore fails to meet man's requirements. Furthermore, even Whitehead's deity is known via intuition, so why not use those intuitions that point to the God of the Bible?

The system itself came under attack. Some believed that Whitehead's deity is too weak to handle the problem of evil, and that there can be no guarantee of God's working in history if he is restricted to persuasion. If the individual is not saved ultimately in some kind of personal survival after death, but only through the "objective immortality" of being included in God's nature, this is not enough.

Others pointed to the principle of creativity as logically prior to God, so that God is reduced to being a principle of limitation. Wieman thought that Whitehead's view of the primordial nature of God as helplessly waiting for creativity to act, as Wieman interpreted it, needed to be revised so that "the order or structure of the creative event is not imposed upon it but is intrinsic to the very nature of such an event and has no source other than the creative work of some lower order of creativity."[68]

Both these criticisms point to the question of whether Whitehead's God has enough power to do what Whitehead said he does. Daniel Day

---

[67] See Langdon Gilkey, *Naming the Whirlwind* (Indianapolis: Bobbs-Merrill, 1969), p. 224.

[68] Henry Nelson Wieman, *The Source of Human Good* (Chicago: University of Chicago Press, 1946), p. 194.

Williams suggested that some concept of coercion is necessary, although not with the thoroughness of Calvin's view.[69] Such criticisms overlook Whitehead's emphasis on God as remorseless or ruthless, however. There is something inexorable in God; "he is that actual entity from which each temporal concrescence receives that initial aim from which its self-causation starts." [70] There is, then, a connection between God's power and activity in the world.

This connection is something that William Temple did not accept. There clearly is relevant novelty in the world, said Temple, but if God is only the ground of possibility this does not tell us how it occurs. To call it God's primordial nature does not get us beyond process and therefore is not an explanation. When Whitehead assigns the quality of love to the action of God's consequent nature, he "surreptitiously introduces thoughts which properly belong to Personality, though ostensibly he stops short at the category of organism." [71] What Temple suggested was that the category of personality was essential to provide for self-transcendence of any organism. Insofar as "God is the great companion—the fellow-sufferer who understands," [72] Temple suggested, "if only Professor Whitehead would for creativity say Father, for 'primordial nature of God' say Eternal Word, and for 'consequent nature of God' say Holy Spirit, he would perhaps be able to show grounds for his gratifying conclusions." [73] Whitehead did not use Temple's personalistic concepts, however, for he interpreted personal order and consciousness within the functioning of an actual entity. Temple did not believe that God as conceived by Whitehead could transcend the actual world or reveal himself as a person, and therefore he moved from Whitehead's position to a more personalistic one. But Whitehead was reluctant to speak of God either as personal or impersonal. He did use personal images in speaking of God, but he made it clear that this was only interpretive discourse. He spoke of God's freedom, his power, and his creativity, but these functions were not unconditioned. It might be suggested that such concepts point to what it means to say that God is personal (but not a person).[74]

Whitehead's God does not provide the guarantees that come from an

---

[69] See Daniel Day Williams, "Deity, Monarchy, and Metaphysics," in Leclerc, *The Relevance of Whitehead*, pp. 364-72.
[70] Whitehead, *Process and Reality*, p. 374; see p. 373.
[71] William Temple, *Nature, Man and God* (London: Macmillan & Co., 1934), p. 260.
[72] Whitehead, *Process and Reality*, p. 532.
[73] Temple, *Nature, Man and God*, p. 259; see p. 298.
[74] See Christian, op. cit., pp. 409-11.

all-powerful God. Whitehead spoke of risk and adventure, of becoming and perishing, of a peace that emerges from suffering and yet passes understanding. A coercive deity provides a different picture of the world from that of a persuasive one. Whitehead spoke of the Galilean vision, which reflected the tenderness of a God of love, yet, like the Gospels, there was a certain remorselessness and inexorableness in God. Perhaps Whitehead was close to the spirit of a passage from *The Epistle to Diognetus*: Did God send Christ

> like a tyrant with fear and terror? Not at all. But with gentleness and meekness, like a king sending his son, he sent him as God, he sent him as man to men; he sent as seeking to save, as persuading, not compelling, for compulsion is not the way of God. He sent him as one calling, not pursuing; he sent him as loving, not judging. For he will send him as judge, and who will endure his coming? [75]

Many criticisms of Whitehead's system are possible, and there are many loose ends. This is what Whitehead would have expected. The point to be insisted on is that Whitehead's thought continues in a significant way the development of radical empiricism, pragmatism, and pluralism as found in the philosophy of William James, placing these insights in a new perspective and a great system that challenges one's powers to think and at the same time appeals to one's experience. Once one grasps Whitehead's fundamental insights, the world, religion and God begin to make sense.[76] Charles Hartshorne, Schubert Ogden, and Daniel Day Williams were three philosophical theologians who moved the argument further.

---

[75] "The Epistle to Diognetus," 7:4-6, in Edgar J. Goodspeed, *The Apostolic Fathers: An American Translation* (New York: Harper & Row, 1950), p. 280.

[76] See William A. Christian, "The New Metaphysics and Theology," *America and the Future of Theology*, ed. William A. Beardslee (Philadelphia: Westminster Press, 1967), pp. 94–111, on how one may be both a speculative philosopher and a theologian.

The Concrete God

CHAPTER 9

THE PHILOSOPHY OF ORGANISM SHOWED PROMISE OF COMBINING empiricism and rationalism with metaphysics and religion, so that it would be possible not only to think about God in the categories of modern scientific thought but also to point to a religiously available deity. Among those who think in these terms, God is both the supreme concrete reality and the supreme abstract principle, available in and through experience on the one hand and through rational thought on the other.

This way of thinking had been established in American thought in the early part of the twentieth century, owing to the impact of Peirce, James, Dewey, and others, and it came to its full fruit in the philosophy of Whitehead. In the meantime, however, Charles Hartshorne was making a similar approach. Some of Hartshorne's most distinctive writing occurred before World War II, but the bulk of his writing has been since then, so that he belongs both to the pre-World War II generation and to the post-World War II philosophers and theologians.

From the beginnings of his philosophizing, Hartshorne emphasized that experience has a social structure, with the emphasis on feeling as something shared. We can and do feel each other's feelings. We participate in the experience of other subjects. But for this plurality of experience to have meaning, there must be something that is all-inclusive. Hartshorne also believed in real freedom and in chance, reflecting the influence of James and Peirce. Peirce and Whitehead reinforced these beliefs, and some others, and led him to a distinction between Peirce's idea of the continuum (the "primordial continuum of indefinite potentiality") and Whitehead's eternal objects, with the result in Peirce's favor.[1]

Obviously Whitehead was the dominant influence in Hartshorne's development, but Hartshorne also had great regard for Peirce, Hocking, Bergson, and many others. Yet as he came to the full flowering of his philosophy, he placed greater emphasis on an a priori ontology and less on descriptive or empirically based metaphysics. On the one hand, he worked over the ontological argument of Anselm and, on the other, he was influenced by Karl Popper's insistence on the possibility of falsification of any genuine empirical knowledge. It is possible to establish necessary truths which are not negated by experience and which tell us nothing about contingent reality.[2]

Hartshorne sometimes saw Whitehead as a corrective of Peirce. For example, Whitehead interpreted experience as "a definite succession of unit events, never more than finite in number in a finite time." [3] What is experienced immediately as concrete is always a past happening. The process of becoming is interpreted as discontinuous. The actual is what is experienced.

The universe, then, is a synthesis of the possible and the actual. The result, for Hartshorne, is a world view known as panpsychism, in which all subjects are units of experiencing and deity is conceived under the term panentheism, with God thought of as including all things and yet not merely the whole of actual things. This view seeks to combine the best of pantheism and of theism, so that God includes everything and yet is independent of particulars. God participates in actuality and is affected by it; he is a dipolar deity, abstract and necessary on the one hand and concrete and contingent on the other.

Hartshorne's name has been associated with Whitehead's, so it is important to note both the similarities and differences. Among Whitehead's chief achievements, according to Hartshorne, are (1) his interpretation of individuality, (2) the "conception of organism, of

---

[1] See Ralph E. James, *The Concrete God* (Indianapolis: Bobbs-Merrill, 1967), p. 33.
[2] See John E. Smith, ed., *Contemporary American Philosophy* (London: George Allen & Unwin; New York: Humanities Press, 1970), pp. 218-20.
[3] Ibid., p. 222. Used by permission.

societies of entities feeling each other, compounded of each other's feelings," [4] (3) the novel intuition that "the many become one and are increased by one," [5] (4) the conception of God as "endlessly enriched by new data" and as "the supreme, but not the sole, case of creative decision," [6] and (5) "the differentiation between the primordial nature and the endless series of consequent natures [or states] of God seems to me easily the most illuminating thing that anyone has contributed to the theological problem for a hundred years." [7]

Hartshorne agreed with Whitehead that aesthetic awareness of the concrete is presupposed in all abstract knowledge. We begin with intuitive awareness of the concrete whole, and all differentiations are abstractions. This is a much broader empiricism than that of most other philosophers and is distinctive of the philosophers of organism. It places the emphasis on becoming, with concepts of being as abstractions. Reality, for both men, is a social process, and from this insight comes the view that an individual is "a form of sequence of particular actualities socially inheriting a common quality from antecedent members; and that personality itself is a special temporally linear case of such social—that is, sympathetic—inheritance." [8]

Hartshorne's appreciation of Whitehead's genius was shown also in the emphasis on the novel intuition that "the many become one and are increased by one." [9] This is a genuine pluralism, and yet a novel unity emerges which is not predictable. It is a creative synthesis by which novelty occurs. "The many *are* not one, they *become* one," [10] and this successive becoming implies freedom. The outcome of this process is not just a rearrangement of the plural factors but the emergence of a new

---

[4] Charles Hartshorne, *Whitehead's Philosophy* (Lincoln: University of Nebraska Press, 1972), p. 55; from *Philosophical Essays for Alfred North Whitehead*, ed. Otis H. Lee (London and New York: Longmans, Green & Co., 1936), pp. 193-220.

[5] Alfred North Whitehead, *Process and Reality* (New York: Macmillan, 1929), p. 32. Copyright 1929 by Macmillan Publishing Co., Inc., renewed 1957 by Evelyn Whitehead. Used by permission.

[6] Hartshorne, *Whitehead's Philosophy*, p. 164; from *Alfred North Whitehead: Essays on His Philosophy*, ed. George L. Kline (Englewood Cliffs, N.J.: Prentice-Hall, 1963), pp. 18-26.

[7] Hartshorne, *Whitehead's Philosophy*, p. 38; from *The Philosophical Review*, vol. 44, no. 4 (July 1935), pp. 323-44.

[8] Ibid., p. 16; from Victor Lowe, Charles Hartshorne, and A. H. Johnson, *Whitehead and the Modern World* (Boston: Beacon Press, 1950), pp. 25-41.

[9] Whitehead, *Process and Reality*, p. 32.

[10] Hartshorne, *Whitehead's Philosophy*, p. 162; from Kline, op. cit., pp. 18-26.

factor. Thus time and reality are conceived as cumulative, both preservative and creative. Nothing is lost in this process as the new occurs.

But Hartshorne was not satisfied with some aspects of Whitehead's philosophy. He took issue especially with Whitehead's concept of eternal objects, for they make possibility as definite as what becomes actual. This is a denial of creation, making it too specific. The eternal aspect, said Hartshorne, must be completely general. This is suggested in Peirce's "primordial continuum of indefinite potentiality." [11] This continuum of possibilities can be conceived only in the vaguest possible way.

Hartshorne did not interpret Whitehead's concept of creativity as a "God behind God." Rather, he saw that the emphasis on creativity allowed for self-creative acts, so that God both makes decisions and accepts and enjoys the decisions of others.[12] This helps one to understand that there is only one God, who is primarily concrete but has primordial or abstract aspects. This difference from Whitehead is a matter of emphasis, so that Hartshorne could speak of God as conscious and personal. But God is conscious of all actual occasions, while man is conscious of very little; God is influenced by the acts of finite individuals; and he has a memory, which is what makes the past everlastingly significant.[13]

Empiricism

It is harder to evaluate Hartshorne's empiricism than Whitehead's. His concern with the ontological argument tended to disguise its empirical base; yet it can be argued that Hartshorne's efforts in the area of ontology have contributed to the development of empirical theology, as indicated in the thinking of Schubert Ogden, John Cobb, and Bernard

---

[11] Charles Hartshorne, *Reality as Social Process* (Glencoe: The Free Press; Boston: Beacon Press, 1953), p. 20.

[12] *The Philosophy of Alfred North Whitehead*, ed. Paul Arthur Schilpp (Evanston: Northwestern University Press, 1941), pp. 526-28; also Hartshorne, *Whitehead's Philosophy*, pp. 72-73.

[13] See Gene Reeves and Delwin Brown, "The Development of Process Theology," in *Process Philosophy and Christian Thought*, ed. Delwin Brown, Ralph E. James, Jr., and Gene Reeves (Indianapolis: Bobbs-Merrill, 1971), pp. 31-32; see also *Two Process Philosophers*, ed. Lewis S. Ford (Tallahassee, Fla.: American Academy of Religion, 1973), for comparisons of Hartshorne and Whitehead.

M. Loomer.[14] Following Whitehead, it is the experience of the whole that is crucial, although the concrete nature of the specific data is not overlooked. It is, as Meland said, "empirical with a difference." [15] The final insistence on the concrete nature of God as religiously available points to intuition, awareness, and experience at the center of religious thinking and living. But empiricism does not establish a "necessary God," and Hartshorne insisted that only an a priori method could achieve this. Loomer suggested that Meland's view is closer to a continuing empirical method than is Hartshorne's.[16]

Behind both reason and faith, according to Hartshorne, there lies an intuition of the wholeness of God. There is an intuitive relation to God, a vague awareness that is inconspicuous in comparison to other intuitions.[17] Yet mere vagueness is not enough. The dimension of experience that Hartshorne stressed takes one beyond the particulars to such characteristics as purposive, emotional, harmonious, discordant, and religious. One does not generalize from such experiences but seeks the generality already in them. There are elements in both the rational and empirical approaches which cannot be denied, and this is the meeting place for an adequate theological method. The point is to avoid both extremes.[18] Yet a priori knowledge can be empty unless it is grounded in experience; and "mere experience apart from any social-sympathetic character is just as unidentifiable as mere being apart from experience. Cosmic being is cosmic experience, is cosmic sociality or love." [19] The vagueness of a faint intuition can evaporate unless it is focused on love.

Experience leads to the concrete God, but this does not establish his existence or eternal character. Because God's existence is necessary, no empirical proof is possible, for there is no way to prove this belief false by appeal to the facts. Hartshorne at this point accepted Popper's definition of empirical in the sense that some experience could falsify a belief. Without an appeal to the necessity of God's existence, our

---

[14] Bernard E. Meland, ed., *The Future of Empirical Theology* (Chicago: University of Chicago Press, 1969), pp. 41-42.

[15] Ibid., p. 54.

[16] Bernard M. Loomer in ibid., pp. 168-69.

[17] Charles Hartshorne, *The Divine Relativity* (New Haven: Yale University Press, 1947), p. 38.

[18] See Charles Hartshorne, *Man's Vision of God* (Chicago: Willett, Clark & Co., 1941), pp. 62-67.

[19] Ibid., p. 347. Used by permission of Charles Hartshorne and Harper & Row, Publishers. See R. E. James, *The Concrete God*, pp. 138-43.

concept of him would be reduced to that of a mere creature or idol. "The empty conceptual knowledge that God exists does tell us that his individuality is actualized *somehow*." [20] But *how* it occurs is an empirical question, for it brings in the question of contingency.

Because neither empirical nor ontological arguments firmly establish belief in God, Hartshorne turned back to faith. "Only the sense, trust, or insight that we really *mean* something by our worship, and are not talking nonsense, or chasing a formless pseudo-conception can give the theistic answer." [21]

The conclusion to which Hartshorne came was as follows:

> What we can clearly infer as to God is only his abstract essence, and the wholly abstract is no actual value. The concrete actuality of God is in us only in so far as we, with radical ineffectiveness or faintness, intuit it. Though it is vastly less true to say that we do than that we do not "have" or include God, both statements are true. God, on the other hand, in his actual or relative aspect, unqualifiedly or with full effectiveness has or contains us; while in his absolute aspect he is the least inclusive of all individuals.[22]

This sets the stage for looking at Hartshorne's rational arguments for God and for the concept that develops from both rational and empirical evidence.

The Ontological Argument

In *Man's Vision of God* (1941) Hartshorne was already at work on revising the ontological argument. He recognized that this was a purely a priori argument, free from empirical evidence and contingency, and a basis only for abstract thinking about necessary existence. It was required, however, by the presupposition of the concrete God at work in contingent events and by the intuitions of faith.

The problem was, first of all, to consider Anselm's discovery, expose its strengths and weaknesses, and reformulate it into a modal argument that could hold together with some kind of logical coherence. Anselm's

[20] Charles Hartshorne, *A Natural Theology for Our Time* (La Salle, Ill.: Open Court Publishing Co., 1967), p. 77.

[21] Ibid., p. 88.

[22] Hartshorne, *The Divine Relativity*, p. 92.

argument had been pretty well destroyed by Kant, and yet it kept emerging as a basis for belief in God. If we conceive of a perfect being, his perfection must include his existence; otherwise there could be something greater. But Anselm interpreted perfection in terms of immutability, so that God could not change; and this led to a concept of an existing, perfect deity without establishing the existence of the deity.

Hartshorne moved in another direction. He reinterpreted perfection in terms of being unsurpassable, and then he broke this down into unsurpassable absolutely (Anselm's view) and unsurpassable except by self, which meant that we could think of both potentiality and actuality in deity. This he called "relative perfection," which could be explained in terms that there is no absolutely perfect being; but that there is a being in some ways perfect and in other ways surpassable (at least by itself).

Rather than think of perfection as complete and unchanging actuality, it is to be thought of as actuality charged with unending potentiality. Every possibility is a possibility of divine knowing, so that what is impossible is the nonexistence of the divine knower.[23] God knows the actual, and he has potential knowledge of everything that is possible. If the word God means this, then he must be logically necessary. This is his a priori definable relation to both actuality and potentiality, a relation both necessary and abstract, and therefore not open to empirical validation. It is something valid for all situations.

It is clear that in this dipolar view God has both an abstract and a concrete nature.

For God as necessary is God considered under an extreme abstraction, God as barely existing somehow, in some state of concrete actuality or other, no matter what. But God cannot be limited to His merely necessary being; He is the individual that could not fail to be actualized in some contingent particular form. This implies an immeasurable superiority; but what actualizes the superiority is God-now, or God-then, not just God at any time or as eternal, which is a mere abstraction. The necessity that there be some contingent actualization is inherent in the unique abstractness of the identifying divine individuality or essence.[24]

---

[23] Charles Hartshorne, *The Logic of Perfection* (La Salle, Ill.: Open Court Publishing Co., 1962), p. 38.
[24] Ibid., p. 102. Used by permission.

The ontological principle is essential to both religious language and to worship. If we are to speak meaningfully of God, we must be able to assert his necessary existence as well as his contingent nature. Much secular language, reduced to implying the contingency of all existence, fails to do justice to the religious dimension. The theistic question, for Hartshorne, is the sole question facing philosophy.[25] When answered in terms of a dipolar deity, it provides a God who can be worshiped "without incongruity." [26] "Worship is either a revelation of necessary truth, or it is confusion, affirming what could not be true." [27]

Abstraction is a common denominator of individual concrete realities. God has always been defined in abstract terms, such as first cause, knower of all, or goodness. "God," said Hartshorne,

> is the only individual identifiable by abstractions alone. . . . What makes him God and no other individual is abstract. . . . The merely relative abstractness of ordinary individual identity becomes absolute in the divine individuality. This is the long missing key to the ontological argument.[28]

When perfection is defined in terms of surpassable by self but unsurpassable otherwise, the ontological argument is strengthened, and Hartshorne found it "intuitively convincing." Ralph James suggests that this appeal to intuition, which is an "immediate experience of the concrete whole," points to the abstract within the concrete "by means of abstract characterizations." This seems to veer away from the strict logical accountability insisted on in Hartshorne's stress on the ontological argument and to point toward an empirical anchor; or, as Hartshorne put it, "we have to heighten our awareness of the intuitive content by reasoning. This is the function of the theistic arguments." [29]

A Dipolar God

The two strands in Hartshorne's concept of God, the abstract and the concrete, provide a single dipolar deity. As Hartshorne put it,

---

[25] Ibid., p. 131; see my *The Language Gap and God* (Philadelphia: United Church Press, 1970), pp. 47-50.

[26] Ibid., p. 40.

[27] Ibid., p. 113.

[28] Charles Hartshorne, *Creative Synthesis and Philosophic Method* (La Salle, Ill.: Open Court Publishing Co., 1970), p. 246. Used by permission of Open Court Publishing Co. and SCM Press Ltd.

[29] See R. E. James, *The Concrete God*, pp. 102-3.

That "God" stands for the supreme reality does not prevent the word from standing also for the supreme abstract principle. If the supreme abstract principle were not uniquely divine, then God would either come under no concept and be inconceivable (and the word "God" without meaning) or He would be but another instance of the principle, which would thus in a sense be super-divine. This seems blasphemous.[30]

God, then, has both an eternal and a temporal aspect. As temporal, relative, and material, he "includes the world." [31] He is conscious and personal and knows all that exists. God not only contains suffering; he also suffers; and this is consistent with his character. Thus, he both affects and is affected by the world, yet he also as a universal and abstract category is unaffected by any factual event.

The abstract perfection which we know a priori as God's necessary existence is included within the whole, rich, concrete nature of God as contingent. "God is more than his absolute character . . . the absolute is, rather, an abstract feature of the inclusive and supreme reality which is precisely the personal God." [32] Thus God is eternal in some aspects and devoid of change; temporal in other aspects and capable of change; conscious and self-aware; knowing the world or universe; and world-inclusive, having all things as constituents.[33] This combination of aspects in God leads to his being volitional, free, and having the power of goodness.

In his concrete nature, God changes, and this enriches the abstract aspect as well, for the abstract is included in the concrete. As Ralph James summarizes it: "The concrete God changes with every historical event; but *that* He is changing never changes." [34] He is involved in history and suffers with its events. God is adequate to every state of the world in being righteous and holy and loving. We do not say he is righteousness or wisdom or holiness. But we do say that God *is* love.

Only "love" is an abstraction which implies the final concrete truth. God "is" love, he is not merely loving, as he is merely righteous or wise

[30] Hartshorne, *The Logic of Perfection*, p. 5.
[31] Charles Hartshorne and William L. Reese, *Philosophers Speak of God* (Chicago: University of Chicago Press, 1953), p. 15.
[32] Hartshorne, *The Divine Relativity*, p. 83.
[33] Hartshorne and Reese, *Philosophers Speak of God*, p. 16.
[34] R. E. James, op. cit., p. 124.

(though in the supreme or definitive way). This is because in love the ethico-cognitive and the aesthetic aspects of value are both expressed. The lover is not merely the one who unwaveringly understands and tries to help; the lover is just as emphatically the one who takes unto himself the varying joys and sorrows of others and whose own happiness is capable of alteration thereby. Of course, one could distinguish between the abstract invariable lovingness of the perfect lover, and the concrete varying love-experiences he has of his objects in different stages. But love is the one abstraction which makes it almost entirely obvious that there *must* be such a distinction between the generic unchangeable factor and the total value enjoyed. It is not an accident that love was the abstraction least often appealed to in technical theology, though frequently suggested in the high points of Scripture and other genuinely religious writings.[35]

A God of love acts through persuasion and does not take away human freedom. Free agents are included within God and still have their freedom, by which God is affected. There is no such thing as a spectator God. As love he is involved with his creatures and shares their joy and suffering. "The denial of divine suffering is 'a profanation.' "[36] God is free to create as he effects "a transition from indeterminate or abstract possibility to concrete actuality."[37] He is free to create anything but, as creative, he cannot choose not to create. God includes the world, and yet he "contrasts to the world as the necessary to the contingent."[38] All these assertions need to be taken as a whole, so that we can speak of God in terms of the contrast between existing necessarily and contingently, pointing to his contingent concreteness, his divine freedom, his divine inclusiveness, and to necessity as applying to God and contingency to the world. Yet there are both contingency and necessity in God and in the world. There is a sense in which God is both the "supreme system of causation which at the same time is the supreme stream of effects."[39]

This leads to a statement of Hartshorne's panentheism. God is both cause and effect, both independent and dependent, he knows and is known, he is good and yet knows evil. All things are literally in God, and yet he has an identity that marks him off as independent. He needs *a*

[35] Hartshorne, *Man's Vision of God*, pp. 111-12.
[36] Hartshorne, *Creative Synthesis and Philosophic Method*, p. 263.
[37] Ibid., p. 264.
[38] Ibid., p. 265.
[39] Hartshorne and Reese, *Philosophers Speak of God*, p. 502.

universe, and contingently he contains this universe. This fits the model of the human organism, which is more than its parts although it includes its members; one's self-identity remains even if some members are missing or changed. So it is with God and nature. Panentheism follows the organic model, so that God both includes and is more than contingent reality; he includes accidents which are integrated into the whole.

God knows all that has been and is, but he cannot know the not yet. He is affected by the past and present of contingent experience, and this affects the interrelationships between man and God in the future. God is eminently social, for all life has a social structure, and the higher in the scale the more social reality is. At the top of the scale, God is supremely social, for he is in relationship by inclusion with the whole of reality.

If reality is conceived as social process or creative synthesis, there is a constant emergence of new constellations of unity. There is still a great deal of permanence which feeds into the new synthesis, but there is also novelty or chance or unpredictability or flexibility. This relative indeterminism does express its data, and it becomes the source for further becoming. The novel includes the permanent, just as the concrete includes the abstract, and contingency includes necessity.[40]

This leads to an understanding of the place of evil in Hartshorne's system.

> If God has eminent power, every creature has some degree (above zero) of non-eminent power. It, therefore, cannot be deduced from the eminent power of God that what happens is his doing, since the totality of causal conditions of an event includes all antecedent creatures as well as God.[41]

If God stopped one evil, he would open the door to other evils. The multiplicity of creative agents makes evil inevitable, but only through this same multiplicity could good become. This leads to the conclusion that absolute perfection is not possible for moral agents, for infallibility is a divine attribute. Even those who achieve moral stature are subject to chance events, and people are affected greatly by the process of growing up. Beyond all this, God chooses to act by persuasion, thus guaranteeing

---

[40] Hartshorne, *Creative Synthesis and Philosophic Method*, pp. 165-66.
[41] Ibid., p. 237.

the freedom that makes morality, risk, and adventure possible. God wills particular goods, but creatures are free to do as they please, and it is they who particularize God's aim.

There are many individual decisions (whether moral or immoral is irrelevant at this point), and when they are brought together in a composition, events simply happen by chance or luck. This is true even of atoms and electrons. It accounts for certain kinds of illness, widespread failures of harvests, and death. God does not will such events, but the world is such that they occur. "The world is somehow a joint product of the two forms of creativity, and is not uniquely or unilaterally determined by either." [42] This is the key to the problem. Possibilities come into actuality, and some of them are not intended by God or man but are due to accident or chance. Both God and man respond in their own ways, and God both knows actual events and feels what they mean. This is the source of God's joy and suffering.

Man

Because man has freedom in his relation to God and to others, he also has responsibility as a self-creating agent. He is both dependent on and independent of God, and the particularization of ethical and aesthetic aims is his doing and not God's. Man seeks both to glorify God and to serve him, which means that he seeks to promote the creative process, to increase sociality, to contribute to the common welfare or good, and to love his neighbor as himself. In his sympathy for other human beings and indeed for all creatures, he is loving God, who includes all, and therefore is contributing to the divine life. [43]

Man is always in the presence of God, and prayer is the recognition of that fact, normally through linguistic expression directed to the second person singular. The verbal form is man's "attempt to participate imaginatively in the larger process, to enjoy a sort of social relation with its principal personality." [44] A deity who is unsurpassable except by self is worthy to be worshiped.

The richness of living religiously is one result of Hartshorne's total philosophy. One is never free from the presence of God, who wills our

---

[42] Ibid., p. 270; see Hartshorne, *The Logic of Perfection*, pp. 310-17.

[43] Hartshorne, *The Divine Relativity*, p. 133.

[44] Charles Hartshorne, *Beyond Humanism* (Chicago: Willett, Clark & Co., 1937), p. 78.

good. But all creatures are contingent, and thus they die. They have temporal limitations; they become and they perish. Yet they do not become nothing, for the fact that they have lived remains as part of reality. Before they were born, they were literally nothing, but once they are dead the fact that they have lived remains. We cannot refer to a particular individual who will live in the future, but we can refer to any individual who has lived.

Hartshorne's view of "objective immortality" is much like Whitehead's. What we are lives on in the memory of God, but there is no personal existence after death. This is more than the immortality of influence in history, for we build our own book of life, and as it is being written as well as at the end there is an eternal reader, who is God. "Our adequate immortality is God's omniscience of us. He to whom all hearts are open remains evermore open to any heart that ever has been apparent to Him." [45] Death, then, is not destruction but is the limit of life. "To live everlastingly, as God does, can scarcely be our privilege; but we may earn everlasting places as lives well lived within the one life that not only evermore will have been lived, but evermore and inexhaustibly will be lived in ever new ways." [46]

Significance of Hartshorne

Hartshorne's approach to religion was metaphysical. Consistently, he returned to principles of metaphysical thinking, and always his view of God was within what he called panpsychism. The ultimate is not matter but souls, or units of experiencing, or subjects, as they are related or grouped in communities. He would not go as far as Gustav Fechner, who spoke of the souls of animals and even of an earth soul; but he did think of our feelings as the "pooled feelings of many cells." [47] Reality is social and is related to prehensions or the feeling of feelings. "The lowest known organisms have aspects that deserve to be called social." [48] Once there is emphasis on potentiality, becoming, and growth as primary categories, as Charles Peirce showed, panpsychism provides a world view.[49] William James leaned strongly in this direction, for it

---

[45] Hartshorne, *The Logic of Perfection*, p. 252.
[46] Ibid., p. 262; see my *Live Until You Die* (Philadelphia: United Church Press, 1973), pp. 126-29.
[47] Hartshorne and Reese, *Philosophers Speak of God*, p. 257.
[48] Hartshorne, *Man's Vision of God*, p. 160.
[49] Hartshorne and Reese, *Philosophers Speak of God*, p. 258.

made possible the belief that we are internal parts of God; Hartshorne commented that James pulled away from commitment to panpsychism for pragmatic and empirical reasons and that this weakened his case for a social view of diety.[50] Hartshorne's position tended toward idealism, but his epistemology was realistic; the object is real, the subject depends on its objects, an entity is or will become an object for some subject, and awareness occurs between objects which are also subjects.[51]

Hartshorne, like Whitehead, brought together many strands of the American spirit in theology. The emphasis on pragmatism and empiricism goes back to Charles Peirce and William James, although Hartshorne found what was valid in pragmatism in Whitehead. The pluralistic element in metaphysics, so evident in Hartshorne and Whitehead, can be found in James and Peirce. The denial of determinism and the stress on freedom, wrote Hartshorne, was indicated long ago by James. Hartshorne was convinced by James "that God is not the only agent making decisions which can be attributed neither to any other agent nor to any complex of antecedent causal conditions." James also made clear that "causes are *less determinate* than effects, therefore less rich in value." [52] But Hartshorne was disappointed with James's temporal deity who participates in a pluralistic universe. The category of supreme power, seen as an abstraction from the concrete, did not appear in James's thought because, according to Hartshorne, James never came out for panpsychism.

Hartshorne looked on Peirce as another seminal thinker, because in one sense he was a forerunner of those who conceived God as dipolar; the ingredients were there in the emphasis on potentiality, the primacy of becoming, growth, and panpsychism. Because Hartshorne could not accept Whitehead's view of "eternal objects," the suggestion by Peirce that there was a primordial continuum out of which evolved eternal possibilities became a viable alternative for him. There are still abstract forms, but the "primordial continuum of indefinite possibility" is a corrective of Whitehead.[53] Although Peirce was not a systematic

---

[50] Ibid., pp. 336, 351.

[51] See R. E. James, op. cit., p. 39.

[52] Charles Hartshorne, in Smith, *Contemporary American Philosophy*, p. 214; see Hartshorne, *Beyond Humanism*, pp. 154-55; Hartshorne and Reese, *Philosophers Speak of God*, p. 351; R. E. James, op. cit., p. 39.

[53] Hartshorne, *Reality as Social Process*, p. 20.

thinker, he was the original developer of pragmatism and emphasized that chance and freedom were essential to the understanding of the world. Peirce also saw clearly that the basic intuition behind all thinking has to do with the aesthetic rather than with knowing or goodness. We need to reverse the usual order, so that we have beauty, truth, and goodness, with beauty as the primary category. Truth and goodness are instrumental to aesthetic value.[54]

Hartshorne was not influenced by Dewey or Ames. He agreed with much that Dewey wrote in criticism of traditional or classical theism, but he did not see how Dewey's humanistic theology provided an answer to the problem.[55] Hartshorne found even less substance in Edward Scribner Ames's position, which he dismissed as a somewhat poetic way of talking about God without recourse to metaphysics.[56] Dewey influenced both Ames and Wieman.

Hartshorne equated Wieman's methods with those of Dewey and made the disclaimer that Wieman was not influenced by Whitehead even when he used the term "creativity." Furthermore, Wieman differed from Dewey at many points. Hartshorne's criticism of Wieman was that the concept of man was too passive. Dewey, like Whitehead and Hartshorne, insisted that man must be a co-worker with God and be self-creative in his freedom. Hartshorne also criticized Wieman's concept of God as creativity, for such a deity lacks consciousness, memory, or purpose, and, as we have seen, these are crucial attributes of God in the philosophy of organism. The process theologians see the permanence of values as they exist in the memory of God, and thus Wieman is to be criticized for saying that values cease and become nothing.

Wieman, wrote Hartshorne, could have enriched his views by relying on analogy, especially that of the human organism. We come to knowledge of God as we know ourselves and draw upon analogies to account for concepts that help us relate to God. Such analogies would account for ascribing consciousness, purpose, memory, and sociality to God. We can do this within the framework of a naturalistic theism, avoiding the dangers of classical theology. But Wieman refused to make

---

[54] Hartshorne, *Creative Synthesis and Philosophic Method*, pp. 303, 308.
[55] Hartshorne, *Beyond Humanism*, pp. 39-57.
[56] Hartshorne and Reese, *Philosophers Speak of God*, p. 384.

use of both analogy and metaphysics and therefore never got beyond a barren creativity.[57]

From the point of view of empirical theologians, Hartshorne's reliance on the ontological argument was disturbing. The empiricist looks to experience to establish the reality of what exists. Daniel Day Williams wrote,

> I cannot see what use the ontological argument is to our understanding of God and the world apart from our experience of that "most perfect being" which enters every thought. Is the idea of God equatable with an experience of God? . . . If this be so, then the ontological argument does not move simply from concept to actuality but from a concept which involves experience to a description of what is experienced.[58]

It may be that Williams stressed experience which leads to one side of a dipolar deity and that Hartshorne stressed reason which leads to the other pole, for Hartshorne comes to rely heavily on intuition as a basis for confidence in the ontological argument.

Hartshorne, then, is indebted to some of the key figures in American philosophy, and chiefly to Whitehead, but he is also his own man—a thinker of significant stature. This had led him to make his own original interpretations of Whitehead (some of which have been criticized by other philosophers)[59] and to develop his own position, which has become a central jumping-off point for such process theologians as Schubert M. Ogden and John B. Cobb, Jr. Not only is Hartshorne's creative originality significant but so is his influence on others.

---

[57] Ibid., pp. 396, 404-8.

[58] Daniel Day Williams, in Smith, *Contemporary American Philosophy*, p. 239.

[59] See William A. Christian, *An Interpretation of Whitehead's Metaphysics* (New Haven: Yale University Press, 1959), pp. 291-92, 330-31, 404-7; Brown et al., *Process Philosophy and Christian Thought*, pp. 39-44, 308-13, 320-23. See Eugene H. Peters, *Hartshorne and Neoclassical Metaphysics* (Lincoln: University of Nebraska Press, 1970), for a responsible treatment of Hartshorne's position; also his *The Creative Advance* (St. Louis: Bethany Press, 1966).

Existentialism and Process Thought

CHAPTER 10

SCHUBERT OGDEN HAS ABSORBED MUCH OF THE THINKING OF BOTH existentialism and process philosophy, especially as found in Rudolf Bultmann and Charles Hartshorne. His roots are in the American spirit in theology, and he sees himself aligned with the liberal tradition in Protestant Christianity, and especially with the Chicago school and with Wieman, Macintosh, Whitehead, and Hartshorne.[1] He has enriched this tradition by making clear its relation to existentialism as a way of understanding more clearly the nature of persons while moving toward a metaphysics of process. He takes seriously the significance of scripture and operates as a Christian theologian more than as a philosopher of religion.

For Christian theology to operate effectively, it must be grounded in a theistic metaphysics. The problem of God is a metaphysical one. "The God of theism in its most fully developed forms is the one metaphysical individual, the sole being whose individuality is constitutive of reality as such and who, therefore, is the inclusive object of all our faith and understanding."[2] This opens up the abstract side of philosophical

---

[1] See Schubert M. Ogden, *Christ Without Myth* (New York: Harper & Row, 1961), pp. 131-32. He mentions Bushnell, Clarke, Rauschenbusch, the Niebuhrs; among process theologians, Meland, Loomer, and Williams; from Europe, Schleiermacher, Ritschl, Herrmann, Harnack, Troeltsch, Schweitzer, early Barth, Bultmann in part, and Tillich (or is he American?).

[2] Schubert M. Ogden, "The Task of Philosophical Theology," in *The Future of Philosophical Theology*, ed. Robert Evans (Philadelphia: Westminster Press, 1971), p. 67.

thinking and makes possible the thinking of God as necessarily existing. It also establishes the independence of philosophical theology to deal with the whole of human existence, including the historical evidence from Christianity. So Christian theology properly presupposes a more general philosophical theology, and reflection on experience in the Christian mode will be consistent with the reflection of philosophical theology, although it will recognize that it has its own unique contribution to make to faith.[3]

The empirical, pragmatic, pluralistic, and metaphysical spirit of American theology is reflected in Ogden's thought. His empiricism is derived from Whitehead's broad-based nonsensuous perception, enriched by the existential note.[4] His pragmatism is less obvious, because he interprets the practical reason in more existential terms, but he accepts the moral strenuousness of moral obligation as developed by William James.[5] His metaphysics is derived from Hartshorne and Whitehead, and this leads to the "dismantling" of classical theism and the overcoming of atheistic humanism.[6] What Ogden adds to this picture is his adaptation of the thought of Bultmann and Heidegger to that of Hartshorne, which makes clearer the concrete God in whom we have a "life-trust." Thus the abstract pole of God, as an object of rational understanding, is brought into human existence as a divine subject, and the God of the philosophers is seen also as the God of religious faith.[7]

Prospects for Empirical Theology

Ogden's empiricism is closer to Whitehead's than to Hartshorne's. The stricter empiricists, such as Wieman and Macintosh, could not agree in

---

[3] Ibid., pp. 77, 82.

[4] Schubert M. Ogden, "Present Prospects for Empirical Theology," in *The Future of Empirical Theology*, ed. Bernard E. Meland (Chicago: University of Chicago Press, 1969), pp. 80-88.

[5] See Evans, op. cit., p. 57; Schubert M. Ogden, *The Reality of God* (New York: Harper & Row, 1966), p. 137 note.

[6] Schubert M. Ogden, "Beyond Supernaturalism," *Religion in Life*, vol. 33 (Winter 1963-64), pp. 15-16.

[7] Schubert M. Ogden, "Bultmann's Demythologizing and Hartshorne's Dipolar Theism," in *Process and Divinity*, ed. William L. Reese and Eugene Freeman (La Salle, Ill.: Open Court Publishing Co., 1964), pp. 507-8; see my interpretation in *The Language Gap and God* (Philadelphia: Pilgrim Press, 1970), pp. 63-76.

their interpretation of the evidence. How much reduction of belief is necessary to maintain a rigid empiricism? How much must empiricism be expanded to provide evidence for Christian beliefs? Yet, Ogden claims, an appeal to scripture requires an empirical theology. The transcendent God of the New Testament is also immanent, and thus if anything can be experienced God is the necessary ground. Even wicked men can know God, "for what can be known about God is plain to them, because God has shown it to them." He "has been clearly perceived in the things that have been made (Rom. 1:19-20)." Ogden concludes, "If God were not somehow experienced by us in our experience of anything whatever, he would not be the God to whom the faith of Scripture bears witness, and that faith could neither be true nor have any consistent meaning." [8]

The empirical theology of the recent past, however, has been caught up in verificational analysis, pointing either to a purely finite process of interaction or to a noncognitive concept of God. This result leads Ogden directly into a consideration of Whitehead's nonsensuous empiricism, which is "an intuitive awareness of our own past mental and bodily states and of the wider world as they compel conformation to themselves in the present." [9] The primary experience is of a vague totality from which details are derived by abstraction. Because Ogden uses the word empirical in this broad sense, he is now inclined to speak of theology as "experiential" or "existential." [10] His position is a reassertion of Whitehead's emphasis on the subjectivist principle and reflective understanding, as one comes to know himself as an experiencing self.[11] This takes Ogden beyond James's radical empiricism toward an even more undiscriminated feeling which provides "that self-evidence which sustains itself in civilized experience." [12] We experience being and value without distinction between them, and this awareness is of more than our selves and other creatures, for it includes a sense of the

[8] In Meland, op. cit., p. 74.

[9] Ibid., pp. 81-82.

[10] Schubert M. Ogden, "The Reformation We Want," *Anglican Theological Review*, vol. 54 (Oct. 1972), p. 264.

[11] Schubert M. Ogden, in *Language, Truth and Meaning*, ed. Philip McShane (Notre Dame, Ind.: University of Notre Dame Press, 1972), pp. 225-26.

[12] Alfred North Whitehead, *Modes of Thought* (New York: Macmillan, 1933), p. 106. Copyright 1938 by Macmillan Publishing Co., Inc., renewed 1966 by T. North Whitehead. Used by permission.

whole in which we are included. There is what Whitehead called "the intuition of holiness . . . which is at the foundation of all religion," [13] and this leads to an "awareness of ourselves and the world as of worth to God." [14]

There is a question whether such claims for empiricism can be justified, although Dewey held a similar view. We cannot avoid reflecting on experiences which we all share, and these include experiences which for Ogden lead to a conception of God. If we cannot avoid inner nonsensuous perceptions of the whole and sensuous perceptions where we discriminate, it becomes difficult to eliminate *a* concept of God, although it is likely that we will cease to accept the classical concepts. Or can we still accept an atheistic or secular account without ignoring or eliminating certain types of experience? Ogden maintains that the reality of God becomes a necessity of thought both as ultimate and abstract and as contingent and loving, but it remains necessary that God be contingent.

The Reality of God

Like Bernard Meland,[15] Ogden is aware of the radical changes in culture and of the influence of the process of secularization on religious beliefs. He distinguishes between "secularization," which reflects a method of dealing with reality, and "secularism," which makes the findings of science the only knowledge there is. The first way of thinking leads to theology which reflects a world view that is consistent with the findings of science; the second makes any theology or religious belief impossible. But even secularity leads to theological difficulties for many.

The problem, as Ogden sees it, is that we have inherited a supernaturalistic theism with premises that no modern mind can accept: the idea of creation out of nothing, the static God of classical theology, the doctrine of last things, the miracles, and the metaphysical outlook that accompanies such beliefs. The attempt to combine the loving God of scriptures with the immutable God of the Greeks leads to a conclusion that is logically incoherent. The "death-of-God" theologians

---

[13] Ibid., p. 120.

[14] Schubert M. Ogden, in Meland, op. cit., p. 87.

[15] See Bernard E. Meland, *The Secularization of Modern Cultures* (New York: Oxford University Press, 1966).

and the logical positivists are right: such a concept fails to point to a reality we can believe in.[16]

Building on the analysis of Stephen Toulmin, Ogden says that the first function of religion is the reassurance of our own worth. Confidence in one's self, seemingly inborn, is often threatened by persons and events, and religious assertions have a "re-presentative" character that relates us to the ground of our confidence. We then presuppose that this ground is "somehow" real. This confidence in one's worth becomes the basis for moral action.

> I hold that the primary use or function of "God" is to refer to the objective ground in reality itself of our ineradicable confidence in the final worth of our existence. It lies in the nature of this basic confidence to affirm that the real whole world of which we experience ourselves to be parts is such as to be worthy of, and thus itself to evoke, that very confidence. The word "God," then, provides the designation for whatever it is about this experienced whole that calls forth and justifies our original and inescapable trust, thereby meaning existentially, as William James once said, "You can dismiss certain kinds of fear." [17] From this it follows that to be free of such fear by existing in this trust is one and the same thing as affirming the reality of God.[18]

This special mode of reasoning reflects the moral optimism of Macintosh and the will to believe of James, but even though it is tied in with existence and moral experience, it is hard to see that this is enough to establish the reality of God. Ogden claims that any consideration of moral experience at depth leads to talk about God, so that faith in God becomes unavoidable. We become selves because of this faith in God, and therefore we come to believe in his reality. All so-called proofs of God are secondary as support for this faith.[19]

This argument appeals to experience, but it is not empirical. It is, says Ogden, "experiential" in that it applies to some possible experience and

---

[16] See Delwin Brown, Ralph E. James, Jr., and Gene Reeves, eds., *Process Philosophy and Christian Thought* (Indianapolis: Bobbs-Merrill, 1971), pp. 176-81, 184; Ogden, *The Reality of God*, pp. 16-20.

[17] William James, *Some Problems of Philosophy* (New York: Longmans, Green & Co., 1911), p. 62.

[18] Ogden, *The Reality of God*, p. 38.

[19] See ibid., pp. 135-42; compare Antony Flew, "Reflections on 'The Reality of God,'" *Journal of Religion*, vol. 48, no. 2 (Apr. 1968), pp. 150-61.

because it is metaphysically basic to all experience.[20] It is not an empirical claim that can be falsified but a metaphysical one. Just as we can say that the universe or reality exists without fear of falsifiability, so can we speak metaphysically of God if he "is that order fully understood" and thus encompasses whatever we mean by reality.

The New Theism

It is helpful to keep Whitehead's and Hartshorne's thinking in the background when one considers Ogden's view of God, although Ogden's position is enriched by his understanding of existentialism and his concern that theology be grounded in scripture. The originality of Ogden lies in his creative use of sources, looking on the existential emphasis of Bultmann and Heidegger from the perspective of process metaphysics.

Ogden's starting point is the secularity of our current culture. "Secularity as such, as distinct from secularism, is simply the emphatic affirmation that man and the world are themselves of ultimate significance." [21] Secularism, on the other hand, is an enemy of belief in God and leads to a denial of classical theism. But classical theism is also impossible to maintain in the light of secularity, and therefore we need to take a close look at the newer theism.

God, conceived in terms of secularity, "is the ground of confidence in the ultimate worth or significance of our life in the world." [22] To make this concept intelligible, we are led to think of God in relational terms, affected by his relations to our actions and yet in some sense existing for himself. Existence as an abstract constant is contrasted with actuality as an abstract variable. Thus, God's existence is necessary but his actuality is the way he behaves in relationships. This leads to the concept of a dipolar deity, both supremely absolute and supremely relative, reflecting Whitehead's primordial and consequent and Hartshorne's abstract and concrete poles of God's nature.

This kind of thinking is metaphysical, speculative, and imaginative, using the organic self in relation as a model. There are relations within one's own body and with other selves and ultimately with a larger

[20] See Schubert M. Ogden, "God and Philosophy," *Journal of Religion*, vol. 48, no. 2 (Apr. 1968), pp. 172, 175.
[21] Ogden, *The Reality of God*, p. 44.
[22] Ibid., p. 47.

whole. These temporal relations are what constitute the self, and yet there is a self-identity arising out of moments of decision as we act out our own creativeness. The chief category for this process is creative becoming. This kind of analysis is applied to God by means of analogy.

If God is the exemplification of metaphysical principles, as Whitehead claimed, it is possible to make use of a strict analogy that implies anthropomorphism.[23] Yet "God is not a self in univocally the same sense as man," for God is always present and is eternal. God is dependent on the world as a self is dependent on others, and yet he is in his abstract essence dependent on nothing. As the self not only acts overtly but also intends to carry out its subjective aim or purpose, so God is conceived by strict analogy as a self who loves. God

> constitutes himself as God by participating fully and completely in the world of his creatures, thereby laying the ground for the next stage of the creative process. Because his love, unlike ours, is pure and unbounded, his relation to his creatures and theirs to him is direct and immediate. . . . Because his love or power of participation in the being of others is literally boundless, there are no gradations in intimacy of the creatures to him, and so there can be nothing in him corresponding to our nervous system or sense organs.[24]

The creativity of God is always mixed with the creativity of human beings, and thus they influence each other, but God's influence is that of love while men's motives are always mixed and often opposed to what God intends. This leads the religious man to seek to align himself with the overall purpose of God, "who accepts us without condition into his own everlasting life, where we have a final standing or security that can nevermore be lost." [25]

God, as he works in time, remembers the past, experiences the present, and anticipates the future. Yet he is not bound by time in the way that human beings are, for the latter's becoming and perishing include a beginning and an end, while God is everlasting. Man as finite is limited in both time and space, and God is free of limitation in both aspects. This qualitative difference shows that even a strict analogy may

---

[23] Ibid., p. 175.
[24] Ibid., pp. 177-78.
[25] Ibid., pp. 178-79.

not hold absolutely. In this sense, we may say that God transcends time and space, just as we may claim that God transcends history. Yet, insofar as God is creator and redeemer, he works in and through history in at least two senses.

First, God acts in and through creatures within the framework of time and space. It is in this sense that God is concrete, is actualized, is contingent, is experienced. Even in this relationship, however, God's acts are conditioned by man's freedom of choice. In the immanent interrelationships, we may distinguish God's act and man's act, but the concrete event is always a mixture of the two.

Second, "what constitutes religion as one form of culture alongside of others is man's attempt to express the ultimate meaning of his existence by grasping the divine *logos* that he encounters in his experience and re-presenting it through appropriate symbolic means." [26] Thus man's action reflects God's action or even, we may say, "actually *is* God's action." Certain events in history may be interpreted as God's action in this sense, and some events are uniquely suited to such interpretation.

It is this element of particular events that gives rise to particular religions and moves us from consideration of religion in general and the more abstract concepts of philosophical theology to specific religious beliefs, symbols, and practices. Any specific theology presupposes a theistic metaphysics but moves to interpretations based on particular revelations.[27] This leads into the question of the place of Jesus Christ in Christian theology.

There are many claims, religious and otherwise, on our lives. If the divine Logos is discernible everywhere, there is still the need to decide between conflicting claims about its representation. Jesus has "decisive revelatory power," and thus the Christian community says

> that *Jesus* is the decisive act of God . . . that in him, in his outer acts of symbolic word and deed, there is expressed *that* understanding of human existence which is, in fact, the ultimate truth about our life before God; that the ultimate reality with which all men have to do is God the sovereign Creator and Redeemer, and that in understanding ourselves in terms of the gift and demand of his love, we realize our authentic existence as men.[28]

---

[26] Ibid., p. 181.
[27] See Evans, op. cit., pp. 72-82.
[28] Ogden, *The Reality of God*, pp. 185-86.

Christians find in Christ what God means to them. Ogden writes that in Paul's mythological language about Jesus as Lord there is the "same existential significance," so that the same word addressed to all men becomes particularized for us in Christ. This word is expressed as promise and demand, as death and resurrection, as through kerygma and sacraments we live out our lives under "the love of God in Christ Jesus our Lord (Rom. 8:39)." [29]

The stress on God's love leads to an understanding of death and resurrection in terms of what they mean for God as well as for man. If God is love, he not only affects all things but is affected by all things. This means, first, that we have some degree of influence on God and that God has an eminent influence on us, and therefore prayer and worship make sense as man's action in relation to God and in his response. But it also means that because we are objects of God's love, God overcomes our death and our sin by accepting us into his everlasting life.[30] This, of course, is the idea of objective immortality as developed by Whitehead and Hartshorne. If every moment lives on in God, there is reason also to believe that our experiences are resurrected or restored.[31] What we have been and are remain known in the memory of God, to put it in Hartshorne's terms.

Existentialism

We have said that there is an existential element in Ogden's position that gives it a cutting edge. Ogden's earliest writings dealt with Bultmann as contrasted with Wieman and Hartshorne, and *Christ Without Myth* is a distinguished interpretation of Bultmann's position. Near the conclusion of that book, Ogden wrote that "until process philosophy is informed by the insights of existential analysis, its lack of an explicit anthropology, which handicaps it for theological employment, can hardly be remedied in keeping with its own implicit principles." [32] Thus we find comments on Bultmann and Heidegger, and sometimes incisive treatments of them, throughout Ogden's writings.

---

[29] Ibid., p. 203.
[30] Ibid., p. 223.
[31] Ibid., p. 226; but Ogden qualifies his conclusion by saying that this "leaves completely open whether we somehow manage to survive death and continue to exist as experiencing subjects as is claimed by conventional theories of immortality" (p. 229).
[32] Ogden, *Christ Without Myth*, p. 152.

186

However, existentialism is not a satisfactory philosophy in itself. Important as existential analysis is, it needs the fulfillment and enrichment that can be provided by process philosophy. The distinction between essence and existence, as found in the thought of Bultmann and Heidegger, needs to be supplemented by the concept of actuality as used by Whitehead and Hartshorne. Hartshorne pointed up three weaknesses in Heidegger's thought: first, because of a failure to see the connection between philosophy and mathematics, there was an inadequate use of the concept of structure; second, there was insufficient interest in aesthetic phenomena; and third, there was a refusal to grasp "in our sensory contact with reality the blurred sympathetic intuition of the feelings of other individuals." [33] These points are clearly accounted for in process thought.

Ogden believes that much can be made of Heidegger's interpretation of temporality as an enrichment of or support of a process theology. He builds his interpretation from a footnote in Heidegger's *Being and Time*, which criticizes the traditional concept of eternity and suggests that it might be interpreted as "a more primal and 'infinite' temporality." [34] Heidegger did not develop the implications of this note, but Ogden believes that it has implications for a contemporary doctrine of God.

Philosophy is an ontological task, dealing with the overall picture rather than with the personal understanding of the individual in his concrete experiences. There is a difference between a philosophical and a confessional theology, between a reasoned statement and a proclamation, although there must be consistency between them.

When Heidegger speaks of God's "more primal" or "infinite" temporality (what Hartshorne calls "eminent" temporality),[35] it opens up a strict analogy not only between kinds of time but also between man and God. At least, Ogden thinks we can presuppose such a strict analogy, and thus we can reason from an existentialist analysis of man to a concept of God in which "eternity" is construed as "eminent" temporality. If man is related to others, then God is to be conceived as

---

[33] Charles Hartshorne, *Beyond Humanism* (Chicago: Willett, Clark & Co., 1937), p. 304; see Ralph E. James, *The Concrete God* (Indianapolis: Bobbs-Merrill, 1971), pp. 17-29.
[34] Martin Heidegger, *Being and Time* (New York: Harper & Row, 1962), p. 499, note xiii; cited in Ogden, *The Reality of God*, p. 145.
[35] Charles Hartshorne, *Creative Synthesis and Philosophic Method* (La Salle, Ill.: Open Court Publishing Co., 1970), p. 84.

"essentially related to a world of others in whose being he actively participates by reason of a similar basic structure of care."[36] Such a God has a past and future as well as a present, just as man finds his meaning in all three dimensions of time. Yet God is different from man, because his temporality is "infinite," while man's is finite. Likewise, following the same strict analogy with man, Ogden believes that for Heidegger God is related to all others, and that this defines his absoluteness. These characteristics are conceived in man in their finite mode and in God in their eminent or primal mode.[37]

Heidegger, so interpreted from a single footnote, seems to have a position that parallels those of Ogden, Hartshorne, and Whitehead. The question arises as to whether Heidegger's position is needed at this point, or whether Ogden has simply shown how Heidegger may be interpreted in process terms.

The same question occurs when Bultmann's position is considered. Thomas Oden suggests that "Ogden's romance with process philosophy and theology has largely shaped his perception of the issues relating to Bultmann."[38] It is evident that Ogden is a creative theologian in his own right, and that Bultmann's interpreters vary in their conclusions, some being more Lutheran and kerygmatic than others, but *Christ Without Myth* has its own virtues in making sense out of Bultmann for many readers.[39] Ogden does not make a process theologian out of Bultmann, but he uses some of his insights as a basis for a creative synthesis.

Ogden claims that demythologizing must be taken seriously and that Bultmann, by stopping with the kerygma, has placed a limit upon the process. Myths may continue to be used "only if they are constantly *interpreted* in nonmythological (or existential) terms."[40] Therefore,

statements about God may be interpreted as statements about man. By this we mean *not* that theology may not speak directly about "God and his activity," but simply that whenever it does so speak, its statements must be at least implicitly about man and his possibilities of self-under-

---

[36] Ogden, *The Reality of God*, p. 150.
[37] Ibid., pp. 152-57.
[38] Thomas Oden, "The Alleged Structural Inconsistency in Bultmann," *Journal of Religion*, vol. 44, no. 3 (July 1964), p. 193.
[39] See my *The Language Gap and God*, pp. 62-68.
[40] Ogden, *Christ Without Myth*, p. 128.

standing if they are not to be incredible and irrelevant. In *this* sense, "statements about God and his activity" *are* "statements about human existence," and *vice versa.*[41]

Ogden is concerned that a theocentric emphasis precede any adequate Christology, which opposes him to Bultmann and Barth, among others. The general possibility of salvation lies in God's purpose for man. Ogden appeals to the New Testament for support.[42] The New Testament does not say that salvation became possible in Jesus Christ but that it became *manifest.* Thus, for the Christian, the event of Jesus of Nazareth, conceived as a historical occurrence as well as an act of God in history, is essential but not exclusive. Being confronted with Christ is the way in which we come to understand ourselves existentially; in him the reality of God is "actually present 'in, with, and under' the statement that seeks to express it."[43] This demands our decision, and therefore we are responsible.

Oden suggests that Ogden has presented "an unchristological solution to a problem which can only be solved, as Bultmann insists, christologically." What we have is a "decisive affirmation of the grace of God as Creator."[44] But Ogden would say that an adequate Christology must be centered on the reality of God, and that the dipolar God of process thought is both redemptive and creative. For Christian theology (as distinct from philosophical theology in general), writes Ogden, "the sole norm of every legitimate theological assertion is the revealed word of God declared in Jesus Christ, expressed in Holy Scripture, and made completely present in the proclamation of the church through its word and sacraments."[45] When this statement is understood within the perspective of Ogden's use of demythologizing, strict analogy, and process theology, it has promise of value in communicating the gospel in a secular society.

Some Criticisms

Ogden's argument for believing in the existence of God in his title essay, "The Reality of God," is based upon the presuppositions of a man

[41] Ibid., p. 137; see Ogden, "The Significance of Rudolf Bultmann for Contemporary Theology," in *The Theology of Rudolf Bultmann*, ed. Charles W. Kegley (New York: Harper & Row, 1966), pp. 104-26.
[42] Ogden, *Christ Without Myth*, pp. 141-44.
[43] Ibid., p. 161.
[44] Oden, op. cit., p. 200, note 41, and p. 198.
[45] Ogden, *Christ Without Myth*, p. 138.

concerned with his own worth and with the validity of his moral activity. It echoes the moral optimism of Macintosh and the will to believe of James, although it finds its roots in Toulmin's analysis of moral language. As one reflects upon his presuppositions and his moral experiences, he finds that he believes in God.

But there are moral men without such presuppositions, there are those who do not recognize any "unconditional significance" in their decisions, and it is not clear what are the common experiences upon which we must reflect. So far, we have certain necessary presuppositions and beliefs, but Ogden allows that a theological or metaphysical assertion is false if it "misrepresents the common structure of all our experiences . . . and thus is falsified by any one of them we choose to consider." [46] But, as Flew claims, Ogden does not consider any experiences that would falsify his conclusions. [47]

Ogden, in spite of his well-placed criticisms of classical theism, makes one bad slip that Flew points out. In true process style, he claims that God "is not utterly immaterial or bodiless" and he is clear that God is, to use Hartshorne's term, "surrelative" or "relatively perfect" but that the only thing changeless about God is that he changes. He is "the *eminently* incarnate one." [48] Then he reintroduces the Absolute as "in a literal sense 'eternal,' 'immutable,' 'impassive,' 'immaterial.'" God "includes the Absolute." [49] This does not seem to me to be the claim that Whitehead makes for the primordial nature of God or Hartshorne for his abstract necessary existence. [50]

According to Eric Mascall, Ogden's position in *Christ Without Myth* is more extreme and dangerous than those of John A. T. Robinson or Paul van Buren. [51] Perhaps this is because Mascall looked at Ogden through the criticisms of van Buren. Mascall's criticisms from the standpoint of neo-Thomism stand outside the mainstream of the American spirit in theology, but van Buren, although influenced by Barth and British logical empiricism, is very much within the American stream.

---

[46] Ogden, *The Reality of God*, p. 93.
[47] Antony Flew, in *Journal of Religion*, vol. 48 (Apr. 1968), pp. 151-55.
[48] Ogden, *The Reality of God*, pp. 58-60.
[49] Ibid., pp. 60-61.
[50] Flew, op. cit., pp. 157-58.
[51] Eric L. Mascall, *The Secularisation of Christianity* (London: Darton, Longman &: Todd, 1965), p. 6.

In *Christ Without Myth*, Ogden was not concerned to develop his process thought but to reflect on the contribution that existentialism, especially Bultmann and to some extent Heidegger, could make to Ogden's general concern for a theology that was relevant in a secular society, especially secular man outside the church. In contrast, van Buren was concerned with a secular man's interpretation of the Gospel in terms of a rather strict linguistic empiricism. Thus, from the beginning, van Buren challenged Ogden's right to speak about God at all.

Ogden asserts that we may speak of God analogically, a claim open to the same criticism that we cannot speak of God at all. Therefore, when Ogden says that "statements about God and his activities *are* 'statements about human existence,' and vice versa," [52] van Buren cites Ronald Hepburn's point that "a translation of words does not change the facts to which they refer." [53] If words about man which can be verified are translated into words about God which cannot be verified, the move is illegitimate. But, on Ogden's grounds, we already may speak about God, and therefore we may speak about a nonmythological anchor in human existence.

There is also the danger that one might mix language categories, and van Buren says that both Ogden and Bultmann are guilty of confusing existential and empirical statements. Van Buren illustrates this confusion of the logical placing of religious language as follows:

> If a man crossing the ocean on a steamer rushes from his cabin shouting that the ship is on fire, he is certainly suggesting a course of action, however implicitly. The suggestion is to be taken seriously, however, only if the situation is as he has described it. A wise officer will begin by investigating to see if there is a fire, not by attempting to understand himself as a man who is on a burning ship. The language of the New Testament is logically of this sort. It proclaims that God has acted, that Jesus has been raised from the dead, that the powers of darkness have been overcome; in a word, that the situation of man has been changed. Something has happened, and the question of an appropriate response is obviously important.[54]

---

[52] Ogden, *Christ Without Myth*, p. 137.

[53] Paul M. van Buren, *The Secular Meaning of the Gospel* (New York: Macmillan, 1963), p. 67; see Ronald Hepburn, "Demythologizing and the Problem of Validity," in *New Essays in Philosophical Theology*, ed. Antony Flew and Alasdair MacIntyre (London: SCM Press, 1955), pp. 227-42.

[54] Van Buren, op. cit., p. 69.

Van Buren suggests that when there is moral repulsion to a story that may be historical, Bultmann talks about "a crude mythological conception of God." Of course it is often a disputed point whether any given biblical account is history, folklore, myth, miracle story, or a mixture of these. The proper question to ask is whether Ogden has discarded stories for which there is historical evidence. Incidentally, it is interesting to note that in van Buren's account the incidents about being raised from the dead or the powers of darkness being overcome are not taken literally later on in his book. About Easter, all that van Buren says is that "something happened" which is not open to empirical investigation. Ogden and van Buren are nearly in agreement on this point.

Van Buren continues with a similar objection to existentialism. Ogden, he says, "replaces the historical event of Jesus of Nazareth by the existential response of the believer." [55] Now it is true that for both Bultmann and Ogden the emphasis is on the existential response, on the significance of the cross as central to man's self-understanding. This need for immediacy is the basis for R. H. Fuller's jibe: "The Christ-event took place not in the years 1-30 A.D. but every time that Bultmann enters the pulpit at 11 A.M. on Sunday." [56] It is interesting to note that Thomas Oden makes exactly the opposite criticism of Ogden: "One might wonder why Ogden chose to point up the *historisch* dimension of the basis for faith, since, as he well knows, Bultmann argues that faith is never attainable through objective historical (*historisch*) inquiry." [57] Both Bultmann and Ogden agree that Jesus of Nazareth existed and died on the cross. The resurrection as recorded in various stories is considered as myth, and van Buren is correct in his criticism at this point, although it is hard to see any difference between Ogden's and van Buren's interpretation of "The Easter faith." "Ogden ends," writes van Buren, "by dispensing with Jesus himself." [58] This is patently a misstatement of Ogden's position, for it is clear that Ogden accepts as historical some of the reports of the life of the man Jesus, in whom is the "decisive manifestation" of God's love. [59]

Ogden can also be criticized, says van Buren, for saying that one can

[55] Ibid., p. 70.
[56] Mascall, op. cit., p. 10.
[57] Oden, op. cit., p. 199, note 21.
[58] Van Buren, op. cit., p. 73.
[59] Ogden, *Christ Without Myth*, pp. 153, 159-64.

reach the same authentic life independently of Jesus. This is not quite what Ogden says, although his theocentric emphasis points in this direction. The saving grace of God is expressed through the concept of Christ or the Logos as God in action. If the cosmic Christ is eternal, if he was offered as part of God's love at every point in time, then in any literal sense we can speak of a Christ (preexisting) as independent of the historical man Jesus, although for Christians Jesus as the Christ is central.

Finally, van Buren claims that "it is Heidegger who gives the final definition of Ogden's 'norm.' " [60] It was already clear in *Christ Without Myth* that Heidegger's existentialism was to be used to enrich Ogden's basic process philosophy, and that speaking analogically was more important than speaking mythologically about God, but this position, made clear in *The Reality of God*, would be equally distasteful to van Buren.

The criticisms of Flew and van Buren are from the standpoint of a strict empiricism that takes seriously the principle of falsification, but Ogden (and Hartshorne) would agree that this kind of limited empiricism does not establish the God of panentheism. The broader type of empiricism, especially the nonsensuous empiricism of Whitehead, is not subject to detailed falsification but is used to account for the vague experience of the whole, and this is close to the use of intuition by Hartshorne and of existential confidence by Ogden.

A criticism from the standpoint of process philosophy has also been suggested. In Ogden's Christology, there is difficulty in understanding how God acted in Jesus other than the way in which he acts in all men. Ogden claims that there is no difference in God's aim for any person, including Jesus, who is a "decisive manifestation." In terms of both Ogden's and Hartshorne's view of God, this is about as far as one can go.

David Griffin suggests, however, that if one takes seriously Whitehead's belief in God's "subjective aim," this is something that can be particularized. If God had an ideal aim for Jesus, and if Jesus in the freedom of his own self-creative decision responded in the light of his inheritance, environment, and the particular situation, we could say that God's aim for him was actualized. Thus, for Christians, we could

---

[60] Van Buren, op. cit., p. 79.

proclaim his necessity as an actual occasion in history.[61] This interpretation of process thought moves in a direction different from Ogden's, for it asserts special acts of God and a supreme act in and through Jesus Christ. Griffin goes so far as to speak of "God's prevenient initiative" as expressed in process terms, while at the same time allowing for Jesus' "free decision." Griffin's conclusion is that *"Jesus was God's supreme act of self-expression, and is therefore appropriately apprehended as God's decisive revelation."* [62] If Griffin is correct, this approach would be more satisfactory to those immersed in the historic Christologies.

Conclusion

As in Hartshorne's thought, so in Ogden's, the American spirit in theology moves toward a greater rationalism, with less emphasis on empiricism and pragmatism, except as these methodologies operate as an explication of one's reflection on existence. Ogden has made much greater use of the insights of existentialism than have the other process theologians, and this has enriched his thought in many ways.

Whitehead expressed severe reservations about the limits of human thought, and Bernard Meland believes that Hartshorne and Ogden have not stayed within these limits in some of their claims. There are still too many unmanageable aspects of experience to be taken into account; there is still much in myth that cannot be reduced to process categories; there are notes of depth and indeterminacy in experience that need greater empirical analysis. Perhaps we need to recapture something of the empiricism and pragmatism and pluralism of William James, and certainly the openness of awareness of Meland.[63] This would not undo the vision of panentheism and process thought, but it would enrich it.

---

[61] See David R. Griffin, "Schubert Ogden's Christology and the Possibilities of Process Philosophy," in Brown et al., *Process Philosophy and Christian Thought*, pp. 347-61; also, John B. Cobb, Jr., in ibid., pp. 382-98.

[62] David R. Griffin, *A Process Christology* (Philadelphia: Westminster Press, 1973), p. 227; see pp. 213-23.

[63] See Bernard E. Meland, in Brown et al., *Process Philosophy and Christian Thought*, pp. 116-27.

An
Empirical Base
for
Process
Theology

CHAPTER 11

THE TRIADIC EMPHASIS OF JAMES INCLUDED RADICAL EMPIRICISM, pragmatism, and a pluralistic metaphysics. If these three elements are manifestations of the American spirit in theology, issuing in a theism that sees God at work in the world in which novelty, chance, and freedom are factors both God and man must deal with, we have the setting for our study. As the story developed, however, some of these elements dropped into the background or vanished altogether. The explicit metaphysics vouched for by James was not present in Dewey, who had no use for antecedent reality. Dewey was primarily an instrumentalist, and this gave a strong pragmatic slant to his empiricism. Gerald Birney Smith, Mathews, and Ames made use of evidence from experience, and Smith spoke of a mystical experiment, but Mathews and Ames never got far beyond the pragmatic value of the God idea. Wieman was the most thoroughgoing of the empiricists, but after an original immersion in Whitehead's process thought, he retained an organic naturalism as a framework for his theology, with the metaphysical structure at a minimum. Macintosh struggled to produce empirical evidence, made some use of pragmatism, and recognized that the completion of his system required a metaphysical superstructure.

With Whitehead, the full triadic emphasis of James reasserted itself, but with a greater emphasis on metaphysics. Hartshorne, however, turned to a more rationalistic emphasis on metaphysics and was seriously critical of the efforts of empirical theology, although his concrete God required some interpretation of experience or intuition. Ogden followed Hartshorne's lead and added ingredients from existential analysis, which from a phenomenological point of view might be considered a nonempirical approach to experience. This is an oversimplified summary, but it points to the next step in our study, the recovery of an empirical base for process thought, a combination of the insights of Wieman and Whitehead, as found in the thought of Daniel Day Williams.

Bernard Meland wrote that "in his earlier years, Williams was the most eclectic of the process group of empiricists in his selection of sources and perspectives." [1] He had a broad sympathy that led him to see the values of other positions. He regarded Christian theology as a distinctive discipline and, as a theologian, spoke from within the Christian community. Therefore, he made a distinction between the disciplines of philosophy and theology, as did Ogden, although both of them recognized the debt of theology to philosophy. With his capacity for fairness and objectivity, he was able to operate as a mediator between various Christian traditions, especially in the successive editions of his *What Present-Day Theologians Are Thinking*. He saw clearly that each person operates from his own perspective, and this relativity of perspectives points beyond any one position to include insights from other ones.[2] Reason, from this way of thinking, is never an abstract activity, although reason is a function which abstracts from experience. Reason, dealing with many perspectives and inconclusive evidence, never leads to a closed system of thought. "Reason has for its field the whole of experience; and this means experience not as an abstract category but as the particularity of concrete events." [3] This includes the events of history, as Christianity asserts.

Williams recognized that this tradition was outside the main theological stream in the Barthian and neoorthodox period. Wieman, especially, stood apart in his continuing assertion of an empirical basis for religious knowledge. Yet Wieman reflected the democratic spirit,

---

[1] Bernard E. Meland, ed., *The Future of Empirical Theology* (Chicago: University of Chicago Press, 1969), p. 46.

[2] See Daniel Day Williams, "Truth in the Theological Perspective," *Journal of Religion*, vol. 28, no. 4 (Oct. 1948), pp. 242-54.

[3] Ibid., p. 253.

pragmatic attitude, and religious feelings of American culture and had an accurate picture of the actual practice of religion even when theological interpretations reflected neoorthodoxy.[4] Certain elements in Wieman's thought need to be lifted up as of special significance. Williams indicated that one of these was the distinction between created and creative good.

> Every human love is a created good and is directed to some created good, that is, some structure of meaning, person or value. The *creative* good is the present working of God, bringing new structures into existence. That working is terrible in its power to shatter old structures.[5]

God is the source of new structures, and man's salvation is to be open to this creative and transforming power. In *Religious Experience and Scientific Method*, Wieman stressed the significance of contemplation and of a "total datum" in all its richness as a basis for religious knowledge, but this got lost in his later thought owing to his virtual abandonment of metaphysics.[6]

Williams was critical of Wieman for his reliance on definition as a way of establishing an empirical basis for belief in God, for his lack of metaphysics, for his too-literal description of God and his ignoring of metaphor, analogy, and symbol, and his refusal to make full use of historical concepts which could be blended with his current interpretation.[7] In spite of his able interpretations of social responsibility, he lacked a doctrine of vocation. It is clear that Williams accepted much of what Wieman wrote but objected to what he left out.[8]

It is the positive side of Wieman's thought that should be stressed, "the essential rightness of Wieman's insight into the ultimate problems of man's existence under God," which sets "us free to think about God's presence in a dynamic history."[9] Whatever our concept may be, we

---

[4] Williams, in *Charles Hartshorne and Henry Nelson Wieman*, ed. William S. Minor (Carbondale, Ill.: Foundation for Creative Philosophy, 1969), pp. 55-57.

[5] Daniel Day Williams, *The Spirit and Forms of Love* (New York: Harper & Row, 1968), p. 210; used by permission. See also Williams, in *Contemporary American Philosophy*, ed. John E. Smith (London: George Allen & Unwin; New York: Humanities Press; 1970), p. 245.

[6] Williams, in *The Empirical Theology of Henry Nelson Wieman*, ed. Robert E. Bretall (New York: Macmillan, 1963), p. 93.

[7] Bretall, op. cit., p. 91.

[8] Minor, op. cit., p. 58.

[9] Bretall, op. cit., pp. 95-96.

need to know God as "he is experienced as a process in existence," to whom we may respond as he works in his sovereign goodness and power.[10]

Williams also was greatly influenced by Hartshorne and Whitehead. He saw how the concept of God viewed from the perspective of process philosophy is freed from the positivistic criticisms of traditional theology, so that we can claim that "God conceived as metaphysically creative activity, as becoming, does enter into the processes of human society, and his being lends its structure and value to the forms of human readiness." [11] There is a broad view of religious experience that ties in with process metaphysics. This metaphysics is conceived as a social doctrine of reality, a term which Williams preferred to organic, for it is more obviously pluralistic. Whitehead, however, did not make clear the way in which God is fully actual in experience, and in his insistence on God's persuasion he may have missed the note of coercion which Williams believed is also essential to understanding how God works.[12]

We cannot say that God acts in the same way that science can say that one body acts on another, and yet we cannot say that God's acts make no difference. Whitehead pointed to a middle position, so that we can say that God's primordial nature

> acts only by being presented to creatures as the integrity of the order of possibility by virtue of which there can be a world. No specific action is completely determined by the primordial order. . . . The consequent nature acts by being concretely apprehended in feeling in such a way that God's specific response to the world becomes a constitutive function in the world. . . . God's causality is exercised in, through, and with all other causes operating.[13]

Thus the meaning of every occasion can be transformed.

We are working here with real, vague and obscure data so that

---

[10] Minor, op. cit., p. 60.

[11] Daniel Day Williams, "A Philosophical Outlook," in J. E. Smith, *Contemporary American Philosophy*, p. 230. Used by permission.

[12] Daniel Day Williams, "Deity, Monarchy, and Metaphysics," in *The Relevance of Whitehead*, ed. Ivor Leclerc (London: George Allen & Unwin, 1961), pp. 370-71.

[13] Daniel Day Williams, "How Does God Act?: An Essay in Whitehead's Metaphysics," in *Process and Divinity*, ed. William L. Reese and Eugene Freeman (La Salle, Ill.: Open Court Publishing Co., 1964), pp. 178-79.

concepts cannot be readily verified or falsified. Yet the empirical note dominates, for "verification must take the form of observable results in cosmic history, in human history, and in personal experience," but we still must consider "the meaning of the whole of experience." [14]

Williams, we have said, had an appreciation for many perspectives in theology, and in his first chapter of *God's Grace and Man's Hope* he indicated the values of both neoorthodoxy and liberalism. No simple choice between them is necessary, for both attempt to include elements of experience vital to our total understanding, but both are one-sided in their views of man and God, of sin and redemption, and therefore we need a more adequate theology to take account of the realities of experience.

Empiricism

"All knowledge, without exception, is derived from a critical interpretation of what is given in human experience." [15]

> The experience is the concretely felt bodily being-in-the-world and grasping the aliveness, the becoming, the give and take with a real world in the total complex functioning of the animal body and its conceptual apparatus. The flow of experience is the stream of qualities coming into our bodily perceiving. We "cut up" the world through the functioning of our perceptive apparatus. We screen out much of it. Our bodies take in more than our consciousness ever grasps. But we really perceive the world of things which have their life, their qualities, their impingement upon our receptive organism.[16]

This organic empiricism includes sense data and nonsensuous intuition. It points toward the grasping of possibilities as a new pattern for satisfaction. This feeling for the realm of structures is the "conceptual pole," although we may not always be conscious of it. We bring abstract structures to concrete experience for verification. "All knowing is evaluation," for we select from the wide scope of possibilities as we come to know any occasion. Such knowledge is always tentative

[14] Ibid., p. 179.
[15] Daniel Day Williams, *God's Grace and Man's Hope* (New York: Harper & Row, 1949), p. 41.
[16] Williams, in J. E. Smith, op. cit., p. 232.

and subject to further testing and correction, for we can never exhaust the concreteness of reality.[17]

We know God as we know anything or anybody else, and yet he is both hidden from us and pervasive of our experience in a way that is unique. There needs to be an element of discernment of what is "beyond, behind, and within, the passing flux of immediate things." [18] It is not something that we come to easily, and yet it can only come through particular experiences. Our knowledge is historical, in the sense that anything experienced is already past, as we have encountered the world.

> Where there is no sensitivity there is no experience. We ourselves have to be equipped and transformed so that we can respond to what is given to us in our total experience. Our knowledge of God is the case par excellence of this necessity for sensitive discrimination and responsiveness. There are conditions of mind and spirit for recognizing the presence of God, as there are analogous conditions for recognizing the structure, the beauty, and the spirit of a symphony.[19]

Empiricism has a pointing function. "Wieman's way of pointing to the presence of God as the creative event in experience is the foundation of empirical theology." [20] It is possible to analyze many aspects of experience from a phenomenological approach to get at the dimensions of suffering, anxiety, and other elements in one's response to life. To get beyond this point in our thinking, we need to bring in metaphysical categories, which in Whitehead's case were derived from experience but which are so general that they do not depend on any one experience for their verification. This brings us to the use of analogy as a way of thinking and speaking about God. Williams used the concept of "community of analogous structures," which recognizes the social nature of reality with structure, process, and valuation as "the ultimate metaphysical elements." Thus we can understand the formal mode of

---

[17] Ibid., p. 233; Meland, op. cit., pp. 176-77.
[18] Alfred North Whitehead, *Science and the Modern World* (New York: Macmillan, 1925), p. 275. Copyright 1925 by Macmillan Publishing Co., Inc., renewed 1953 by Evelyn Whitehead. Used by permission. See Williams, *God's Grace and Man's Hope*, pp. 46-47.
[19] Williams, *God's Grace and Man's Hope*, p. 49.
[20] Williams, in Meland, op. cit., p. 190.

God as primordial, as "the indispensable metaphysical participant in every world." [21]

Williams believed that we can reach this position without relying on the ontological argument, thus agreeing with Whitehead against Hartshorne. If the appeal to experience is futile, as Hartshorne contended, then the ontological argument may be necessary. In the development of it, Hartshorne contributed mightily to our understanding of perfection and unsurpassability, which is a helpful concept for interpreting experience, but Williams wrote that "I cannot see what use the ontological argument is to our understanding of God and the world apart from our experience of that 'most perfect being' which enters into every thought." [22] In other words, for Williams, "in every experience we are, however dimly, aware of the sustaining, value-producing, goal-ordering reality at work in all things." [23]

This does not limit the work of reason; in practice it places a greater demand on its functions, for reason needs to deal with experience and reflect on it, and in doing so it is concerned with emotion and intuition, subconscious processes, and moments of insight. It moves beyond rational intellection and purely logical relations toward a more complicated process. Reason always operates from a perspective (which may take in account other perspectives), for it is your reason or mine, and it is the reasoner who has a bias, or blik, or perspective which may need challenging. Reason can be informed and rational or it can be used to protect prejudices.

Reason does deal with abstract processes, and much of Hartshorne's discussion of the ontological argument may be helpful at this point. But reason needs to find its abstractions in the rich processes of experience, just as God as abstract needs to be seen as an element in the total becoming which is his full nature. Thus our thinking needs to be constantly revised by a return to experience as well as by continuing reflection.[24]

Metaphysics

Williams shared Whitehead's vision of metaphysics. The philosophic

[21] Ibid., p. 191.
[22] J. E. Smith, op. cit., p. 239.
[23] Ibid.
[24] Williams, *The Spirit and Forms of Love*, pp. 284-86.

mind develops categories which reflect the structure of the creative becoming which is our basic experience. Thus the vision is judged by its adequacy for illuminating actual experience.[25] Metaphysical statements are not scientific ones, but provide a description of the generality which applies to all possible experiences, and in principle can be verified in every experience.[26]

One does not rely on intuition for evidence, although intuition may provide the vision. The evidence is indirect, and there is never enough evidence for adequate certainty, although potentially there is a wealth of evidence if it could be properly selected. But finite man must be satisfied with his limited experience. Then he comes to his conclusions on the basis of three criteria: consistency, applicability, and adequacy. Religious experience is brought into this process, but one must guard against any exclusiveness of one's perspective or bias, so that metaphysical inquiry will transcend in part the cultural and religious conditioning of the inquirer.[27]

Williams' approach to process metaphysics was in terms of specific Christian concepts: the idea of God, man's responsibility and vocation in relation to the Christian hope, the analysis of the meaning of love, the crucial aspects of suffering. These ideas are spelled out from the standpoint of process metaphysics and are then related to the theological problem of the thinking and behavior of the Christian in the world today. As a result, many of the technical aspects of the analyses of Whitehead and Hartshorne were bypassed, although other essays by Williams dealt with evaluations of their thought as such.[28]

God

Briefly, it was Williams' intention to interpret the concept of God emerging from Whitehead's writings, with only minor changes. Thus, God is dipolar. In his primordial nature he is "the ordered realm of abstract structure" which is unchanging and which is the source of potentiality. It cannot be acted upon and does not suffer. It is a structure of possibilities. But God also participates in the lives of all creatures, and

---

[25] Ibid., pp. 10, 109, 291.
[26] Ibid., p. 9; J. E. Smith, op. cit., p. 235.
[27] See J. E. Smith, op. cit., pp. 235-36.
[28] See Williams, "How Does God Act?" in Reese and Freeman, *Process and Divinity*, pp. 161-80, and "Deity, Monarchy, and Metaphysics," in Leclerc, op. cit., pp. 353-72.

thus he shares the power of his being and responds concretely to their feelings, taking every event into the content of his own life. He shares in our sufferings and joys, and his life is enriched as he surpasses himself in perfection. In his consequent nature he is conscious and personal.[29] He participates in our lives as "the immanent structure-giving actuality, participating in all becoming, and moving from actuality to new possibilities with the life of the world." [30] God's actions, however, are his and not man's, so that his immanence is a sharing but not identification.

Williams did not distinguish between God as primordial and the principle of creativity (as did Whitehead), so he spoke of God as creator or as creative order. God binds together the total society of being and is the thrust toward more meaningful and complex societies. But his creatures have their own powers of creativity and freedom of response to the lure of fulfillment. So God is not completely in control, and evil for which he is not responsible results. When there are novelty, chance, and freedom in the world, there is always the risk that things will go wrong. In such situations, God is not helpless.

Williams emphasized the redemptive element in God's nature. Although God acts primarily through persuasion, the structural principles of his nature can be opposed only at the risk of losing the good, and this can lead to destruction and misery. This evil can be transmuted into new goods and higher fulfillment. Whitehead and Hartshorne claimed that this happens within the nature of God who shares all that we do; Williams said we can express the meaning of this claim only by analogy, but we do know that in some cases such transmutation of evil occurs.[31]

Williams moved another step in this direction with the doctrine of God's forgiveness, as a continuing quality of his love. Williams saw this as happening within the Christian community as a community that has already experienced forgiveness and is able to share it. "We come to know the forgiveness of God primarily through those personal relationships in which love is experienced as a mercy in which we are moved by a power greater than ourselves." [32]

The emphasis in Williams' thought points toward the same qualities

---

[29] Williams, *The Spirit and Forms of Love*, pp. 108-9.
[30] J. E. Smith, op. cit., p. 238.
[31] Williams, *God's Grace and Man's Hope*, pp. 53-54.
[32] Ibid., p. 55.

in God that Whitehead underscores: a love that is patient, forgiving, suffering, and affected by what his creatures do. He acts primarily by persuasion, but Williams questioned whether this is enough. Tenderness and persuasion are important, but "no organism would survive five seconds on the exercise of tenderness alone." [33] There is too much experience of force and coercion in life for us to ignore the elements of coercive power in God. Williams suggested that, in Whitehead's insight, "abstract structure can be causally efficacious" and, in the "disclosure of the divine initiative in religious experience" (which Whitehead may have underestimated), there is a basis for belief in "the priority, the initiative, and the efficacy of the divine power." [34] But Williams agreed with Whitehead in keeping power subject to love and persuasion. "It is the power to do everything that the loving ground of all being can do to express and to communicate and fulfill the society of loving beings." [35] There are consequences when we try to go beyond the limits of possibility, and these are more than persuasion. This is a far cry from the concept of the divine monarch of traditional theology; it is the very vulnerable deity who receives into his being those occasions which can hurt and hinder or support and further his aims for the world.

Man

The essential nature of man is that he belongs to a society and participates in a complex of relationships that includes God's activities. There is "a stream of conditions and events" which affects him, includes him, and which he contributes to. He is capable of free choice in both thinking and action, and yet he is limited by what he has been and is becoming. He lives by the consequences of his own actions and the actions of others.[36] Essential to this is the need to belong, to have a sense of his own value because he is wanted, to be secure within a community, to experience communion with God and neighbor. This is more fundamental than the will to power or the ultimate concern of Tillich.[37] It is a process of becoming that includes elements of both determination

[33] Williams, in Leclerc, op. cit., p. 370.

[34] Ibid., pp. 370-71.

[35] Williams, *The Spirit and Forms of Love*, p. 137; see Williams, in Reese and Freeman, *Process and Divinity*, p. 177.

[36] Williams, *God's Grace and Man's Hope*, p. 117.

[37] Williams, *The Spirit and Forms of Love*, pp. 146, 153, 205.

and freedom; it includes risk and adventure and promises elements of security, and at the end gives nothing but "perpetual perishing" that points to our "objective immortality" in God.

The anxiety of loneliness is a threat to our security, and this leads to desperation to protect what little security we may have. This can cause a disorder of the intellect and the will, so that our life becomes a meaningless thrashing about. Our basic humanity is partially destroyed by our own actions, as we betray what is best in us. This leads us to exploit others for our own seeming security. Thus we lose both our innocence and our freedom to love, and our true security turns to anxiety and a sense of separation from God and others.

Because God works through love, we may be able to look on ourselves as we are. Such disclosure is always painful, and unless it occurs in an atmosphere of acceptance in spite of sin, it is likely to be rejected. Judgmental assertions rarely lead to repentance. Often the pointing to what is right is more effective than exposure of what is wrong. Yet as we realize that what we do affects God, that his love takes upon itself our wrongdoing and suffering as well as our goodness and our joy, we may see ourselves in a new light.[38]

This, however, is not the end of the process. For many people, most of their behavior supports their will to belong, at least to a small group and sometimes to the community at large, and these people do not always realize that each development of the life of the spirit brings new temptations. We tend to think too highly of ourselves and then to be subject to temptation when our guard is down.[39] So whether we are lost in our loneliness or rich in achievements, we are not free from temptation to use our creativity in opposition to the love of God.

This is where the religious dimension becomes crucial.

The love which is revealed in Christ is a love which seeks the fulfillment of all things in such a relationship to one another that what flows from the life of each enriches the life of all, and each participant in the whole life finds his own good realized through the giving of self to the life of the whole.[40]

---

[38] Ibid., pp. 148-50.
[39] Williams, *God's Grace and Man's Hope*, pp. 192-93.
[40] Ibid., p. 78.

It is a love that reveals both the creativity and the redemptive action of God in the lives of men.

Love

John B. Cobb has said that Williams' *The Spirit and Forms of Love* is "the first major process systematic theology." [41] In this study, Williams has taken the concept of love and interpreted it from within a process perspective. In an especially eloquent passage he wrote:

> Love does not put everything at rest; it puts everything in motion. Love does not end all risk, it accepts every risk which is necessary for its work. Love does not resolve every conflict; it accepts conflict as the arena in which the work of love is to be done. Love does not separate the good people from the bad, bestowing endless bliss on one, and endless torment on the other. Love seeks the reconciliation of every life so that it may share with all the others. If a man or a culture is finally lost, it is not because love wills that lostness, but because we have condemned ourselves to separation and refuse reconciliation. We make our hells and we cling to them in our lovelessness. . . . Love means to will the freedom of the other, the acceptance of the consequences of relationship to another, and the vulnerability which goes with that acceptance. [42]

There is an asymmetrical relation between God's love and man's love, for God is necessary to man and yet no particular creature is necessary to God's existence. His love is perfect and ours is not, and our capacity for love depends on his love. His love is evident to us in our experiences of him as temporal and related to us. Love in its concern for the other conserves the individuality of both. Love cannot be coerced but is freely offered and received, although conditioned by the physical, emotional, and historical situation. Love is action, and this means suffering, "the capacity to be acted upon, to be changed, moved, transformed by the action of or in relation to another." [43] It is a matter of feeling and caring. Because love has an effect, it exemplifies causality, responding both to what is in the past and to what is possible in the future. "In love we impose conditions upon one another both intention-

[41] John B. Cobb, Jr., *Journal of Religion*, vol. 50, no. 2 (Apr. 1970), pp. 199-206.
[42] Williams, *The Spirit and Forms of Love*, pp. 138, 162.
[43] Ibid., p. 117.

ally and unintentionally." [44] This can lead to the transformation of the self. Love may provide new insights, but it is not a substitute for impartial and objective analysis.

God also is an individual, having his being in relation to actual entities other than himself. He is not "being itself." God recognizes the freedom of his creatures in their response to his love. God is never impassible but always responds in love to man's condition; thus he is a suffering God. It is "the acceptance in the divine of the tragic element in the creation, a patience and bearing with the loss and failure, and ever renewed acceptance of the need for redemptive action." [45] God, however, still remains invulnerable in his primordial nature. God has power which is more than persuasion (cf. Whitehead), but it includes involvement that is consistent with love. We can speak of God's suffering love as a process that goes on all the time, but it is not the end of the matter, for love points to the transmutation of suffering, and this leads to hope as "a critical issue for empirical theology." [46]

Hope

Hope sees the past merging into the future and assumes that the future is relevant to the present. Therefore, it becomes the basis for evaluating the present. It avoids both the pessimism that the present is everything and the optimism that progress is certain, for it sees God at work against opposing factors. It recognizes that novelty and chance are factors in predicting the future, but that something deeper is at work. Risk and adventure, which give zest to life, are meaningful because the whole process has meaning and value.

If God is at work in our midst and therefore shares in the time process of duration, while he also stands apart, we can see that this life has meaning now. Our life, like God's concrete life, is faced with opposition. There are possibilities that are unrealized for a number of reasons. There is actual evil. This is the point at which Williams developed the metaphor of "the embattled reign of Christ" as a symbol of what the revelation culminating in Jesus Christ means. Our lives have

[44] Ibid., p. 119.
[45] Ibid., p. 127.
[46] Williams, "Suffering and Being in Empirical Theology," in Meland, *The Future of Empirical Theology*, is an interpretation parallel to his treatment of love. See p. 192. Also, Williams, "Tragedy and the Christian Eschatology," *Encounter*, vol. 24, no. 1.

208

the potential for being transformed as we see God anew through the Christ figure and we come to participate in the victory of good over evil. There is a battle, and God works with and through us in seeking for victory.

This is not a utopian view of a perfect society but a vision of the potential movement of society in the right direction. The sources of this hope are found in the potentiality in our natural existence, especially as we come to recognize our ecological responsibility for this earth; it is sustained by our participation in the struggle for a better social order; and it is found in Christian teachings about the kingdom of God. If this sounds a little like a restatement of the social gospel, the answer is that while the good society is not the kingdom of God, we are obliged to create the good society for the sake of the kingdom of God.[47]

Concerning death, Williams seemed to agree with the other process theologians that there is an "objective immortality." Williams spoke of "belonging" not being destroyed by death. "The future for the self is the whole of its meaning in the everlasting life." [48] We entrust our conscious personality to God without knowing what will happen. Our death is a getting out of the way so that God may get his work done, but "even in death God draws us to Himself." [49]

Against this background, Williams developed a doctrine of vocation, which is our free response to a loving God who is working in human history as creator and redeemer. Working for real goods against opposition involves us in sacrifice, in compromise, and risk. We need to guard against irresponsibility and hopelessness while being realistic about possibilities. So we respond to God's demand, even though feebly and uncertainly, as we seek that knowledge and skill which will enable us to increase our effectiveness in our vocation.[50]

Jesus Christ

Williams, like Ogden, struggled with the meaning of Christology in a process theology.[51] He developed his view in terms of God's love,

[47] Williams, *God's Grace and Man's Hope*, p. 176.
[48] Williams, *The Spirit and Forms of Love*, p. 212.
[49] Williams, *God's Grace and Man's Hope*, pp. 197, 164.
[50] Ibid., pp. 147-57.
[51] Other important contributions include W. Norman Pittenger, *The Word Incarnate* (New York: Harper & Row, 1959) and *Christology Reconsidered* (London: SCM Press, 1970); David R. Griffin, *A Process Christology* (Philadelphia: Westminster Press, 1973);

which, he said, has rarely been made central in doctrines of the incarnation. God acts decisively for the world's redemption, and we see the central evidence of this in Jesus Christ, through whom God has provided "what is needed to heal the disorders in the human spirit, and to inaugurate a new possibility for every life." [52] In the union of the freedom of God and man there is conformation to God's will. Jesus, who in John Knox's well-known categories was remembered, interpreted, and known still,[53] is thought of as "God's elect man," [54] through whom God seeks to persuade the human spirit. It can be asserted that "history is changed by what Jesus has done. . . . God now has a new history to deal with because it is history with Jesus' action in it, with all the consequences of that action and God's response to it." [55] In the experience of the Risen Christ, we have a sign that God's work inaugurated in Jesus is continued in humankind and in the new community.

But not only does God have a new history to deal with, man has a new history to work in which includes what Jesus has done. "Atonement is that working of love in which the meaning of being human is made plain. . . . It is an act of human loyalty which discloses the divine loyalty." [56] If the suffering of Jesus is a disclosure of the suffering of God, as process theology holds, we come upon the mystery of reconciliation. The language of forgiveness becomes performative and therefore becomes adequate for achieving reconciliation. This is continued in the life, work, and worship of the Christian church.[57]

Process Theology

Process theology is a vision to be shared, not a dogmatic pattern to be imposed. Effective beliefs, whether philosophical or theological, emerge

---

Peter N. Hamilton, "Some Proposals for a Modern Christology," in *Christ for Us Today*, ed. Norman Pittenger (London: SCM Press, 1968), pp. 154-75; articles by Thomas W. Ogletree, David Griffin, Peter Hamilton, John B. Cobb, Jr., and Ralph E. James, Jr., in Brown et al., *Process Philosophy and Christian Thought*.

[52] Williams, *The Spirit and Forms of Love*, p. 155.

[53] Ibid., p. 156; see John Knox, *Christ the Lord* (New York: Harper & Row, 1945).

[54] Ibid., p. 160.

[55] Ibid., pp. 166-67.

[56] Ibid., pp. 181-82.

[57] God's love can work effectively outside the Christian tradition and with no knowledge of the historic Jesus. At this point, Williams agreed with Ogden, Hartshorne, and Whitehead. See ibid., p. 191.

from the behavior patterns and the experiences of men. As Whitehead wrote, "the intolerant use of abstractions is the major vice of the intellect." [58] But if one shares the vision, what then? Is it possible to grow in grace?

Williams asserted that we can accept the concept of growth toward maturity, and that there are steps in the process whereby God brings about a transformation. There is no sudden break with the past, no matter how dramatic the change may seem, for we always deal with what the past has to offer to the present as well as with new possibilities. He set forth five principles, which are not separate moments and may occur in various orders.

There is a beginning, when faith is born and we are free in a new way to commit ourselves to the working of God in our midst. Faith is a response to grace, man's trust in the loving, persuasive, creating, and redeeming deity. Faith is a gift which man can refuse, but man cannot create faith by an act of will. And it is difficult to judge whether a person has faith by any outside criteria.

What is actualized is a new way of looking on life, a new and deeper way of devotion to God's service, and a profounder participation in the working of God. There is much room for interpretation at this point. A new vision can bring about a reorientation of behavior. We may fall from grace and suffer from loss of faith, but our moments of faith remain part of us.

We have already indicated that, at each stage of development, there may be a failure in meeting new temptations. The claim to perfection discloses the sin of pride that can destroy the good that has been achieved. Goodness leads to increase of power, political, ecclesiastical, economic, or otherwise, and this increases the danger of corruption.

Real development toward Christian maturity is possible. "Christian maturity means progress in self-understanding which is one of the prerequisites of works of love." It "involves the development of the skills and intelligence through which love can do its work. It is here that much of the responsibility of Christian education lies." [59]

Love as *agape* introduces a radically new element into the understanding of love. It is not opposed to *eros*, although it may lead to a degree of

---

[58] Whitehead, *Science and the Modern World*, p. 26.
[59] Williams, *God's Grace and Man's Hope*, pp. 194-95.

tension. Growth in love is never a simple progression but involves a break because of our self-centeredness, which tries to take over. *Agape,* a love offering forgiveness, enriches and redirects the pilgrimage in a new way. Thus, *agape*

> is the love which underlies all others. We discover it at the boundary of our existence, in the experience of crisis, and in the overwhelming goodness for which we give thanks, or at the abyss of despair toward which we plunge. Agape is the affirmation of life, the forgiveness of sin, the spirit in which the self can give itself away and yet be fulfilled.[60]

In this way, human and divine love are united in the mystery of grace.

Thus, as a result of growth in grace, the person of genuine faith can face death without fear. As we grow in love for all "the goods of mortal life," we find that we can put them away with a certain detachment, yielding them all to God, who in his love will keep them in his memory. "The wisdom of life lies in the discovery that joy belongs only to him who can submit all his own hopes to the cause of the great community of good which life on earth can never fully define or capture." [61]

Conclusion

If we are seeking for a theological position that commends itself to the twentieth-century scientific-minded person, we may do well to start with experience, see that certain concepts work out satisfactorily, and place the thought system within the framework of a metaphysics. There is a sense in which any philosophy is a vision that appeals to self-evidence rather than to proof. In the light of experience, one responds to suggestions that become self-evident; then one returns to various experiences with the concepts that are developed. "Pragmatism," wrote Whitehead, "is simply an appeal to that self-evidence which sustains itself in civilized experience." [62]

There is a kind of empirical argument that appeals to specific experiences against the background of a transcendental deity, and

---

[60] Williams, *The Spirit and Forms of Love*, p. 210.
[61] Williams, *God's Grace and Man's Hope*, p. 197; see *The Spirit and Forms of Love*, pp. 212-13.
[62] Alfred North Whitehead, *Modes of Thought*, (New York: Macmillan, 1938), p. 106. Copyright 1938 by Macmillan Publishing Co., Inc., renewed 1966 by T. North Whitehead. Used by permission.

against such arguments the death-of-God theologians had a point. A revealed God cannot be falsified by specific experiences. But none of those attacking these arguments ever considered the works of Macintosh and Wieman, who believed that a critical interpretation of experience could lead to an immanent God as process, and that other processes pointing away from such an immanent God could be considered as evidence of something other than God.[63] James's more limited God in a pluralistic universe was even more immune from such judgments. But Whitehead's empiricism moved beyond the specific experiences of particulars to a vague experience of the whole, and reflections based on such nonsensuous perception would come under the rubric of being self-evident.

Whitehead was interested in the penetration of self-evidence, so that it operated at a deeper level. It is self-evident that reality is process, for our experience makes clear that "we are in the present; the present is always shifting; it is derived from the past; it is shaping the future; it is passing into the future. This is process, and in the universe it is an inexorable fact." [64] But in order to think about these things, man is capable of abstraction, so that he can abstract particulars from the vague totality of experience. This capacity can lead to the intellectual love of God, whereby we think of him in his ultimate or primordial state, as "the fulfilment of the mind's search for what is real." [65] The exercises of theological and philosophical thinking can be a source of joy.

There is a sense in which Williams' theology is self-evident, but like Whitehead he also turned back to history and experience as the basis for his beliefs. Williams was a student of Wieman as well as of Whitehead and Hartshorne, and therefore he kept looking back to his empirical base as well as forward into abstractions that illuminate the total landscape. We are helped in understanding him by our previous chapters on Wieman, Whitehead, and Hartshorne, for Williams did not detail his metaphysical arguments and therefore we can fill in some of the gaps with our previous knowledge. However, he also went beyond these mentors with his more careful concern to interpret specific Christian doctrines in terms of a process metaphysics and empiricism.

---

[63] Daniel Day Williams, *What Present-Day Theologians Are Thinking*, 3d ed., rev. (New York: Harper & Row, 1967), p. 98.

[64] Whitehead, *Modes of Thought*, pp. 53-54.

[65] Williams, *The Spirit and Forms of Love*, p. 300.

We can say, then, that Williams was in one sense the current fulfillment of the American spirit in theology, rivaled perhaps by Schubert Ogden. John B. Cobb, Jr., was working in the same direction, but he was closer to Hartshorne in his more rational approach. Bernard Meland, with his rich insights into experience as appreciation and his strong sense of the situation in various cultures, all against a background of his own independent interpretation of process metaphysics, was of great importance to the understanding of this whole movement.

There are other approaches to experience, there are different ways of considering pragmatism, and there are ways of enriching process thought with further insights from the Christian tradition, all of which we need to look at in the final chapter.

CHAPTER 12

BERNARD MELAND RECALLS THE ORIGINAL IMPACT OF WHITEHEAD'S *Religion in the Making* on the Chicago group in 1926. Although in the empirical tradition, Shirley Jackson Case, Shailer Mathews, Edward Scribner Ames, and Gerald Birney Smith could not understand Whitehead. They were troubled both by his vocabulary and by his interpretations, and they tended to dismiss him as another muddle-headed philosopher until Mathews invited Wieman to interpret the book. Wieman did this in a masterly fashion, so that some at least of Whitehead's concepts were translated into the thought forms of the Chicago schoool.[1]

Without taking anything away from Whitehead, we need to recall that he was not primarily an innovator but a systematizer and that his thinking emerged from the evolutionary, empirical, and intuitional approaches of Henri Bergson, William James, Lloyd Morgan, S. Alexander, and Jan Smuts.[2] This led to a language problem which the Chicago school did not immediately understand, for Whitehead's prose was complicated because of what he was trying to describe. Instead of

---

[1] See Bernard E. Meland, *The Realities of Faith* (New York: Oxford University Press, 1962), pp. 109-11; Meland, ed., *The Future of Empirical Theology* (Chicago: University of Chicago Press, 1969), p. 33.

[2] See Meland, *The Future of Empirical Theology*, p. 30. Plato, Aristotle, Locke, and Leibniz influenced Whitehead also.

216

the two-termed relation of subject and predicate, Whitehead was attempting to describe a many-termed relationship. We have immediate experience, as James showed, of "an all-embracing continuum within which differentiated many-termed relational perishing particulars come and go." [3] Whitehead saw this clearly, but he also agreed with James that at the periphery of experience there was a sense of the vague, indeterminate, and timeless, the all-embracing continuum F. S. C. Northrop calls "the undifferentiated (impressionalistically) aesthetic continuum." [4]

Like Whitehead and Hartshorne, Northrop develops a parallel to knowledge through radical empiricism by turning to abstract thought. He points out that there is a realm of logical knowledge, which is also many-termed and relational, by which we think in nonimage, nonpropositional terms. This requires us to go beyond normal language and to use the symbolic logic of mathematical physics and of legal science when interpreted in terms of logical realism. In the field of metaphysics and religion, this leads to the concept of "Logos," interpreted as "ratio" or "word." This conclusion remains purely speculative, unless it is "epistemically correlated with radical empiricism," [5] and is therefore verified in some kind of empirical test.

The sources of Northrop's approach are not different from those of Whitehead. Both men took seriously the Principle of Relativity and Quantum Theory, which allow for chance and novelty in their world view. Thus, there is an understanding of the meaning of freedom and of the working of evil in our experience. God is love, conceived both as "an eternally-now, logically realistic relation between beloved creatures" and as "the undifferentially emotive love." [6] These are "the two components of His creativity." [7]

Using "mysticism" in Wittgenstein's meaning, Northrop indicates the limitations of language by reminding us that words can only point or

---

[3] F. S. C. Northrop, in *Religion and the Moral Predicament of Modern Man*, ed. Benjamin F. Lewis (Brooklyn: Pageant-Poseidon, Ltd., 1972), p. 108.

[4] Ibid., p. 108; see F. S. C. Northrop, *Man, Nature and God* (New York: Pocket Books, 1962), pp. 188-90; see my *The Language Gap and God* (Philadelphia: United Church Press, 1970), pp. 40-45.

[5] Northrop, in Lewis, ed., op. cit., p. 114.

[6] Northrop, *Man, Nature and God*, p. 236.

[7] Ibid., p. 237; see Northrop, "The Relation Between Naturalistic Knowledge and Humanistic Intrinsic Values in Western Culture," in *Contemporary American Philosophy*, ed. John E. Smith (London: George Allen & Unwin, 1970), pp. 107-51.

show, rather than say anything. Our radical empirical concepts can only point; our imageless postulations can only show. Our pointing is to a world of perishing particulars in their many relationships; and this forces us to be suspicious of ordinary language that fails to get beyond subject and object in a one-way relationship. Our showing is purely abstract and relies on its self-evidence for its sense and ultimately on a return to experience for its verification.

The Religious Dimension

One problem facing Christianity is that its doctrines claim no one metaphysical foundation, and yet we have to fit it into some metaphysical scheme in order to understand these doctrines in our own day. John E. Smith claims that there is a religious dimension of experience which holds for all religions, and yet we understand this dimension within a particular tradition. So the Christian theologian seeks for a world view compatible with Christianity.[8] This leads one to consider ways in which religion can be made intelligible as reflection on experience.

In the American tradition in philosophy, these studies emerged in the philosophies of Peirce, James, and Dewey. Their radical empiricism has led us to consider the relation between the language-using animal (man) and his environment, so that experience is a medium of disclosure about the nature of the world, pointing to what is beyond nature as well as in it. Experience always includes valuation and some degree of thought (although much influences the subconscious), and thus there is selection of data from experience. Because experience is many-relational, we have to consider findings from aesthetics as well as science, economics as well as ethics, religion as well as secular studies. These experiences flow into each other and affect each other, and our response is an imaginative and speculative reconstruction of our experience in terms of concepts and beliefs. We are not passive observers but active participants.[9]

As John E. Smith develops this approach, he claims that "experience is disclosure of a reality transcending the experience of each individual," by which he means that "one and the same such object can be ingredient in the experience of many different individuals, and the

---

[8] John E. Smith, *Reason and God* (New Haven: Yale University Press, 1961), pp. 155-56.
[9] See John E. Smith, *Religion and Empiricism* (Milwaukee: Marquette University Press, 1967), pp. 44-50.

object clearly cannot be identified with the experience of any one of them." [10] When we face the "quality of our life *taken as a whole,*" we come upon the sense of devotion, concern, and transformation.

Experience is understood as encounter. There is a reality independent of that which is encountered and of the one who encounters. This distinction is important. This guarantees a realistic epistemology and enables the one who encounters to stand over against the other. Because that which is encountered is given, the one who encounters is not responsible for what is there, except insofar as he acts upon it to alter it.

If experience is to have meaning, it needs interpretation. There is valuing in this process as well as analysis, for we make decisions about what may be trivial or important among our experiences, and through such grading we come to conclusions about what is most relevant or important. But we still need to include what is of less value in our total scheme of things.

Such gradations of value lead to areas of experience which are said to be holy or sacred or religious. The sacred is not distinguished from the secular by any sharp lines but is discerned within the totality of all experience. Thus there is a religious dimension to experience, and God is disclosed in the midst of experience rather than directly or immediately known. At this point, Smith takes issue with James, claiming that James made too great a distinction between immediate experience and inference.[11] So Smith does not speak of religious experience but of the religious dimension of experience, through which we see our life "as having a ground and a final purpose." [12] As we run up against the crises and contingencies of life, as we realize our responsibilities, our weaknesses and failures, and finally our deaths, we see signs of our encounter with God.[13]

But to see God in such situations, we need already to have some idea of God. The idea of the holy or sacred or numinous is found in some form in every culture, so that the idea is present as various cultures interpret the meaning of deity for their own purposes. The experience of the holy within all experience is responded to in terms of celebration

---

[10] Ibid., p. 53.

[11] John E. Smith, *Experience and God* (New York: Oxford University Press, 1968), p. 52.

[12] Ibid., p. 63.

[13] Ibid., p. 151.

or ritual. These celebrations are normally associated with the crises of life: birth, puberty, marriage, sickness, and death. They may be happy or sad, but their main purpose is to point to the religious dimension in life in both a public and private way. Such rituals arouse the sense of awe or mystery or wonder in the face of events with particular meaning.

Such experiences are of necessity vague, and they point to encounter with a reality other than self, but in order to render such responses and our understanding of the reality of the religious object intelligible, we resort to analogy. The deepest religious emotions, when left unanalyzed, do not provide direction or meaning for living but can evaporate into sentimental nothingness. Because the religious dimension of experience cannot be reduced to the merely finite or controllable, we need to move into an area where we can say that the religious object is *similar* but not identical to man's concepts. The love that we ascribe to God is similar to and yet different from love as experienced in interpersonal relations between human beings. Smith develops this argument in a sophisticated manner, for he is convinced that we cannot be naïve in religion any more than in scientific thinking. When theology is oversimplified or isolated from the mainstream of culture, it becomes a foreign body within the culture.

As Christians, says Smith, we are concerned to relate the religious dimension of experience to the Christian revelation as received in history. He speaks of God as having *"a center of intention,"* drawing upon the analogy of presupposing such a center of intention in another self. We can also speak of God as a center of concern, in like manner. For our evidence in the tradition of Christianity, we can turn to the prophetic voice, conscience, and Christ. "Behind these phenomena stands the transcending center of intention," for these portions of evidence "are supposed to *point to or mean God.*" [14] Thus a Christology develops which asserts that God is mediated to us through Christ who is the final manifestation of God. The reality of Christ is experienced in the "beloved Community," which "is the unique habitat of the Spirit." In all these ways, we reach the conclusion that God is a suffering and redeeming deity of love who reaches out to humankind in healing and power.

---

[14] John E. Smith, *The Analogy of Experience* (New York: Oxford University Press, 1973), p. 99.

Smith makes use of the major thinkers of the American spirit in theology, most notably James, Dewey, Peirce, and Whitehead, but he develops his empiricism with a different emphasis that can be contrasted to the others, and thus he comes to conclusions which relate more easily to the Christian tradition. Like Ogden and Williams, he is willing to place his empiricism in the service of Christianity and its tradition, and thus he makes constructive suggestions for our overall consideration.

A Neglected Argument

This kind of reflection took a slightly different turn in what Charles Sanders Peirce called "A Neglected Argument," which has continued to be so, appearing as a reference most often in footnotes.[15] He suggested that this argument arises from "musement," a playful working of the mind as it runs on without any rules and leads us into aesthetic contemplation or wonder. There are three areas or "universes" upon which musement may play: potentiality, actuality, and generality. As one appreciates the rich variety and simplicity of structure of the developing universes, he sooner or later comes upon a concept of God as an explanation or at least an "attractive fancy." "The more he ponders it, the more it will find response in every part of his mind, for its beauty, for its supplying an ideal of life, and for its thoroughly satisfactory explanation of his whole threefold environment." [16] This leads at least to an explanatory hypothesis which is highly plausible.

In this way, Peirce became certain of God's reality, but he was reticent about claiming what were God's characteristics, seemingly mixing classical and panentheistic concepts with a degree of uncertainty. His conclusions were more practical than logical and not thoroughly thought through, but Hartshorne suggested that the dominant elements were panentheistic, so that we can believe that the universe exists in the mind of God, that we can allow for freedom and chance, and that the divine purpose works through generalities.[17] But the main point is that the kind of musement which Peirce described is a kind of free-play meditation that accounts for the meaning of many of our experiences.

---

[15] As in ibid., p. 57 note.

[16] Charles Sanders Peirce, in Charles Hartshorne and William L. Reese, eds., *Philosophers Speak of God* (Chicago: University of Chicago Press, 1953), p. 261; see pp. 258-68.

[17] Ibid., p. 269.

The Appreciative Consciousness

Bernard Meland sees a movement of thought coming from James and Dewey, but he properly distinguishes between the more hardheaded instrumentalism of Dewey and the more creative and aesthetic appreciation of James. There is a line of inquiry leading from James's "deeper empiricism" "through the creative thought of Bergson and the British philosophers of emergence, into the metaphysics of Whitehead, and the present-day Chicago school of religious empiricists." [18]

Meland takes the concept of "lived experience" from James and in a magnificent essay develops his theme of "The Appreciative Consciousness." [19] There is in any culture a developing sense of wonder that leads to religious sensibility pointing both to the mysteriousness of "A-More-Than-Human-Reality" and to one's fellow creatures. This provides a restraint on the egoistic drives and makes possible a genuine sense of community.[20]

Time as it is lived is dynamic and in flux as part of the becoming and perishing which is basic to existence. There is a creative advance into novelty, and yet the past contributes to the present and the future. Meland, basing his thought on Bergson and James at this point, stresses the dynamic nature of the conscious process as active and purposeful. This stream of consciousness has its luminous and dark moments; it is selective and yet open to novel experience; it is volitional, and yet at the fringe it picks up vague impressions that affect its subliminal functions. Clarity often is achieved at the expense of the richness of impression and awareness. Meland, like James and Whitehead, is suspicious of too much clarity.

Perception, or awareness, or appreciation occurs within a context. It is, says Meland, a "richer, thicker form of experience" of the "individual-in-community," which is where religion emerges, because one understands himself in terms of ultimate meanings.[21] It starts with *open* awareness, which is "receptiveness to the full datum of experi-

---

[18] Bernard E. Meland, *Higher Education and the Human Spirit* (Chicago: University of Chicago Press, 1953), p. 45; see Meland, *The Future of Empirical Theology*, p. 285 note.

[19] See Meland, *Higher Education and the Human Spirit*, pp. 48-78.

[20] See Bernard E. Meland, *The Secularization of Modern Cultures* (New York: Oxford University Press, 1966), pp. 136-40.

[21] Meland, *Realities of Faith*, p. 199.

ence," limited always by structure, but which can push through to a new dimension. It becomes more positive as it becomes *appreciative* awareness, because it reaches out toward knowledge of what is beyond oneself. Finally, it may become *creative* awareness, which is "wonder becoming a creative force." [22] The distinctions between these three stages are slight, but as one moves through them he comes to a greater appreciation that issues in increased energy moving toward greater capacity for decision.

In these and other ways, Meland shows his kinship with James, Wieman, and Whitehead, stressing the "immediacy of lived experience" so that all that has occurred in history

> transpires as concrete occurrence, merging in the distillations of history as lived with an emerging present, and carrying the import of both immediate and ultimate demands. The "thickness" and "rich fullness" of this primal datum, the empirical theologian would observe, must forever put one on guard against venturing heedlessly into capturing it as a clear and distinct formulation. [23]

Meland uses organismic imagery in the Whitehead tradition to spell out his concepts, and relates them to Christian beliefs.

In doing this, Meland pays a great deal of attention to culture and to the nature of faith. He is aware of both the great varieties of cultures and to the increased secularization of all cultures. We are products of our own culture, and therefore we have to work with the structures of experience which that culture makes available. It determines how we use our myths. "The ancient tales communicate this relationship in the imaginative vivid language of myth and poetry; modern metaphysics employs its modern myths to articulate on a vaster scale than the descriptive word affords the scope of human destiny." [24]

But Meland sees culture also as an enemy of faith, and therefore he turns to Christianity as a kind of subculture which can provide hope. This forces him to an analysis of faith as a source of insight and to the myths of the Christian heritage as a means of understanding. Faith

---

[22] Bernard E. Meland, *Faith and Culture* (New York: Oxford University Press, 1953), pp. 162-63.

[23] Meland, *The Future of Empirical Theology*, p. 290.

[24] Bernard E. Meland, *Seeds of Redemption* (New York: Macmillan, 1947), p. 41.

becomes for him "an attitude of trust assuming explicit cognitive concern." [25] Without sacrificing his empiricism or his process metaphysics, Meland develops a theory of revelation within the Christian tradition and expands his view of a creative and redemptive God at work through Christ and the church.

Meland asserts that the Judaic-Christian *mythos* cannot be excised from our culture. Furthermore, "there are resources within the culture that lend a sense of reality to this gospel of grace and judgment to which the church bears witness, but to which, the church as *church*, and Christians as *Christians*, may be but vaguely attuned." [26]

Meland's background includes strong influences from Gerald Birney Smith and Wieman, with Whitehead always in the picture. He moves away from Smith's mystical naturalism and from Wieman's naturalism, and he modifies his inheritance from Whitehead's Platonism with his insistence on the biblical tradition without losing his stress on process philosophy. His empiricism, expressed in many ways, still shows his indebtedness to James and Wieman, especially Wieman's *Religious Experience and Scientific Method*. In these ways, he demonstrates the thesis of this book, that there is a continuing American spirit in theology, expressed in its empiricism, pragmatism, and pluralistic metaphysics, and skeptical of any finished systematic structure.

A Vision for Theology

Behind the empiricism of all the thinkers mentioned in this book is theory, either clearly asserted as in Whitehead's writings or at least presupposed. Philosophy is always in the service of a vision; it is an imaginative reconstruction of what is likely to be so; we can speak of it as "speculative empiricism" by which we develop abstract theories, open up new alternatives, and present novel ideas which lift us out of the deadly or even irrelevant repetitions of past ideas. Such speculation, however, is grounded in perceptual and nonperceptual intuitions and must conform to the demands of logical coherence and consistency. [27]

---

[25] Meland, *Faith and Culture*, p. 120.

[26] Bernard E. Meland, "How Is Culture a Source for Theology?" *Criterion*, vol. 3 (Summer 1964), p. 19.

[27] See Bernard M. Loomer, "Whitehead's Method of Empirical Analysis," in *Process Theology*, ed. Ewert H. Cousins (New York: Newman Press, 1971), p. 72 (reprinted from unpublished Ph.D. dissertation, Divinity School, University of Chicago, 1942).

There is a basic model or key analogy for this kind of thinking: the human body. "For just as the body is one and has many members, and all the members of the body, though many, are one body, so it is with Christ. . . . If one member suffers, all suffer together; if one member is honored, all rejoice together. Now you are the body of Christ and individually members of it (1 Cor. 12:12, 26-27)." We see the human body as becoming and perishing and yet with an identity running through moments of change, and in which finally the perishing overcomes the becoming. Between persons as members of the body of society, we see a mutual interpenetration of empathy or feeling or prehension, so that we can speak of "knowing" another; yet this word, "knowing," can also apply to "knowing" God in the biblical use or in Abraham's "knowing" Sara in the sexual (and biblical) meaning. The fourth Gospel reflects this when Jesus is represented as saying, "If you had known me, you would have known my Father also; henceforth you know him and have seen him. . . . Believe me that I am in the Father and the Father in me. . . . You will know that I am in my Father, and you in me, and I in you (John 14:7, 11, 20)."

Survival depends on becoming a society of organisms modeled after the organic body. This is true of ants or bees or chimpanzees as well as of human beings. Yet man, to a greater degree than other creatures, has the capacity of mind: to think, to invent, to innovate, and to control his environment. He operates in terms of freedom and purpose as a self-creative agent. Therefore, he is important, even though he exists in a world which is not the center of the solar system. As Whitehead wrote,

For animal life the concept of importance, in some of its many differentiations, has a real relevance. The human grade of animal life immensely extends this concept, and thereby introduces novelty of functioning as essential for varieties of importance. Thus morals and religion arise as aspects of this human impetus towards the best in each occasion. Morals can be discerned in the higher animals; but not religion. Morality emphasizes the detailed occasion; while religion emphasizes the unity of ideal inherent in the universe.[28]

---

[28] Alfred North Whitehead, *Modes of Thought* (New York: Macmillan, 1938), p. 28. Copyright 1938 by Macmillian Publishing Co., Inc., renewed 1966 by T. North Whitehead. Used by permission.

This kind of thinking is directly relevant to the findings of modern science and evolutionary theory. We observe in the evolutionary process a large element of waste, of mutations which have not worked out but have been destroyed; we see chance variations which turned out to have high survival value; we see mutations of human genes which lead to distortions of human growth and to disease; and at the same time we see creative forces at work following unpredictable lines that seem to be mere chance, and yet we see a control and limitation of that creativity which makes it possible to avoid chaos and to live in a cosmos that fits our rational empiricism.[29]

Insofar as our culture fits with and reflects a scientific view of the world, process philosophy presents an interpretation of nature and God that is consistent with that culture. Harold Schilling has spoken of "the new consciousness in science and religion" and points out how an empirically based process view reflects both empirical findings and the thought process and vocabulary of this consciousness.[30] But it does more than this; it brings our thinking about nature and God together in a unified whole of our thinking, so that we can have an overview of the world and God in a consistent metaphysics.

For those who have been affected by the death-of-God literature, with its attack on a concept of God foreign to process theology, the alternative of a process metaphysics has hardly been considered. Yet, like the death-of-God writers, Whitehead and his followers have been critical of classical theism, which they see as culturally conditioned and outmoded, but instead of announcing the death of the reality of God they have redefined this everlasting reality in terms that can point to him in today's culture. For anyone who has been influenced by the new consciousness in science, this new consciousness in religion is a viable option.

Strangely, however, much that passes for theology has not been influenced by this new consciousness. It is as if the scientific revolution in human thought had never occurred. The largest, strongest, and fastest-growing churches in America are militantly conservative, rejecting even such minor concessions to modernity as new translations of the

---

[29] See Peter Hamilton, *The Living God and the Modern World* (Philadelphia: Pilgrim Press, 1967), pp. 38-72.

[30] Harold K. Schilling, *The New Consciousness in Science and Religion* (Philadelphia: United Church Press, 1973), pp. 244-55.

Bible or forms of worship. They reflect a subculture that finds the reality of religious living divorced from the scientific and technological culture that bombards them from every side. The ethnic group or subculture which affects their religious thinking has no connection with a scientific view of the universe, and the focus of their beliefs, while demanding a high personal morality, is on otherworldly concerns. Their language and ways of thinking are, from a modern point of view, mythological and poetic, and yet they would insist that their beliefs are to be taken literally. It is clearly possible, then, to subtract religion from the dominant notes of a culture and to feed it on the subculture which reflects a previous tradition. Religion's basically conservative bent is protected by a mentality of restricted relevance.

That this is not a satisfactory outcome for many in the traditionally oriented churches is evident from the response to J. A. T. Robinson's *Honest to God*. Here was a questioning approach to religion, and the questions threatened traditional beliefs and thus freed many lay people to ask their own questions. It is significant that Robinson soon moved beyond his dependence on Bultmann, Bonhoeffer, and Tillich to a position of panentheism, which was very close to the fundamental thrust of those represented in these chapters.[31] Panentheism, suggested Robinson, provides a basis for understanding the incarnation.

The incarnation can be considered as a novel event, in that it had not occurred before and had a unique revelatory significance. Yet its meaning depended on past events in the history of the Hebrews, and it erupted in the fullness of time. It changed the structure of consciousness of a subculture within the surrounding culture. In Whitehead's language, we can say that Jesus "prehended" God, grasped the fullness of God's meaning to the utmost. Yet Jesus was fully human, a contingent actual entity within the temporal realm. God provides every entity with its "initial subjective aim," and this can be particularized rather than left as a generality. Thus we can say that Jesus was an exemplification of the metaphysical principle in terms of immanence and the consequent nature of God. The risen Christ is understood as objectively immortal in the consequent nature of God, and thus can be prehended by us. What is revealed through the total impact of Jesus is

---

[31] John A. T. Robinson, *Exploration into God* (Stanford, Cal.: Stanford University Press, 1967), p. 86.

the working of a creative and redeeming God who suffers. The persuasive love of God is revealed on the cross.

In one way, we can assert that God did not become more sensitive or loving because of Jesus Christ; he was disclosed as such through Jesus Christ. But this is not a strictly empirical assertion, for if on the grounds of process thinking God is influenced by man's prehensions of him, he was changed by what happened to Jesus, sharing in both the suffering and the joy of his life and death. These happenings occurred within history, and as what Jesus was became part of the memory of God, it affected human history not only in man's memory but also through the possibilities released in God's loving persuasion, which includes the possibility of man's redemption.

Thus God is the "fellow sufferer who understands." [32] Suffering is not interpreted simply as bearing pain but means "being acted upon. It is conformation to requirements imposed by something which reshapes the self. It means to bear." [33] One faces the tragedies of life, the "dark realities," as Wieman called them.[34] These can be shared, and in process thought they are shared by God. "The discovery of the other who bears the consequences of my suffering and shares my condition is a powerful mode of personal communication and healing." [35]

> Empirical theology points to the fact that what works in human existence, so as to bring suffering into creative communities of value, is not primarily human will, action, or design, but the action of God. We experience the weaving together into one community of being of many strands of action, feeling, pain, language, memory, and expectation. Man is in the weaving, but he is not the weaver.[36]

God and man are both released from suffering through the creative, active love of God.

---

[32] Alfred North Whitehead, *Process and Reality* (New York: Macmillan, 1929), p. 532. Copyright 1929 by Macmillan Publishing Co., Inc., renewed 1957 by Evelyn Whitehead. Used by permission.

[33] Daniel Day Williams, "Suffering and Being in Empirical Theology," in Meland, *The Future of Empirical Theology*, p. 181.

[34] See Henry Nelson Wieman, *Man's Ultimate Commitment* (Carbondale, Ill.: Southern Illinois Press, 1958), ch. 3.

[35] Daniel Day Williams, in Meland, *The Future of Empirical Theology*, p. 188.

[36] Daniel Day Williams, in Meland, *The Future of Empirical Theology*, p. 190.

Empiricism, Process, and Education

There are implications in this approach to theology for education. Whitehead wrote that "the essence of education is that it be religious." [37] By this he meant that the inculcation of duty and reverence was central. Because process philosophy deals with concepts that reflect our experiences and we have potential control over events, we have responsibility to be knowledgeable within a frame of reverence. The problem is to make practical use of ideas as elements in decision-making and creative activity, and to escape from the prison of inert ideas. This is not an easy task, but it is what education is about.

Knowledge as such does not have value. "That knowledge which adds greatness to character is knowledge so handled as to transform every phase of immediate experience." [38] This can lead to freedom, but along the way there needs to be discipline and even "a certain ruthless definiteness" in order to provide for direction and pace in learning. What needs to be avoided at all costs is a premature definiteness or conclusion leading to dogmatic certainties; and where precise knowledge is available it needs to be so paced that it can be retained for immediate use.

When a young child starts to learn, the ideas should be few and worthwhile, mixed in every possible combination and applied by the learner to his own life. No barren or inert ideas have any conceivable worth and therefore can be ignored. There can be theoretical ideas, as the child becomes capable of theory, but even these must be immediately applicable in order to avoid becoming inert. Only as learners sense the importance of what they are doing can they be encouraged to use their own initiative.

Ultimately, such education can lead to wisdom beyond knowledge and to a style of living based on duty and reverence. Religious education has not achieved this goal, except in rare cases, chiefly because it has been caught up in dogmatism and petty moralism and the static concepts of traditional theism. It has never had or has lost the sense of adventure. "Whatever be the right way to formulate religious truths, it is death to

---

[37] Alfred North Whitehead, *The Aims of Education* (New York: Macmillan, 1929); Mentor ed., p. 26.

[38] Ibid., p. 43.

religion to insist on a premature stage of precision. The vitality of religion is shown by the way in which the religious spirit has survived the ordeal of religious education." [39]

Education always occurs in a context, even if it be only the relation of teacher to pupil. The interrelationships by which we prehend each other, feel each other's feelings, reflect on experiences we have in common, and then share in the dialogue by which we come to abstract concepts about the meaning of our experiences are part of the educational process. There is a creative togetherness in such experiences which can be understood, in Wieman's terms, as the creativity that leads to specific created goods. Wieman knew that many students fail to take full advantage of their opportunities, learn little or just enough to get by, or learn so much that it "becomes like surplus flesh on a man who is overweight." [40] But there are those who learn in order to expand their vision and deepen their sense of community with others. They absorb what they learn from the past into their own lives, they see history as their personal history, they suffer from the evils which they read about, and they take into themselves values that are worthwhile. No matter what the subject matter, they discover the creative power of the human mind, the goals of high purpose, and those structures in experience which bring new possibilities into being. Education means power and results in activities that bring out potentialities for good or evil. What the student gains from the educational process is both more and less than the aims of the educators and the institution, but the basic goal is truth about reality. A commitment to this truth stands at the center of the educational process. "No matter what a man's theological beliefs may be," said Wieman,

> this creativity of interchange is the only way to communicate his faith, whether he believes in a supernatural Person, a trinity, a cosmic process, the power of being, some vision of ideal possibility, or this very creativity itself, without further metaphysical interpretation. In any case, rituals of commitment to this creativity are required. [41]

In this way, education can be a means of promoting spiritual values, in which all other subject matter is to some degree involved.

---

[39] Ibid., p. 50.
[40] Henry Nelson Wieman, *Religious Inquiry* (Boston: Beacon Press, 1968), p. 159.
[41] Ibid., p. 177.

It is in this sense that all education is religious. Man's enduring life of the spirit is expressed through his creative activity, which is a process of becoming and perishing and which is fed or starved by his environment. In the full appreciation of his environment, he needs that art which provides vivid and transient values, so that he not only understands the sun but also appreciates the sunset, and sees in both the creative activity of deity. This pushes man via the aesthetic way into an appreciation of a dipolar deity which inspires man's worship.

This way of thinking is grounded in experience. As we examine and interpret the whole field of experience, plus the specifically religious experience, and treat it in a manner analogous to scientific thinking, we become aware of the primacy of the flow or process of reality. Yet this process has a degree of structure that makes it intelligible beyond the moment of perception, so that we can speak of continuity along with becoming and perishing.

The key concepts point to becoming, creativity, participation, potentials, universe including others, and love. When we speak of God as love, we are making a great claim that needs some unpacking. Love involves some kind of mutual interaction, some sharing of suffering and joy, some tender care that includes direction, some creative activity in relation to another. Such a deity is influenced by what is going on, and because God is love he works through persuasion without denying man's freedom. He does not coerce us but he is with us and about us, and occasionally he is opposed to us. "God is *in* the world, or nowhere." [42]

Such a concept of God, as long as the vocabulary of process thinking is used, does not get caught in the imagery of the male orientation of biblical and traditional language. "The principle of concretion" does not have to be translated as "Father." The Logos which is incarnate in the man Jesus is not identified as masculine, although Jesus is completely male. The imagery surrounding God and the trinitarian formula does not have to be sexist, either male or female. It is obvious that deity is not subject to sexist categories. Process theology should have a special appeal to women theologians, for it provides an opportunity to rethink the categories by which we describe deity. We are free to develop new

---

[42] *Dialogues of Alfred North Whitehead*, recorded by Lucien Price (Boston: Little, Brown & Co., 1954), p. 297.

analogies, images, and symbols in order to talk about God. It is possible to think of God as entering into personal relations with human beings without using personality terms, although this is difficult in the light of our cultural history. There is a sense in which human analogies for God, especially the more anthropocentric ones, are like graven images, for they substitute a mental idolatry for the concrete reality. The proper use of all analogies, images, symbols, and myths is to point to the reality about which we are speaking and never to substitute them for the real entity.

Process theology also has special promise for black theology, for the concerns of black theologians overlap the concepts of process thinking. Basic to black theology are the problems of evil and suffering. If evil is seen as resulting from a mixture of chance and freedom in a world in which God's persuasive love is operating, and if suffering is shared by God's love, then we can live with some degree of sanity and faith in a world in which evil and suffering are experienced in an unbalanced proportion by segments of human society. Furthermore, such a world offers the promise of liberation and deliverance. If God's subjective aim is the fulfillment of human destiny, and if freedom is a gift to all mankind, then we may properly hope that human efforts can achieve a higher degree of liberation and a resulting deliverance from injustice. There is evidence in history that an Israel can achieve a sense of peoplehood in devotion to a God of love and can experience liberation from slavery. But races and classes of people have been subjected to many forms of injustice, and ultimately it is the transforming power of God's creative and loving grace that makes possible the achievement of humankind's hopes. Thus we are turned back to a consideration of what kind of deity is essential on the basis of empiricism and whether such a deity makes hope possible.

As with women and their concern that our imagery about God not be dominated by masculine concepts, so with blacks and third-world cultures there is concern that such imagery be freed from an undue emphasis on European and other white racial concepts. Process thought makes possible a rethinking of these images, so that cultural and racial expressions of deity and Christology become suitable for religious experience, as long as such imagery is never taken literally.

There is also an interpretation of nature in process thought that should affect theology. No longer can we think of humankind as dominating nature. Technology has sought to subdue the earth, and biblical religion has often been interpreted in a like manner, but this has led to the destruction of nature's resources and to a denial of man's essentially animal dependence on nature. Process thought, with its views of the interrelationships and mutual interdependence of all actual entities, whether human or animal or nonorganic, provides a world view in which human beings are both dependent on nature and responsible for nature's ecology. Such an approach may help to reverse the thinking of some Christian theologians, as well as technocrats, that human beings have an inalienable right to exploit nature's resources.

Concepts derived from process thought, however, have some religious limitations. Because they reflect the many-relational aspects of experience, they are not easily reducible to simple subject-predicate terms, and when they are so reduced they fail adequately to point to the multiple relations through which deity works. They are not easily adaptable to liturgical practices. Yet liturgical formulas, insofar as they are biblical, are not only one-to-one relational but are almost cravenly masculine in their imagery (with the exception of devotions to Mary) and in any case are guilty of approaching image formation that seems like idolatry. It would sound strange to begin a prayer with the ascription, "O Principle of Concretion" or "Divine Cosmic Whole" or "O Primordial and Consequent Deity" or "Blessed Dipolarity" (which is no worse than "Blessed Trinity").

Yet worship is at the center of process theology. This should be abundantly clear in our reports on all the theologians we have examined. It also is the anchor of all empiricism in theology. James and Wieman are as insistent on this point as are Whitehead and Meland. The power of God is not only discovered by men through worship, but God's capacity to inspire worship is the power of his persuasive love. Process thought, then, only threatens the idolatrous uses of worship and the forms which illustrate this. Process thought provides a way of thinking about God that is suitable not only for the forming of concepts but also for directing our worship. It teaches ways of thinking and worshiping according to a world view in which God is seen as dynamic, loving, creating, and transforming, as a process who guides the world and who is the potential to be actualized in the future.[43]

---

[43] See my "Whitehead and Religious Education," in *Religious Education*, vol. 68 (May-June 1973), pp. 315-22; "Process Theology and Religious Education," *The St.*

Empiricism, Process Thought, and Christianity

In order to understand the function of empirical and organic theology in relation to Christianity, we need to take a look at certain presuppositions. The first of these is that natural theology, as understood historically by the Christian tradition, is a continuing possibility. Second, this natural theology derives its knowledge from human experience as found in all human cultures and therefore is relevant not only to Christianity but to all religions in their own cultural habitats. Third, the methodology of natural theology is akin to the methodology of any other discipline, not only science but also aesthetics, ethics, literature, and philosophy. Fourth, religious experience and knowledge contribute to the totality of man's knowledge and must be considered as significant in man's metaphysical thinking. Fifth, specific religious traditions have their own integrity and are to be examined within their own frameworks but with consideration of the factors previously listed.

This avoids immediately the problem of those who say that the only way to knowledge of God is through Jesus Christ, which may lead to the claim that there is no God but that Jesus Christ is his only son! We cannot make this approach, any more than we can say that the general study of religion may be valid but that it does not apply to Christianity because Christianity is not a religion. On these points, process theology is opposed to those who claim a unilateral revelation in Jesus Christ that makes all other religions invalid. In order for there to be an incarnation, say the process theologians, there must be a deity who is capable of ingression, of becoming ingredient in the processes of becoming, or being incarnate in a human being. This concept of deity is essential to an empirical process theology.

Process thought, furthermore, makes possible the Christian concept of "the living Christ." According to the interpretation of "objective immortality" as proposed by Whitehead and Hartshorne, it is possible to think of what Jesus stood for as being everlastingly present in the consequent nature of God. The resurrection points to the conservation of the values of the incarnation and the revelation of Jesus as the Christ, so that the indwelling or ingressed Logos (which is both primordial and

Luke's Journal, vol. 16 (Mar. 1973), pp. 3-10; in *Dimensions in Religious Education*, ed. John R. McCall (Havertown, Pa.: CIM Books, 1973), pp. 177-82.

consequent) may be thought of as never ceasing to be, although the human Jesus went through the process of becoming and perishing and then became "everlasting" as we can become "objectively immortal."

There is a sense also in which Jesus lives on in the church, through its preaching, its memory, and its sacraments. "In memory of me" takes on additional meaning when we tie the phrase in with "the memory of God." The idea of process, which destroys the distinction between materialism and mentalism, finds sacramentalism as valid as incarnation. When deity is thought of as immanent and as processive in its consequent nature, we can conceive of sacraments as acts of men whereby God expresses his immanence either in the figure of Jesus Christ or through the power of the Holy Spirit. Thus a dipolar deity is known in various ways, although he remains one God.

The Lord's Supper in all its forms and traditions is always a memorial, but, as Williams writes,

> it is not only a memorial of the past. It is a celebration of the continuing action of God who gave his Son for the world, who continually offers men the mercy of forgiveness, and calls them to become members of the living body of their Lord. The sacrifice does not repeat the sacrifice of Jesus. That was once for all. Bu there is an important truth in the traditional Catholic language about "repetition." The suffering, atoning, and redeeming love of God is remembered and represented ever anew when the sacrament is celebrated, and, we most certainly add, when it is received in faith.[44]

It is good process theology to speak of the church as "the body of Christ," for the organismic imagery fits our experience. The impact of the Christ event culminated in the church, arising out of that early community of disciples as a result of the resurrection experience and of Pentecost. Within the community they experienced the indwelling or ingression of the Holy Spirit or the presence of the living and risen Christ. The language by which the story is told is mythological and supernatural, but if we have a theory of evolutionary emergence of novelty, a creativity that makes all things new, we can account in some degree for this new creation.[45]

[44] Daniel Day Williams, The Spirit and Forms of Love (New York: Harper & Row, 1968), pp. 189-90. Used by permission.
[45] See Meland, The Realities of Faith, pp. 287-96.

There is no doubt in my mind that the church takes on the coloration of the culture which surrounds it. It is this, Whitehead pointed out, that led to the view of God as a monarch and tyrant and, to some extent, to the powers of ecclesiastics which denied men their proper freedom. Today, likewise, the church in America reflects a democratic culture, sometimes carrying it to such extremes that God is stripped of his power to govern. Certainly, as churches reflect ethnic subcultures and racial ghettoes, there is a lack of concern for those who are different, and thus racism becomes more rampant in the churches than in the culture as a whole. But, as Meland pointed out, there is a cultural witness from the church that helps to transform a culture, and the church becomes a persuasive power even when it is opposed to its surrounding culture. Just as the church went underground in Roman times, so it seems quiescent in Communist countries today; but this is better than selling out to the dominant elements in a culture, which so often is the case.

The church is "a cultural organism." But also it

is a distinctive and exceedingly precious instrument of grace, being the organic, cultural carrier of the revelatory event in all the ways that are suggested by a concern with doctrine, worship, pageantry, creative art, and the ministry of prophetic action as these persist through the care and dedicated labours of the believing community.[46]

Yet the church is fallible, and its failings contribute to the suffering of God. Christians and their churches are divided; the churches fail to take those steps of simple community that bring human beings together; the churches spend their time on trivia when there are important tasks challenging them. But this behavior does not hide its fundamental mission, which is to be a beloved community in which the transforming and creative power of God is at work in a humanly available manner. It is the responsibility of the church to point to the ways in which God's power may be released in human relations in every aspect of life, for God is not restricted to the church. For all its cultural limitations, the church stands over against culture because its roots are empirically grounded in the creative working of God.

The good is subsumed under beauty, for the harmony of intensity for

---

[46] Meland, *Faith and Culture*, p. 202.

actual entities is God's subjective aim. As process theology has been developed, it becomes possible to understand God's personal involvement through his consequent nature as a dynamic source of value, providing an initial aim for individuals.[47] "There is evil when things are at cross purposes." [48] The key concepts of goodness are love and justice as known in our experience. However, because God's persuasive power may be opposed by creatures, the future is not guaranteed. Novelty, chance, and risk point to an open future.

Both good and evil, as experienced by creatures, are prehended by God, are taken up into his life, and may be transformed there. In this sense, we seek "a kingdom not of this world." [49] But there is still God's influence on the world; Whitehead writes, "For the perfected actuality passes back into the temporal world, and qualifies this world so that each temporal actuality includes it as an immediate fact of relevant experience. For the kingdom of heaven is with us today." [50] So whatever is taken up into God is transformed and then becomes a new influence on us. This becomes the gift of peace.

James saw the implications for ethical behavior of religious faith. He distinguished between the easygoing and the strenuous mood, between the ones who give up and the ones who respond heroically. When God is "one of the claimants," there is a new perspective on ethical activity, for the horizon widens. "Even if there were no metaphysical or traditional grounds for believing in God, men would postulate one simply as a pretext for living hard, and getting out of the game of existence its keenest possibilities of zest." [51] The heroic example is one source of new life, for often "our faith is apt to be a faith in someone else's faith. . . . Thus not only our morality but our religion, so far as the latter is deliberate, depend on the effort which we can make." [52]

---

[47] See Lewis S. Ford, "Divine Persuasion and the Triumph of Good," in *Process Philosophy and Christian Thought*, ed. Delwin Brown, Ralph E. James, Jr., and Gene Reeves (Indianapolis: Bobbs-Merrill, 1971), pp. 287-304; from *The Christian Scholar*, vol. 50 (Fall 1967).

[48] Whitehead, *Religion in the Making*, p. 97. Copyright 1926 by Macmillan Publishing Co., Inc., renewed 1954 by Evelyn Whitehead. Used by permission.

[49] Whitehead, *Process and Reality*, p. 520.

[50] Ibid., p. 532.

[51] William James, "The Moral Philosopher and the Moral Life," *The Will to Believe* (New York: Longmans, Green & Co., 1897), p. 213.

[52] William James, *Psychology: Briefer Course* (New York: Henry Holt & Co., 1892), pp. 459-60.

This emphasis on man's effort is not a denial of God's creative power but points to the way in which God's presence influences man in his freedom. The responsibility is man's, but man cannot rely on his own resources. Man has a social dependence on other creatures and on God. Without love, we cannot continue any meaningful existence, so that Meland can speak of living "upon the grace of one another." [53] Our common life together creates both the harmony and the dissonance of the meaning of life. Ultimately, this points beyond the social reality of human beings in community to the sensitive working of God in our midst. A "goodness which is beyond our ken, but which nevertheless affects our existence, is the source of a beneficence that we do not seek, do not plan for, and often are not ready to receive." [54] This, in Wieman's terms, is creativity which works in and through us. It is both creative and redemptive and supplies energies which otherwise remain latent within us. It is experienced as forgiveness and reconciliation, as support and dynamic for action, as an awakening of consciousness or a deepening of it, as a divine MORE at the fringe of consciousness, as the opening of our actual selves to the everlasting potential hidden in the abstract nature of a primordial deity. God not only is "the valuation of the world" but also the source of "the energies of men." [55]

Conclusion

It has been our thesis that there has been an American spirit which uses empiricism, pragmatism, and process metaphysics in a variety of ways in theology. This is a typically American way of thinking in other fields, especially philosophy, and only in a minor way has it affected theology as taught in the churches. Insofar as theology reflects dominant ways of thinking in a culture, thereby appealing to those influenced by secularized and scientific views, this approach to religious belief has

[53] Meland, *Faith and Culture*, p. 177.

[54] Ibid., p. 179.

[55] W. Norman Pittenger has written a number of small books relating process thinking to Christian doctrines. Among them are *The Word Incarnate* (New York: Harper & Row, 1959), *Christology Reconsidered* (London: SCM Press, 1970), *Process Thought and Christian Faith* (New York: Macmillan, 1968), *Christian Faith and the Question of History* (Philadelphia: Fortress Press, 1973), *The Christian Church as Social Process* (Philadelphia: Westminster Press, 1971), *Goodness Distorted* (London: Mowbray, 1970), *"The Last Things" in Process Perspective* (London: Epworth, 1970), *Trying to Be a Christian* (Philadelphia: United Church Press, 1972), and *The Holy Spirit* (Philadelphia: United Church Press, 1974).

found a welcome. This is evident not only among Protestants but also among those Catholics who are influenced by Teilhard de Chardin, Gregory Baum, Eugene Fontinell, Leslie Dewart, and others. The chief influence, however, has come from the Chicago school of theologians whose forebears were William James, Charles Sanders Peirce, and John Dewey.

We have traced this development. Already in its earliest form, in James, the full development was anticipated in his psychology, radical empiricism, pragmatism, and pluralistic metaphysics. Dewey's instrumentalism retained James's interest in empiricism and pragmatism but not the metaphysics or religion. The Chicago development lacked the rich dimensions of James's empiricism, placing it more in the one-to-one relationship of subject-object language, which is why Smith, Mathews, and Ames had difficulty with the many-termed relational thinking of Whitehead.

The two giants of empirical theology, especially in the late 1920s and throughout the 1930s, were Douglas Clyde Macintosh and Henry Nelson Wieman. They were single-minded in their concern for empirical method, and at this point they reflected the secular culture more than the religious dimensions not particularly influenced by that culture. Wieman's strength lay in his critique of nontheistic humanism, because he took their empirical thinking seriously and provided evidence for theism on their grounds. Macintosh was more in the tradition of apologetics, looking at experience within the Christian tradition as a basis for making empirical assertions about the nature of God; thus, he did not stop with results based on his religious empiricism but moved to various overbeliefs based on reason and surmise which rapidly reinserted most of the traditional Christian beliefs. Thus, although sympathetic with Whitehead's process philosophy, he never moved far enough away from classical beliefs to deal resolutely with neoclassical theism. Wieman, at first, was open to an interpretation of religious experience which paralleled some of Whitehead's interpretations of consciousness and which was very close to that of James, thus pointing toward a pluralistic process metaphysics, but he backed away from this in terms of a naturalistic theism which was restricted to interpersonal relationships and creative interaction at that level. Thus, although significant for later developments, his thought was pretty much limited to interpersonal realities.

We can speak quite properly of a flowering of James in the philosophical vision of Whitehead. Whitehead's view was more complex than that of James, but for both men there were disclosures of reality that needed new forms of expression. Philosophy for Whitehead was akin to poetry, and he even called it mystical, "for mysticism is direct insight into depths as yet unspoken. But the purpose of philosophy is to rationalize mysticism: not by explaining it away, but by the introduction of novel verbal characterizations, rationally coördinated." [56]

Quite properly, Whitehead's philosophy provided the stimulus for additional developments in which there was enrichment. Hartshorne's emphasis on the theological and the rational added greatly to the logical possibilities of thinking about God within process metaphysics, and his influence carried over to John B. Cobb, Jr., Schubert Ogden, and Daniel Day Williams. Cobb is a blend of Whitehead and Hartshorne, with his own independent judgments as additional contributions; Ogden's existentialism is consistent with Hartshorne's use of Heidegger and others, but Ogden has made more use of empiricism and existentialism within the process framework. Daniel Williams was closer to Wieman in his empiricism, was more concerned with the relation of process thought to Christianity, and had at least begun to develop a systematic process theology.

F. S. C. Northrop was influenced by Whitehead, but his approach has reflected many other influences. He is probably more astute than most in his acquaintance with and evaluation of other religions, he has brought together insights from Wittgenstein and modern physics to help in fitting together empiricism and process thought. John E. Smith continues strongly in the empirical tradition, but does not make as much use of Whitehead's process thought; James, Peirce, and Dewey are predominant in his thinking as interpreters of experience. The impact of culture upon the whole course of development is found in Bernard Meland's impressionistic and profound analysis of empiricism and process. Closely aligned with Wieman and sympathetic with Whitehead, Meland seeks, like Williams, to bring about a clearer connection between empiricism, phenomenology, and Christian faith; he has carried out such an analysis in relation to other cultures, especially India, as well as to the scientific and technical cultures of the West. Thus, his

[56] Whitehead, *Modes of Thought*, p. 174.

utilization of the contemporary American spirit in theology has a particular relevance for those who are concerned about the relationship between theological thinking and the dominant notes of the particular cultures of the twentieth century.

This concluding section, which is a kind of summary roll call of the theologians and philosophers selected for this book, is obviously an incomplete one. Hartshorne, especially, produced many students who have carried on in his spirit, as Wieman did before him; and many younger theologians are looking to Whitehead as a primary inspiration. Already we are coming to a third generation, as students of Ogden, Cobb, and Williams begin to contribute to the now-established American tradition of empiricism, pragmatism and pluralistic process metaphysics.

No predictions are possible, especially for process thinkers who tell us that the future is open. It is clear that this approach to religion has great appeal to a few people, because it reflects a kind of thinking that fits certain aspects of our culture. It almost caught hold in the 1930s, when Whitehead, Macintosh, and Wieman were in their prime; but the new note was that of neoorthodoxy. Today, again, some people find empirical process thinking the best way to get at a meaningful and relevant religious truth, but there are those who are using their subcultures and ethnic groups as a way to escape from the pressures of our culture, and they have set up protective devices to keep religious thinking out of the clutches of empirical findings, partly because of their rejection of certain aspects of the culture. Because religion has the capacity to sit in judgment on culture as well as to benefit from it, this is to be expected. But there are those who agree with Erasmus that the new learning must not be identified with heresy, because that makes orthodoxy synonymous with ignorance.

For More Information

THERE ARE MANY SIGNIFICANT BOOKS COVERING THE PERIOD FROM BEFORE 1900 to 1970 and dealing with some of the same thinkers we have considered in this book. One of the best is *The Spirit of American Philosophy* by John E. Smith (New York: Oxford University Press, 1963), especially for his chapters on James, Peirce, Dewey, and Whitehead. Smith establishes through his interpretation of these writers an American way of thinking about the nature of things, and although the emphasis is not especially religious it is significant for the overall argument.

American Religious Thought: A History, by William A. Clebsch (Chicago: University of Chicago Press, 1973), goes farther back and deals with the scope of such thinking from Edwards through James. Clebsch places each person in his setting and then pinpoints where the major influence was. There are major chapters on Edwards, Emerson, and James, but some of the vignettes in the connecting chapters are equally valuable, especially those on Horace Bushnell, Walter Rauschenbusch, and H. Richard Neibuhr.

For some of the earlier American thinkers, there is valuable material in *The Modern Movement in American Theology* by Frank Hugh Foster (New York: Fleming H. Revell Co., 1939), with some brief treatments of the earliest empiricists such as Lewis F. Stearns and William N. Clarke. Sydney Ahlstrom's essay, "Theology in America," in *The Shaping of American Religion*, ed. James Ward Smith and A. Leland Jamison (Princeton: Princeton University Press, 1961), pp. 232-321, is a magnificent treatment of the whole period but does not go directly into the movement in American theology as we have defined it. Two

242

other essays in the same volume, "Religion and Science in American Philosophy" by James Ward Smith, pp. 402-42, and "Tradition and Experience in American Theology" by Daniel Day Williams, pp. 443-95, come closer to our interests and provide important perspectives on such thinking. There are some similar essays in *Protestant Thought in the Twentieth Century*, ed. Arnold S. Nash (New York: Macmillan, 1951), especially "Can the Philosophy of Religion Be Theologically Neutral?" by George F. Thomas, pp. 73-101, "Liberalism Chastened by Tragedy" by Walter M. Horton, pp. 105-21, and "Do Progressive Religious Educators Have a Theology?" by H. Shelton Smith, pp. 225-46. James, Dewey, Macintosh, Whitehead, Wieman, Hartshorne, and George Albert Coe keep popping up in these essays.

It is clear that James, Peirce, Dewey, and Whitehead are the most influential American philosophers when one peruses *Contemporary American Philosophy*, ed. John E. Smith (London: George Allen & Unwin, 1970; New York: Humanities Press, 1970). See especially Charles Hartshorne's "The Development of My Philosophy," pp. 211-28, and Daniel Day Williams' "A Philosophic Outlook," pp. 229-47. The picture of American theology in the early 1930s is illustrated by *Contemporary American Theology*, ed. Vergilius Ferm (New York: Round Table Press, 2 vols., 1932, 1933). Autobiographical essays by Macintosh, vol. 1, pp. 277-319, Wieman, vol. 1, pp. 339-51, Ames, vol. 2, pp. 1-29, and Mathews, vol. 2, pp. 163-93, are particularly important as background material for various chapters in this book. Additional help may be found in *The Impact of American Religious Liberalism* by Kenneth Cauthen (New York: Harper & Row, 1962), especially the chapters on Mathews, Macintosh, and Wieman, pp. 147-206. A critical study, *Empirical Philosophies of Religion* by James Alfred Martin, Jr. (New York: King's Crown Press, 1945), deals in some detail with the positions of Macintosh and Wieman, pp. 64-109. For the basic flavor of the empirical evaluations of the total scene in 1936, see *American Philosophies of Religion* by Henry Nelson Wieman and Bernard E. Meland (Chicago: Willett, Clark & Co., 1936), who provide a perspective on supernaturalism, idealism, romanticism, and naturalism and deal briefly with many thinkers we have not mentioned.

The Writings of William James, ed. with introduction by John J. McDermott (New York: Random House, 1967; Modern Library ed., 1968), is a good introduction to most of James's ideas. *In the Spirit of*

William James by Ralph Barton Perry (New Haven: Yale University Press, 1938) is something of a classic as an interpretation of both the man and his message. There are many good books and essays on James. The essay by James Dittes, "Beyond William James," in *Beyond the Classics?* ed. Charles Y. Glock and Phillip E. Hammond (New York: Harper & Row, 1973), pp. 291-349, is particularly brilliant in its insight into the Jamesian way of doing things.

There are many collections of Dewey's writings and many studies of various aspects of his thought. For an overview of his life and his thinking, *The Life and Mind of John Dewey* by George Dykhuizen (Carbondale, Ill.: Southern Illinois University Press, 1973) strikes me as particularly helpful. However, it does not provide either a detailed summary or a critique of his religious position. Perhaps more help can be found in *American Pragmatism: Peirce, James, and Dewey* by Edward C. Moore (New York: Columbia University Press, 1961).

The best single treatment of the Chicago school is the essay by Bernard E. Meland, "The Empirical Tradition in Theology at Chicago," in the book he edited, *The Future of Empirical Theology* (Chicago: University of Chicago Press, 1969), pp. 1-62. The whole volume is important, for it covers both the past and the future expectations of empirical theology and process thought. See also *The Realities of Faith* by Bernard E. Meland (New York: Oxford University Press, 1962), pp. 109-36, for a similar story but with other details.

On Wieman see *The Empirical Theology of Henry Nelson Wieman*, ed. Robert W. Bretall (New York: Macmillan, 1963; Carbondale, Ill.: Southern Illinois University Press), especially for the articles interpreting his position by Miller, Williams, and Meland; the whole book is important both for the essays and for Wieman's replies. *The Nature of Religious Experience*, ed. J. Seelye Bixler, Robert L. Calhoun, and H. Richard Niebuhr (New York: Harper & Row, 1937), is by former students of Macintosh and is highly critical. Macintosh's responses can be found in *Review of Religion*, vol. 3 (May 1939), pp. 383-99, vol. 4 (Nov. 1939), pp. 23-44, vol. 4 (Jan. 1940), pp. 140-58, and vol. 4 (May 1940), pp. 434-37.

"The Development of Process Theology" by Gene Reeves and Delwin Brown, in *Process Philosophy and Christian Thought*, ed. Delwin Brown, Ralph E. James, Jr., and Gene Reeves (Indianapolis: Bobbs-Merrill, 1971), pp. 21-69, is an excellent introduction to the topic;

indeed, the whole book is a fine collection of essays from many sources. It contains an excellent bibliography, pp. 475-89. Hartshorne's relation to Whitehead is clear in *Whitehead's Philosophy: Selected Essays, 1935-1970*, by Charles Hartshorne (Lincoln, Neb.: University of Nebraska Press, 1972). For a different interpretation of Whitehead, see *An Interpretation of Whitehead's Metaphysics* by William A. Christian (New Haven, Conn.: Yale University Press, 1959, 1967). One of the most thorough attempts to relate Whitehead's metaphysics to Christian thought is *A Christian Natural Theology* by John B. Cobb, Jr. (Philadelphia: Westminster Press, 1965). For college courses, one of the best introductions is *The Living God and the Modern World* by Peter Hamilton (Philadelphia: United Church Press, 1967). Another simple introduction is *Process Theology*, ed. Ewert H. Cousins (New York: Newman Press, 1971), which contains excellent essays and a good bibliography. For those who want to dig more deeply, *The Philosophy of Alfred North Whitehead*, ed. Paul Arthur Schilpp (New York: Tudor, 1941), is an excellent collection of essays, as is *The Relevance of Whitehead*, ed. Ivor Leclerc (New York: Macmillan, 1961). Both Whitehead and Hartshorne are evaluated in *Process and Divinity*, ed. William L. Reese and Eugene Freeman (La Salle, Ill.: Open Court Publishing Co., 1964).

The best way to come to an understanding of any of these thinkers is through their own writings, most of which are mentioned in footnotes throughout the book and so are not given in this brief bibliography. A considerable critical literature has grown up around the older thinkers, but so far there is not much available which is critical of Schubert M. Ogden, Daniel Day Williams, John B. Cobb, Jr., Eulalio Baltazar, Ian Barbour, Gregory Baum, Charles Birch, Delwin Brown, Kenneth Cauthen, David R. Griffin, Eugene Fontinell, Lewis S. Ford, Peter Hamilton, Eugene H. Peters, Norman Pittenger, and Gene Reeves, so watch for critical analyses of these writers. Some of them will produce major books dealing with specifically Christian doctrines, such as Griffin's *A Process Christology* (Philadelphia: Westminster Press, 1973) or Pittenger's *The Holy Spirit* (Philadelphia: United Church Press, 1974).

Index

(Bold-faced numerals indicate the more important items.)

About the Author

RANDOLPH CRUMP MILLER, A NATIVE OF FRESNO, California, is a well-known religious educator and pastor, editor of *Religious Education*, and author of numerous books, including *Living with Anxiety*, *Live Until You Die*, *The Language Gap and God*, *Education for Christian Living*, *Your Child's Religion*, *The Clue to Christian Education*, and *Christian Nurture and the Church*.

An ordained clergyman in the Episcopal Church, Dr. Miller is Horace Bushnell Professor of Christian Nurture, Yale Divinity School. He is a graduate of Pomona College and Yale University (Ph.D.) and lives in New Haven, Connecticut. He has also taught theology, philosophy, and education courses at the Church Divinity School of the Pacific, the Episcopal Theological School, and Andover Newton Theological School.